Moral Enterprise

For BLP:

*Wilt thou not ope thy heart to know
What rainbows teach, and sunsets show?
Verdict which accumulates
From lengthening scroll of human fates,
Voice of earth to earth returned,
Prayers of saints that inly burned,—
Saying, What is excellent,
As God lives, is permanent.*

Moral Enterprise

Literature and Education in Antebellum America

Derek Pacheco

THE OHIO STATE UNIVERSITY PRESS
COLUMBUS

Copyright © 2013 by The Ohio State University.
All rights reserved.

Library of Congress Cataloging-in-Publication Data
Pacheco, Derek Andrew, 1976–
  Moral enterprise : literature and education in antebellum America / Derek Pacheco.
    p. cm.
  Includes bibliographical references and index.
  ISBN-13: 978-0-8142-1238-7 (cloth : alk. paper)
  ISBN-10: 0-8142-1238-7 (cloth : alk. paper)
  ISBN-13: 978-0-8142-9340-9 (cd-rom)
  ISBN-10: 0-8142-9340-9 (cd-rom)
 1. American literature—19th century—History and criticism. 2. Popular education—New England—History—19th century. 3. Literature and society—New England—History—19th century. 4. Mann, Horace, 1796–1859—Criticism and interpretation. 5. Hawthorne, Nathaniel, 1804–1864—Criticism and interpretation. 6. Peabody, Elizabeth Palmer, 1804–1894—Criticism and interpretation. 7. Fuller, Margaret, 1810–1850—Criticism and interpretation. I. Title.
  PS208.P33 2013
  810.9'3557—dc23
                            2013023700

Cover design by James A. Baumann
Text design by Juliet Williams
Type set in Adobe Caslon Pro

∞ The paper used in this publication meets the minimum requirements of the American National Standard for Information Sciences—Permanence of Paper for Printed Library Materials. ANSI Z39.48–1992.

9 8 7 6 5 4 3 2 1

CONTENTS

List of Figures and Tables — vii
Acknowledgments — ix

INTRODUCTION
Education and the "Alexandrian Library" — 1

CHAPTER 1
Bibliographic Nationalism: Marketing America in Horace Mann's *School Library* — 17
    Schools, Authors, and Economics — 20
    "Respectable" Publishing — 28
    Bibliographic Nationalism — 34
    Conclusion: "Grandest Moral Enterprise" — 46

CHAPTER 2
"Disorders of the Circulating Medium": Hawthorne's Early Children's Literature — 50
    "Benumbed Fingers" — 53
    "Disorders of the Circulating Medium" — 55
    Grandfather's Love — 63
    Loving "Sam" Johnson — 70
    Conclusion: "Very Capital Reading" — 75

CHAPTER 3
"Contact with the World": Elizabeth Peabody's West Street Bookshop   79
- Engendering Controversy   83
- "No Worthless Books"   90
- Transcending West Street   97
- Conclusion: "Transcendental Exchange"   103

CHAPTER 4
"Conversation of a Better Order": Margaret Fuller from the Classroom to *The Dial*   105
- Conversations in Providence   107
- Boston and the "Animating Influences of Discord"   113
- Fuller, Emerson, and *The Dial*   118
- Conclusion: "Old Gentlemanly Pace"   132

CODA
"The Sun is but a Morning Star"   137

Notes   147
Bibliography   181
Index   194

FIGURES AND TABLES

Table

1.1	Volume Titles in *The School Library, Adult Series,* and *Juvenile Series.*	19

Figures

1.1	Facsimile autographs in *Lives of Eminent Individuals: Celebrated in American History.*	31
1.2	"Plainly" and "substantially" bound volumes of *The School Library. Adult Series.*	33
1.3	Title Page for Sarah J. Hale's *Things by Their Right Names, and Other Stories, Fables, and Moral Pieces.*	35
1.4	"Plainly" and "substantially" bound volumes of *The School Library. Juvenile Series.*	40
1.5	Frontispiece for *The School Library. Juvenile Series.*	41

ACKNOWLEDGMENTS

THIS BOOK owes its existence to the support of many excellent academic colleagues. It began its life as a dissertation under the direction of Barbara Packer, an advisor so immeasurably generous with her time that she once penned pages of handwritten commentary for one of its chapters while on vacation, sitting in a Venetian gondola. I also owe a deep professional debt to Michael Colacurcio for years of guidance, as well as to Eric Sundquist and Naomi Lamoreaux for their careful reading of the book's early drafts. Additionally, I am grateful to have had the assistance of two ideal readers in Denise Cruz and Nush Powell, who combed through the book's chapters on multiple occasions, suggesting improvements on each read-through from the first to the fifth. I am indebted to friends and faculty members from the University of California, Los Angeles, including Helen Deutsch, Chris Looby, and Felicity Nussbaum for advice honing the book's arguments through various incarnations from job materials to campus talks; Nicole Horesji, Reggie Allen, Sean Silver, and Geneva Gano for reading early versions of chapters; and Julia, Erin, Luke, Heather, and Rhonda for football at The Shack.

Of course, the research for this book would not have been possible without numerous library archives, as well as the expertise of their library staff, and the permission of the libraries to quote from their collections. Therefore, I wish to thank the Massachusetts Historical Society; the American Antiquarian Society; the Houghton Library and Gutman Special Collections at Harvard University; the Sophia Smith Collection at Smith College; the Boston Public Library; the College Library, the Southern Regional Library Facility, the Charles E. Young Research Library, and the Special Collections Department at the University of California, Los Angeles; the Pollack Library at California State University, Fullerton; the Humanities, Social Sciences, and Education Library, Hicks Undergraduate Library, and Hicks Repository at Purdue University; and the prompt interlibrary loan services available to me at these institutions. I am also grateful for the research fellowships and travel grants provided by the Massachusetts Historical Society; the Department of English at the University of California, Los Angeles; the Graduate Division at the University of California, Los Angeles; the Department of English at California State University, Fullerton; and the English Department at Purdue University. I would also like to thank Gutman Special Collections and the Massachusetts Historical Society for their permission to reproduce images in this book.

Beginning it as a Ph.D. student at UCLA, I finally completed the manuscript at Purdue University. In the English department, I have been blessed with a vibrant community of early and nineteenth-century Americanist colleagues, including Kris Bross, Bob Lamb, Chris Lukasik, and especially Ryan Schneider, who always gives good advice. I would also like to extend my gratitude to Sandy Crooms, Maggie Diehl, Martin Boyne, Malcolm Litchfield, and others at The Ohio State University Press for shepherding the manuscript through to print, and also to my anonymous readers for their enthusiasm, as well as their advice on how to make the manuscript better. A version of chapter 2 first appeared as an article, "Disorders of the Circulating Medium': Hawthorne's Early Children's Literature," in *ESQ: A Journal of the American Renaissance* 53.3 (2007): 282-319, copyright 1984 by the Board of Regents of Washington State University; I thank the publishers for their permission to reproduce it here, and the essay's readers and editors for their assistance in refining its argument.

Finally, as in all things, I am thankful for the support of my spouse—my confidante, reader, editor, thesaurus, wordsmith, satirist, and inspiration—not only without whom this book would never have been completed, but also without whom I would probably still be lurking amongst the cubicles of Royce Hall, dreaming of a degree, a job, a home, and a life (having never planned beyond my thirtieth year); half of all my good ideas come from her, and none of my bad ones. Of course, I would be remiss if I did not also thank Henry and Pickles: Henry for being awesome, and Pickles for being tolerable.

INTRODUCTION

Education and the "Alexandrian Library"

AN ADVERTISEMENT quoted in the September 1839 issue of the *Christian Examiner* trumpets the fact that *The School Library*'s publishers would include a "Book-case, with a lock and key . . . *gratuitously*, to all who take the Library."[1] This is from the "Prospectus" for Horace Mann's *The School Library*, a series of books endorsed by the state Board of Education for use in Massachusetts' newly formed district school libraries. The promotion of the bookcase is interesting not only because it positions the series as an effort to control the dissemination of literature in a burgeoning antebellum print culture—the series' contents appear complete and self-contained in its case, while the lock and key determined who could take books out and when—but also because it, along with the *Christian Examiner*'s singling it out, acts as an argument for the series' moral and economic worth. The locked case intimates that someone may want to steal the contents inside it, which, in turn, reinforces the notion that the books are actually *worth* something; they are, quite literally, valuable commodities. The notice concludes with the series' "Introductory Essay" and the words of William Penn: "For learning be liberal. Spare no cost; *for by such parsimony all is lost that is saved*. But let it be useful knowledge, such as is consistent with TRUTH and GODLINESS."[2] That the case, therefore, is "gratuitous" implies both the publishers' generosity in giving it away for free and also the readers' own economic liberality, the kind of excessive economic expenditure ("Spare no cost") they hope "all who take the

Library" will make when they purchase it at a price commensurate with its moral worth (its "TRUTH and GODLINESS").

This book investigates the intersections of authorship, education, and the literary market in antebellum New England. It examines a coterie of what I call "literary reformers"—including canonical figures (Nathaniel Hawthorne), those less so (Elizabeth Peabody), those more recently inducted into the canon (Margaret Fuller), and still others influential but nonetheless overlooked by current literary scholarship (Horace Mann)—to argue that antebellum writers came to see in educational reform, and the publication venues emerging in connection with it, a means to encourage popular authorship while at the same time validating literary work as a profession. In attempting to forge literary careers, would-be writers had to confront an ambiguous set of notions surrounding an idea of authorship that was at an intermediate stage, shifting between older notions of writing as a largely amateur enterprise undertaken by the gentlemanly classes as an expression of civic duty, and the more modern possibility of a professionalized, commercialized, mass-market career. Considering this coterie's efforts (like *The School Library* above) as what Elizabeth Palmer Peabody termed "great moral enterprise[s]," this book emphasizes the ways in which they articulate interlocking moral and economic imperatives in their search for educational commodities that could help them navigate a still-amorphous literary market.[3]

"Moral," in this sense, encompasses the literary practices of self-culture that were the cornerstone of what one critic calls a "national culture obsessed with values of education and personal betterment through autodidacticism," and that are still a topic of perennial interest to modern scholars of Jacksonian America.[4] In the last decade alone, scholars have delineated an antebellum culture that placed enormous faith in the transformative power of the printed word, in which the everyday disciplines of writing and reading crystallized individual character in an uncertain economic world, and where the seemingly ubiquitous discourse of self-culture was literary discourse, since popular literature often provided narratives of self-improvement that modeled the processes of self-reform.[5] "Enterprise," appropriately, identifies these literary endeavors by their dual valence as simultaneously bold, reformist undertakings and economic ventures. Participating in the great plan for mass education helped conscientious New Englanders validate market exchanges on moral grounds, while at the same time enabling them to shape the circulation of goods and ideas in an increasingly democratized culture by cultivating audiences complicit in the systems they sought to establish. As the "moral enterprise" of the four figures in this book suggests, the line between profit and pedagogy in antebellum America was a fine one indeed; while literary men and women aimed to do good, they felt justified in demanding a share of the profits increasingly available within the nation's print economy, and could not help feeling a twinge of bitterness if such rewards did not materialize.

In its emphasis on moral and ethical concerns, this book complements recent scholarship on the antebellum marketplace, such as *Literary Dollars and Social Sense* (2005) and *The Business of Letters* (2008), both of which characterize literary enterprises as "socially embedded exchanges" in an economic system hurtling toward "impersonal transactions."[6] Ronald and Mary Saracino Zboray argue that the antebellum market is best understood in terms of "social sense" precisely because profits were so fleeting, and they depict a culture still dominated by writing for social ends: for self-edification or self-improvement, to help or eulogize loved ones, to propagate ideas, to fulfill social obligations, or to serve the public good.[7] But while fame and riches remained elusive for the majority of Americans, and while social sense remained the predominant motive for authorship, the antebellum era witnessed an important "first" in our nation's literary history: the very real possibility that writers might do social good *and* make money. Put another way, it presented not merely the novel possibility that an individual might make money *by* writing, but also that a writer might make a living precisely by making a difference.

In reassessing antebellum authors' moral and ethical engagements with the market, for its case study the book turns to a constellation of transcendentalists beyond the usual Emerson-centered one. While, in more exaggerated accounts, the Concord sage could not help but draw "bats and owls, and the whole host of night-birds" to his luminous intellect, one might characterize the group detailed in these pages as Elizabeth Peabody's rather than Emerson's immediate circle.[8] It is she who provides the nucleus around which this narrative coalesces, as it tells the story of literary men and women engaged in ethically redemptive work, writing, collaborating, and even marrying (Hawthorne would wed one of Peabody's sisters, Sophia, while Mann would marry the other, Mary) as they wrangled with the intersections of literature, education, and the marketplace. Unlike older studies that depict romantic authorship as solitary and alienating, this book shows how educator status enabled a practice of authorship that is both redemptive (because of its collective focus) and financially possible (because it offered the support of networks that one needed to survive in a newly commercialized environment).[9]

It is, by now, a truism to call 1836 transcendentalism's "*annus mirabilis*," as Perry Miller once did: the year saw Emerson publish *Nature*, Frederick

Henry Hedge conduct the Transcendental Club's first meeting, the miracles controversy erupt between transcendental and traditional Unitarians, and Bronson Alcott release the first volume of *Conversations with Children on the Gospels*, each event announcing to New England that the "Newness," as it was often called, had arrived.[10] But the period 1839–40 was yet another wonderful time for the circle of literary educators this book examines. In the summer of 1840, Peabody opened in Boston her bookstore and foreign circulating library at 13 West Street, which quickly became a locus of transcendental hustle and bustle. Similarly, in late 1839, Fuller inaugurated, in the front parlor of Peabody's soon-to-be store, her now-famous Conversations for Boston's education-minded ladies, and, in 1840, she began editing the equally famous transcendental periodical *The Dial* (1840–44), published by Peabody herself between 1842 and 1843. The year 1839 also marked the appearance of Mann's ambitious *The School Library*, attempting, along with the common schools and district libraries that incorporated it, to reform, standardize, and centralize American education. Finally, in late 1840, Peabody published Hawthorne's first children's book, *Grandfather's Chair*, originally intended for *The School Library*. It was the first of six such books Hawthorne would write over the next decade, marking a turn to the children's fiction genre that would culminate in his *A Wonder Book for Girls and Boys* (1852) and its sequel, *Tanglewood Tales* (1853), imaginative stories of myth and fantasy that scholars have identified as foundational in helping to transform American children's literature for the better.

In a sense, this book depicts enterprises defined both by Peabody's Boswell-like investment in friends' literary careers and by her efforts to further these careers through the "moral enterprise" of education reform, helping her friends navigate a market culture still dominated by traditional, but fast-dissolving, social bonds and sensibilities. When Mann, directionless after his beloved first wife Charlotte's death, met Elizabeth and her sister Mary in 1832, he had little interest in education. By 1837, however, he would be the state's first Secretary of Education, having consecrated himself "High Priest" of the sisters' most sacred cause. Likewise, when Peabody "discovered" Hawthorne in late 1837, having read with rapture his anonymous tales as they appeared in the *New England Magazine* but attributed them mistakenly to his sister, Elizabeth, she immediately took it upon herself to let him know such genius had "no right to be idle" and to direct his attention to children's literature as an outlet for his talents. Peabody's friendship with Fuller lacked the intimacy she enjoyed with these two men. But even though their differences would lead Fuller to disclose in 1844, "I admit that I have never done you justice. There is so much in you that is hostile to my wishes," she also confessed herself "always . . . in your debt" for Peabody's unflagging support, even in those times when it was least deserved. Indeed, they were continual collaborators, from Peabody acting as "faithful booster"—soliciting magazine employment for Fuller, introducing her to Emerson, hosting her Conversations at 13 West Street, publishing her work—to their efforts to keep the financially troubled *Dial* afloat. Ultimately, Peabody would outlive them all (Fuller died tragically in 1850, Mann in 1859, and Hawthorne in 1864, while she lived until 1894), producing a remarkable career of educational and social advocacy that saw the full range of nineteenth-century preoccupations, including teaching, writing, feminism, utopianism, abolition, Indian rights, and, her most influential and cosmopolitan legacy, importing Froebel's kindergarten model to America.[11]

In detailing this circle's educational enterprises, the book's coterie focus provides a useful opportunity to "revitalize" and "revise" two essential and intertwined categories of transcendentalist scholarship: the national question and the ideology of democratic reform.[12] *Moral Enterprise* thus investigates four literary schemes—Mann's district school library series (chapter 1), Hawthorne's early children's fiction (chapter 2), Peabody's West Street bookshop and foreign circulating library (chapter 3), and Fuller's periodical, *The Dial* (chapter 4)—enacted in the 1840s as means to reform national print culture, and suggests how the realities of the industry both challenged and spurred these efforts. Through them, it addresses an irony integral to antebellum education, transcendental or otherwise; excoriating coterie interests that could retard the processes of self-culture, promote undemocratic elitism, or act as an obstacle to wider success by offending specific audiences, these figures' pedagogical enterprises inevitably relied upon coterie practices common in a culture still defined by the ethos of social authorship.[13] David Dowling has demonstrated how coterie identities functioned for antebellum authors as strategies for negotiating nascent market culture, the clannish allegiances functioning as the "symbolic and cultural capital" allowing them to reach wider audiences.[14] Even as they reproduced these practices, then, the transcendental figures in this book simultaneously expressed discomfort with the term "coterie" in so far as they aligned it with precisely the sorts of insular market tendencies their values stood to correct. Through universal education, for example, Mann hoped to subordinate local economic, religious, or political self-interests to what he saw as higher duties to state and nation. Similarly, Fuller's and Peabody's own vigorous pedagogical critiques of what Fuller termed "coterei [*sic*] criticism" suggest that women's self-consciousness of its ideological dynamics could lead them to less dogmatic (and more "transcendental") practices, and to visions of free markets they aligned with self-culture and self-expansion. In examining their reform commitments, then, this book tracks instabilities in how these figures construct themselves as architects of American print culture, reading their enterprises as stages that play out moments of specific national, racial, class, and gender definition at times challenging and at others rendering invisible formations within Unitarian self-culture.

Although, as *the* national center for *belles lettres* publishing, Boston would not come into its own until the 1850s, antebellum New England was at the forefront of educational reform. As such, the region is ideal for examining the intimate relationship between popular education, literary production, and dissemination in the period. Print enterprises such as the *American Annals of Education,* the *Common School Journal,* and a thriving schoolbook industry had established Boston as a veritable "hub" (to use Oliver Wendell Holmes's formulation) of literary-pedagogical activity. By 1840, 82 percent of the region's white children were enrolled in some form of schooling, and the white adult literacy rate had reached 90 percent. As a result, New England faced a more extensive set of reform concerns than many of its regional counterparts, who lagged behind substantially in even these two basic areas.[15] The transcendentalists themselves were deeply committed to education—so much so, in fact, that the transcendental movement "might just as fairly be defined as an *educational* demonstration" as a literary, philosophical, or religious one.[16] In a sense, their literary ambitions benefited from the still-amorphous relation between "schooling" and "education" at the time; even as New England witnessed the growth of the tax-supported, centralized, and bureaucratized school systems that would dominate the second half of the century, most Americans still sought education in voluntary associations and private institutions encouraging self-improvement through reading and writing, library membership, lyceum attendance, participation in book clubs or literary societies, and other acts constituting an individual's "pursuit of knowledge under difficulties."[17]

As the four enterprises examined in this book attest, educational reform could function in competing ways: while it could be progressive, seeking to create institutions or remold them anew, it also could be conservative, merely nostalgic, or restorative.[18] Mark Vásquez argues that, in antebellum America, self-culture seemed to democratize traditional forms of authority, putting the tasks of personal and social reform into the hands of the individual, even as it functioned as a social control mechanism because it advocated individual responsibility for social ills and thus helped maintain the status quo. In espousing the ends of self-culture, popular literature both "encouraged and controlled the interpretive authority of the reader," enacting "psychological, didactic exercises . . . under the guise of 'self-culture' and autonomy," even as "real authority was still located in the preacher, the teacher, and the writer" peddling their messages through it.[19] If some literary reformers, therefore, aimed to obliterate the old ways in favor of the new, others also saw reform as a means to help preserve social order, to combat emerging trends they believed threatened deeply cherished values and institutions, or to seek what stability they could in a culture in flux.

I use the term "literary reformers" to indicate the ways in which these writers aimed not merely at social reform *through* literature but also at the reform of literature. In this sense, I build upon what María Carla Sánchez has described as a "would-be literary revolution" attempting to "alter the institutions, systems, and processes that order our lives, and to alter them profoundly, in the here and now" by reforming the written word.[20] But whereas Sánchez examines fiction's transformative role in social reform, I am interested in a wide array of literary practices—such as authoring, editing, publishing, and disseminating print texts—brought together under the aegis of modern, democratic education. Positing education as an essential feature of this circle's literary efforts, *Moral Enterprise* suggests the way that New England's "culture of pedagogy" (Ginsberg, 47) invigorates authorial production in the age of reform. Education, in other words, became a means for writers to reconcile deeply held democratic sentiments about the purpose of authorship with concerns over a literary market that fostered all manner of competition from other texts, as well as the ever-changing demands of a growing reading public. Even as other transcendentalists participated in abolition or utopianism, the men and women in this study dedicated their reformist energies to the printed page; seeking to use educational literature to alter the patterns of production, circulation, and consumption that constituted American print culture, they thus hoped to reform the dynamics of the literary market itself.

Moral Enterprise first and foremost asserts that, by the 1840s, literary reformers like Mann, Hawthorne, Peabody, and Fuller had come to see great potential in educational literature, believing it might be an entry point into, and a means to tame, what Mann called the "Alexandrian library" of American print culture. Writing to Elizabeth Peabody about *The School Library,* Mann recommends Catherine Maria Sedgwick as an author with "her eye fixed on the true point" of the enterprise, declaring, "Such stories as hers would make be a fire to consume the Alexandrian library of our bookshops."[21] In comparing the nation's bookshops to the great library at Alexandria, he envisions textual abundance as the distinguishing feature of American life, a modern wonder surpassing the ancient seven. In his invocation of consuming fire, however, he articulates unease with, and a desire to destroy, these vast numbers of books circulating in the marketplace. In the antebellum decades, new print and paper-making innovations—including the use of the cylinder press, the production of cheap paper, and the rise of paperback books, as well as improvements in marketing—reduced the cost of books, while new avenues of distribution—including cheaper, more reliable postal routes and new railroad lines crisscrossing the countryside—completely altered the scale of the print landscape.[22] It was, as literary historians have variously characterized it, a "liminal" time in the market's development; a period catering to a multiplicity of "little publics" both courted and cultivated by publishers actively segmenting audiences by age, gender, and genre; and a time before the cultural consolidations of the late nineteenth century, when numerous factors, including the shift in publishing from the "cottage industry" of the early decades to the corporate powerhouses of mid-century, helped foster a more homogenous print culture.[23]

Of course, Mann was not the first to air his ambivalence toward the "silent revolution," as Emerson called these incipient stirrings of the mass market.[24] A few decades earlier, Washington Irving had fretted at the prospect of a world overrun with books, in which new print technologies "made every one a writer, and enabled every mind to pour itself into print, and diffuse itself over the whole intellectual world." He saw "alarming" consequences for what he called the "stream of literature . . . swollen into a torrent—augmented into a river—expanded into a sea," and, anticipating Mann's own formulation, he complained that a "few centuries since, five or six hundred manuscripts constituted a great library; but what would you say to libraries, such as actually exist, containing three or four hundred thousand volumes; legions of authors at the same time busy; and the press going on with fearfully increasing activity, to double and quadruple the number?"[25] Yet these comments must have seemed positively quaint from the perspective of the 1850s, when Samuel Goodrich, the wildly successful children's author, editor, and publisher, estimated that the consumption of books manufactured in the United States was "not far from seventeen millions of dollars annually," and that the nation's periodical press circulated another "six millions of copies, and five hundreds of millions of separate numbers!" Although he championed this proliferation, at the same time he too could not help thinking back with nostalgia to his childhood, when books were "scarce" and "read respectfully," and when "even the young approached a book with reverence, and a newspaper with awe." Faced with this new age of abundance, he could not help but exclaim: "How the world has changed!"[26]

Fueling this explosive growth was fervor for educational reading that caused schoolbooks to multiply unchecked, infecting the market with the same sorts of excesses that reformers were decrying elsewhere. William Alcott, editor of the *American Annals of Education* and cousin to transcendentalist pedagogue Bronson Alcott, worried, for example, that schemes such as school libraries were becoming the "hobby of the day." As a result, there "were one or two classes or occupations of men especially," presumably writers and publishers, "who stood waiting, with eager expectation," although he was not ready to claim that there was yet anyone who should do so "solely with the view of putting money in their own pockets." Beyond similar complaints by Horace Mann (discussed in chapter 1), educational reformers of all stripes expressed concern for the bewildering variety of schoolbooks in New England. One such editorialist declares: "Some, it is well known, regard the multiplicity of school books among us as a serious evil. . . . We will only say that if it be an evil at all, the evil must be seriously felt in Massachusetts. For in no State, perhaps, in the Union, is there a greater or more perplexing variety." Indeed, the market for such books was large, to say the least; Goodrich declared the explosion of schoolbooks "a feature of the era," estimating that, by 1840, the value of schoolbooks accounted for 36 percent of all publishing business, or 2 million dollars out of 5.5 million. By mid-century, the nation was producing more schoolbooks every year than the entire continent of Europe.[27]

The diversity of what constituted a "schoolbook" in the first place only exacerbated anxieties. In the nineteenth century, "schoolbook" was a catch-all phrase that included primers and spellers, readers, arithmetics, histories, biographies, natural histories, geographies, and even fiction, genres that could be meant for use inside or outside the classroom, as well as by children or adults alike.[28] In short, it seemed as if any book whose aims were educational might be arguably categorized as a "schoolbook." In fact, many publications did stake their claims to such a definition. In assessing trends in periodicals across New England, one editorial observes that the "Religious Magazine, the Mercantile Journal, and perhaps a few other papers of this city, frequently contain important articles in the department of education," and that most of the "business papers of Boston and other places, though they are still behind in this matter, are yielding to the popular demand, and slowly coming up to the great cause of human education and improvement." Even *The Lady's Book*, which seemed on the whole "to be going over to the side of fashion and frivolity," contained a "solid article occasionally."[29]

Peabody's circle sought to deal with this "Alexandrian library" in different, though interrelated, ways. For Mann, the answer to the corruptions of an industry affecting even educational books lay in the promise of institutional publishing. He hoped, as his letter to Peabody about *The School Library* suggests, to transform the market through public–private hybrid enterprises that promoted certain literary texts (like Sedgwick's) to specific markets (such as schoolchildren) and inculcated proper values (domestic and religious), what he calls in one lecture a "purer current of thought at the fountain" to "wash the channels clean."[30] Peabody envisioned teachers like herself as best qualified to arbitrate literary-pedagogical merit, going so far as to suggest to Mann that his library series would be better served by a convention of schoolteachers voting upon each of its contributions (*Letters*, 199). Conversely, Hawthorne and Fuller sought to capitalize on the generic diversity of antebellum educational literature, claiming for fiction, on the one hand, and the periodical, on the other, the power to educate New England's reading masses, even as they sought to transform these genres from within. While Hawthorne sought to drink of the same "fountain" as Mann in casting children's fiction as a means to purify successive generations of young minds, Fuller saw great possibilities in the periodical forms already thought to be *the* democratizing force in American education.

In this context, *Moral Enterprise* traces the way New England literary reformers embraced education as a marketable literary commodity that might compete in and revolutionize the crowded marketplace. In doing so, it builds upon the work of Lawrence Buell, Sheila Post-Lauria, Sarah Wadsworth, and others in refusing to condemn literary commercialization without first "investigating [its] causes and consequences—positive as well as negative."[31] As more than one scholar has suggested, literary commodities always retain value exceeding that which the market assigns to them. Thus, while authors and publishers used education to sell texts, they also saw their book as edifying influences raising the sentiments of those consuming them. An editorial in the *American Annals of Education*, for instance, employs the analogy of "Emily," daughter, sister, and "supporter of every benevolent project with which she is acquainted," to expound, ostensibly, upon the role of siblings in family education, but also to point with equal vehemence to its own literary commodity as a vehicle of instruction. The very "pattern of industry and every Christian virtue," Emily is, in this construction, an edifying influence precisely because she is an ideal consumer, someone who "buys and reads good books, and lends or reads them to others; subscribes for and distributes all sorts of newspapers and magazines which she believes useful."[32]

In challenging commercialization as reduction of worth to cash-value or a form of artistic debasement, therefore, this book considers how antebellum literary-pedagogical enterprises had for their aims aspirations more grand than merely monetary profit. In chapter 3, for instance, I address Elizabeth Peabody's decision, as the publisher and copyright holder of William Ellery Channing's *Emancipation* (1840), to allow multiple editions of the text to circulate without regard for sales of its first edition. In this way, she hoped to capitalize upon the "popular tide" of interest in Channing's work, promoting what she called his "dearest end—to serve the Antislavery cause," even if it meant she had to take a financial loss.[33] Certainly, in other instances the commodification of education encompassed financial considerations. In her 3 March 1838 letter to Horace Mann soliciting employment for Hawthorne, to take another example, Peabody marries monetary returns with moral purpose. Claiming Hawthorne "had in his mind one great moral enterprise . . . to make an attempt at creating a new literature for the young—as he has a deep dislike to the character of the shoals of books poured out from the press," she links his entrance into children's literature with a desire for market reform (*Letters*, 200). Concerned for the quality of antebellum juvenile writing, she decries books "poured out," like Irving's "sea of literature," into the world in unregulated volumes. In calling them "shoals," furthermore, Peabody implies these books' poor character; like an ocean vast but shallow, their diffusion is wide and far-reaching, but of little intellectual or moral depth.

Likewise, as she rhapsodizes over the "moral enterprise" of juvenile literature, Peabody's language slips between moral and economic incentive with ease. Asking Mann to read "'the Gentle Boy'—& 'little Annie's Ramble' & 'the Gray Champion' & 'the Maypole of Merry Mount,'" she tells him,

> you will I think see indications of a genius for such an enterprise that could not fail to make *a fortune* at last that would satisfy so very moderate desires as his. . . . He has deep views—thinks society in this country is only to be controlled in its *fountain of youth*. . . . He says that were he embarked in this undertaking he should feel as if he had a right to live—he desired no higher vocation—he considered it the highest. (*Letters*, 200; emphasis in original)

Equating Hawthorne's "genius" for children's literature, as the highest vocation to which a writer might aspire, with inevitable financial success, that is, the "*fortune*" he "could not fail to make," Peabody is nonetheless quick to assert that Hawthorne holds only "very moderate desires" for financial remuneration. In this case, the matter is not merely about money; Hawthorne seeks to use children's literature to build a following among a new audience, so that he can, as Peabody puts it here, "control" society in its "*fountain of youth*." In other words, he desires not only to capitalize upon the reputation earned as these children grow into adults who buy books, but also to regulate the market's future by altering the habits of its youngest consumers.

While this book confines itself to the United States, it nonetheless acknowledges the international dimensions of the market with which these literary reformers wrangled; in building upon the work of scholars such as Michael Winship and Meredith McGill, it gestures to the influence of the transatlantic trade in these "moral enterprises."[34] American transcendentalism was, of course, by definition transatlantic, as evidenced by its European Romantic inspirations, by its sympathy for French and German literature, and by the efforts of those like Peabody and Fuller, who, through the former's foreign circulating library and the latter's translations in *The Dial*, sought to introduce foreign thought into the mainstream American market. Fuller, in fact, considered it the "great object" of her life to introduce into the United States the "works of those great geniuses . . . which might give the young who are soon to constitute the state, a higher standard in thought and action than would be demanded of them by their own time. I have hoped that, by being thus raised above their native sphere, they would become its instructors and the faithful stewards of its best riches, not its tools or slaves."[35] In this way, her essay on "American Literature" (1846) is the culmination of Fuller's commitment to the idea of the professional author as educator, suggesting a program of national identity formation via market reformation in which a new influx of continental literature might wean Americans from their provincial dependence on, and the "excessive influence" of, British literary and cultural forms ("American Literature," 123). Encouraging a younger generation of Americans (those who will "soon . . . constitute the state") to strive beyond national borders in the interests of better understanding their "native sphere," literary reformers like Fuller promoted a cosmopolitan nationalism that was one of the important legacies of New England transcendentalism.[36]

But, as Fuller's concerns about England suggest, efforts to foster an American national print culture were inevitably international, and even the most dyed-in-the-wool variety of American exceptionalism had to confront the problem of British influence. The literary nationalism described in chapter 1, for instance, reveals the manner in which Mann's "moral enterprise" both rejects and embraces England, simultaneously excoriating its influences on American book production while favoring the homogenous national and racial identity that country represents. Similarly, chapter 2 examines Hawthorne's foray into the self-consciously nationalist genre of children's literature, demonstrating the solace he finds in images of authorship ranging from English colonists such as Cotton Mather in the seventeenth century to "classic" British authors such as Samuel Johnson in the eighteenth. Because all attempts to define the American experience are "embedded in—and frequently strain against—a transatlantic literary culture," thus nativist no less than cosmopolitan nationalisms had to negotiate the complexities of the transatlantic trade.[37]

In tracking their "moral enterprises" within antebellum culture's "Alexandrian library," chapters 1 and 2 trace the way in which Mann and Hawthorne both sought to cultivate a distinctly "American" literature as a means to nurture self-restraint in a democratic society, and to create responsible consumers who would exercise caution in their purchasing habits. To that end, they hoped to reduce Americans' consumption of literary texts to what Mann called "a few good books" ("On District School Libraries," 275), a small number of exceptionally produced and yet widely disseminated texts, including his *School Library,* and, in Hawthorne's opinion, *Grandfather's Chair* and *Biographical Stories for Children.* Making his case, Mann argues that, through a library so constituted, "the faculty of the school will be enlarged. It will be made to extend its enlightening influences to the old as well as to the young. . . . Hence the schoolhouse will be not only a nursery for children, but a place of intelligent resort for men" ("On District School Libraries," 290). But if his *School Library* takes as its schoolhouse entire communities of readers, targeting both "nursery" and "resort" through specialized series adapted to children, on the one hand, and adults, on the other, Hawthorne's own children's books aim to grow "nursery" readers into adults who will then seek "intelligent resort" in his fiction rather than in the other works flooding the industry. Sharing what Mann calls "unmitigated anxiety" over the direction of the market, then, he too embraced popular media championed as part of the age's liberalizing spirit while at the same time using them as "defense or barrier" against those unwanted "propensities" he hoped to curtail in the reading public.[38]

Although they shared their male counterparts' dissatisfaction with the state of antebellum print culture, Peabody and Fuller harbored more expansive senses of the possibilities of self-culture. Chapters 3 and 4 thus investigate the way in which the "moral enterprise" of education had as much to do with hopes of negotiating gender boundaries—or the "crowd of books," as Fuller describes them in *Woman in the Nineteenth Century* (1845), committed to delineating in exacting detail "Woman's 'Sphere'"—as with controlling the circulation of printed texts.[39] Examining their enterprises as searches for what Peabody called "contact with the world," and what Fuller termed a desire become a "citizen of the world," these chapters trace their efforts to foster "extensive" practices at a time when other literary reformers encouraged "intensive" ones—careful, continuous reading of a select few texts, like the Bible, held over from times when books were scarce and expensive commodities.[40] In other words, while some pleaded for frugality of reading in the face of antebellum culture's abundance, Fuller and Peabody encouraged a greater liberality of reading bound up in the promise of female intellectual development transcending arbitrary constructions of gender. Eschewing the "literary domestic," the nineteenth-century phenomenon whereby women writers' public visibility was premised upon their celebrating women's confinement to private life, they used education, broadly considered, to find their place in the marketplace.[41]

Attempting to combine pedagogical and material/economic emphases in order to investigate multiple facets of antebellum educational authorship, the book's chapters range from studies in the history of the book to transcendentalist pedagogy; after all, transcendentalism itself was very much a response to material and economic conditions in antebellum New England. As a result, the book's chapters shift focus in accordance with the shape of critical discourse surrounding the figures surveyed. For instance, while there is no shortage of scholarly treatises on Mann as educator (despite what his biographer calls the "relative dearth of philosophical content in his writings," and a career notable as much for its impatience with theoretical debate as for its practical achievements in systematizing public education), critics have tended to dismiss Fuller's school teaching as little more than money making.[42] Therefore, I pay great attention to how literary economics shaped Mann's educational enterprise (and vice versa), while taking seriously the pedagogical investments leading someone like Fuller to seek her living in educational venues from teaching to editorship. Throughout, however, I attempt to think broadly about "literature" as a social field, as well as to consider the meanings of its commercialization as writers, editors, and booksellers like Mann, Hawthorne, Peabody, and Fuller helped institutionalize it across various professional practices.

The dates of this study, roughly the period 1835–45, are significant not only because they saw the rise of the nineteenth-century print revolution, but also because of the growth of New England transcendentalism, bound up as it was in a variety of social and economic reform impulses. In the 1850s, as Anne Rose argues, such interests would be overshadowed by abolition, as well as by the feeling that urban industrial capitalism "was here to stay." What was once a sense of urgency would settle into "deflated hopes and cheerful acquiescence, suppressed doubts and self-congratulation" as the transcendentalists themselves began to change from reformers to "quite respectable citizens."[43] In the early 1840s, however, there still seemed the possibility that the direction of America's social and economic development might be negotiable. As Robert Milder has suggested, what appears in retrospect as "the onrush of the nation toward laissez-faire capitalism seemed to the actors themselves a moment of cultural self-definition . . . with the balance tipped markedly but not irrevocably toward materialism."[44] As the 1840s progressed, each of the writers in Peabody's circle moved on to endeavors beyond the scope of this study: Mann would resign his secretaryship in 1848 to re-enter politics, Hawthorne would return again to adult fiction, Peabody's varied investments would draw her away from the day-to-day operations of her bookstore, and Fuller would join the ranks of professional writers at the *New York Tribune*, first as a literary editor and then as a foreign correspondent. But each of these subsequent endeavors had roots in earlier attempts to justify authorship, to educate democratic tastes, and to effect literary market reform.

Finally, it is true that the transcendental enterprises surveyed in this book initially appear to be what one might term "boutique" by virtue of their intransigence, modest sales figures, or limited market share; still, one must not undervalue the importance of such endeavors in antebellum America. While much work has been done on the major commercial enterprises (such as Harper & Brothers in New York or Ticknor and Fields in Boston) that would come to dominate the market by mid-century, relatively little attention has been paid to the smaller, less commercialized entities that were in fact the norm in the period's early decades. This book addresses this critical gap, using Peabody's circle to consider four distinct facets of book history: institutional publishing (Mann), authorship (Hawthorne), book lending and selling (Peabody), and editorship (Fuller). Examining the manner in which these industry facets worked together, it depicts transcendentalist literary enterprise as something more than a set of religious or philosophical inquiries divorced from the material realities of the trade, and demonstrates the way it encompassed a kind of market ethic grappling with the limitations of literary production and dissemination in New England.

In the process, this book seeks to reinvigorate transcendentalist studies by treating Peabody's circle as literary-pedagogical vanguards even as, critically speaking, the transcendentalists themselves have been brought down, by both canonical revisionism and studies in the history of the book, from their centrality in earlier accounts of the literary marketplace.[45] Antebellum readers were, indeed, more likely to come into contact with transcendentalism by accident or in piecemeal than by direct purchase, although the same could be said for many texts in an age when personal exchange, library borrowing, and periodical reprints constituted the fabric of everyday reading.[46] In examining this circle's practices at a time when the "business" of business was not, invariably or inevitably, to maximize profits to stakeholders above all else (a sensibility the transcendentalists excoriated, as Emerson did when he railed in "Self-Reliance" against that "joint-stock company" willing to sacrifice the all-sacred "liberty and culture" of its "shareholder" for the "better securing of his bread to each"), it demonstrates that the transcendentalists, like so many other of what Peabody termed "small dealers," sought to earn a sufficient living commensurate with ethical practice, while simultaneously setting an example for others to follow.[47] In this sense, the transcendental literary reformers in this book are important precisely because they exist as regional manifestations of a larger antebellum phenomenon: the attempt at local, moral, and ethical enterprise that was still the heart of the literary industry even as it wished to project these models upon larger, truly national markets.

CHAPTER 1

Bibliographic Nationalism

Marketing America in Horace Mann's *School Library*

IN THE PREFACE to *The Juvenile Budget Opened* (1840), the first of three volumes on the selected writings of respected English Romantics Anna Laetitia Barbauld and her brother, John Aikin, Sarah Hale explains that the texts were written "for English children. You must, therefore, expect to find the scenes mostly laid in England, and English character and manners described."[1] Paradoxically, these three editions—*The Juvenile Budget Opened, Things by Their Right Names* (1840), and *The Juvenile Budget Reopened* (1840)—are part of *The School Library*, an ambitious, Board of Education–sanctioned series of books meant by Horace Mann, architect of Massachusetts' public school system, for use throughout all of the state's district school libraries. Commenced in 1839, *The School Library* was a self-consciously literary nationalist enterprise aimed at producing the informed, self-disciplined, and uniform citizenry thought necessary for the success of a free nation. In scope, the series would, according to its "Introductory Essay," embrace "every department of Science and Literature," and be rich in "the history of our own Country; in Biography, particularly of distinguished Americans; in Voyages and Travels; in those branches of Natural Philosophy and Natural History, which are most useful," as well as in the much-overlooked "agricultural and mechanical pursuits." Designed as "*reading*, and not *school, class, or text* books," and, thus, intended for the use of "the *whole* community" rather than just one class of children, it featured volumes prepared by such nineteenth-century

American luminaries as Washington Irving, Sarah J. Hale, Catharine Sedgwick, and other "individuals, distinguished for their learning, superior judgment, and moral excellence."[2] (See table 1.1.)

That Hale's editions, including what Sarah Robbins calls one of the more "appropriative" adaptations of Barbauld's work, *Things by Their Right Names*, which contains her contributions to *Evenings at Home* (1792–96), as well as selections from *Lessons for Children* (1778–88) and *Hymns in Prose* (1781), should find its way into *The School Library* suggests the extent to which such English writings were considered some of the period's indispensable "American" texts.[3] Indeed, declaring that, in her volumes, readers will find "a table to show you the value of English money, compared with that of our own country" (*Juvenile Budget*, 8), Hale suggests that she edits the work in the hopes of translating English worth into American economic and moral value. Hale, the editor of *Godey's Lady's Book*, one of the most popular woman's magazines in the United States, built her career on the arrangement of other writers' work. Her selection of texts for the *School Library* volumes are meant, as she says, to demonstrate "how we Americans differ, in our thoughts and feelings, from the English people" (7), even as she praises their precepts as "particularly suited to our age and country" (4) in both Christian morality and republican sentiment. But these editions are of "value," ultimately, not merely as manifestations of an American literary market that reprinted English authors and encouraged transatlantic piracy, but also as a case study in the intricacies of efforts to teach "American" values through foreign literature.

Not all the library's contents, of course, were foreign in origin; besides new editions of "standard" foreign texts, it included reissued works by respected native authors, as well as original productions by newly home-grown talent.[4] In this regard, incipient government efforts at educational reform provided important opportunities in the development of professional authorship in America, carving out vast new markets for the publishing industry while providing expanded avenues for American authors to disseminate their work. Such efforts demonstrate the extent to which commodity culture was built into educational reform from the start, since the birth of the literary series format itself in the eighteenth century had as much to do with economics as with ideology. In other words, it had as much to do with publisher costs, copyright, and new print technologies as with grandiose efforts to promote a canon of national "classics" that might rival the venerated works of antiquity, or, for Americans, of Europe more generally.[5] Even as the Board of Education disavowed pecuniary motivation, claiming for *The School Library* a "sacred adherence" to the principle of democratic education, economic considerations

Table 1.1

Volume Titles in *The School Library, Adult Series,* and *Juvenile Series*.

The School Library. Adult series.	*The School Library. Juvenile Series.*
Vol. 1. Irving, Washington. *Life of Columbus* (1839)	Vol. 1. Embury, Emma C. *Pictures of Early Life* (1839)
2–3. Bartlett Elisha, M.D. *Paley's Natural Theology* (1839)	2. Hale, Sarah J. *Pleasures of Taste, and Other Stories, Selected from the Writings of Jane Taylor* (1839)
4–6. Sparks, Jared. *Lives of Eminent Individuals, Celebrated in American History* (1839)	3. Sedgwick, Catharine Maria. *Means and Ends; Or Self-Training* (1840)
7–10. Duncan, Rev. Henry, D.D.; Rev. F.W.P. Greenwood, ed; *Sacred Philosophy of the Seasons* (1839)	4. Hale, Sarah J. *The Juvenile Budget Opened; being Selections from the Writings of Dr. John Aikin* (1840)
11–12. Bigelow, Jacob, M.D. *The Useful Arts* (1840)	5. Lee, Mary E. *Social Evenings; Or, Historic Tales for Youth* (1840)
13. Story, Joseph, L.L.D. *A Familiar Exposition of the Constitution of the United States* (1840)	6. Hale, Sarah J. *Things By Their Right Names; selected and arranged from the Writings of Mrs. Barbauld* (1840)
14–15. George Craik; Francis Wayland, D. D., ed; *The Pursuit of Knowledge Under Difficulties* (1840)	7. Marcet, Jane (Haldimand). *Scenes in Nature; Or, Conversations for Children on Land and Water* (1840)
16. Buell, Jesse. *The Farmer's Companion* (1840)	8. Hale, Sarah J. *The Juvenile Budget Re-Opened; Being further Selections from the Writings of Dr. John Aikin* (1840)
17. Lieber, Francis, L.L.D. *Great Events* (1840)	9. Ellet, E.F. *Rambles about the Country* (1840)
18. Phelps, Mrs. Lincoln. *The Fireside Friend; Or, Female Student; being Advice to Young Ladies on the Important Subject of Education* (1840)	10. *The Child's Friend; Being Selections from the Writings of Arnaud Berquin* (1840)
19. Everett, Edward. *The Importance of Practical Education and Useful Knowledge* (1840)	11. Hale, Sarah P. E. *Lives of Columbus and Vespucius* (1840)
20. Olmsted, Denison. *Letters on Astronomy; Addressed to a Lady* (1842)	12. Hale, Sarah P. E. *Lives of Vasco Nunez Balboa, Hernando Cortes, and Francisco Pizarro* (1840)
21. Potter, Alonzo, D. D. *The Principles of Science* (1842)	
22–25. Everett, Alexander, H. *The History of the World* (1840)	
26. Beecher, Catherine. *Treatise on Domestic Economy* (1842)	

were thus inseparable from the shape the series took. The Board insisted that its publisher manufacture "neat" editions as "plainly" and yet "substantially" as possible, producing books affordable enough to achieve the library's democratic purpose (the dissemination of print to what Mann called those "broad wastes" existing beyond Boston), and yet commensurate with—that is, materially adequate to communicating—the moral worth of the lessons they contained.[6]

What makes *The School Library* worth investigating, therefore, is the way in which, as both a self-consciously nationalist enterprise and a literary commodity competing within a market that was transatlantic in scope, it articulates what its architects understand as an "American" social sense that cannot be divorced from the material and economic conditions from which it springs. Building upon what Meredith McGill describes as "the many insights that can be gleaned from an analysis of the formats in which antebellum literature appeared," this chapter examines *The School Library* inside and out, attending to its advertisements, contents, and production values to consider how its editions articulate "Americanness" as a specific kind of moral spectacle within the antebellum marketplace.[7] In this regard, the materiality of the editions— what it meant for consumers to have such "respectable," as the library's architects termed them, objects in their hands—mattered to both the economic and social aims of the enterprise because *The School Library* quite literally sought to manufacture national character through exceptionally produced, widely disseminated editions. Through this spectacle, the volumes ultimately enact what I term "bibliographic nationalism," embodying a desire to cultivate national markets for literary texts, combined with the moral enterprise of nationalism amid anxieties of foreign influence.

Schools, Authors, and Economics

The School Library had its origins in an 1837 Massachusetts state law authorizing each school district to raise $30 by tax for the purchase of library books.[8] The newly established Board of Education deemed it advisable to leave the preparation of volumes to "the enterprise and judgment of publishers, who would, no doubt, find it for their interest" to satisfy public demand (*First Annual Report*, 14). By placing the onus on the industry, the Board relied upon competition to keep prices down and options plentiful, thereby allowing districts to choose from a variety of books suited to their needs. Few districts, however, availed themselves of the opportunity; within a year, there were still only 50 school libraries in the whole state, 15 of which were located in Boston.[9] The Board speculated that the problem might have been the "difficulty of making the selection" amidst the superabundance of texts and with limited funds (*Second Annual Report,* 19), while Mann surmised that districts struggled to select books because of partisan "jealousy" among residents ("On District School Libraries," 270). In March 1838, therefore, he proposed that the Board sanction its own series, adapted to the needs of the state's common schools and "free from objection on account of partisan opinion in politics, or sectarian views in religion," while still leaving it to districts to select their own books (270).

After consulting with publishers, the Board contracted Marsh, Capen, Lyon, and Webb, of Boston, to produce two series of 50 volumes each: a "*Juvenile series*" intended for children "ten or twelve years of age and under," and a series for more "advanced scholars and their parents" ("Introductory Essay," ix). Marsh et al. estimated they could offer the library to schools in accordance with the Board's demand for "neat editions of books" for approximately $57.50, or a discount of 15 to 20 percent on what they charged for publications of a similar quality.[10] In exchange, they would receive the "privilege of preparing the whole series" and the benefit of "an announcement to the public, that the work had the unanimous sanction or approbation" of the Board (Mann, "District School Libraries," 70–71). The firm could expect a significant competitive advantage from such an endorsement, so much so that one editor complained that, by promoting a single publisher's sales, the Board's sanction amounted to unlawful "censorship of the press" and a "sin" against the "dignity and freedom of letters."[11]

While the Board had expected to vet all manuscripts submitted for the series, it quickly became clear this was not feasible, as Mann intimated when he told historian George Bancroft that he had been so inundated with requests to examine manuscripts "*in esse* or *in posse*" that it "would have occupied the time of each member of the Board more than half of the year" to respond to them all.[12] As Marsh et al. had hoped to make such arrangements with the Board in relation to submissions as would "enable us to go on with publishing without interruption" in business, the firm thus proposed to take the task upon itself, occasionally presenting them with lists of texts they intended to publish, books which, "when completed," would then "be subject to the examination of the Board to be modified or rejected" for their sanction. In other words, they proposed they be allowed to solicit and publish what made the most financial sense to them, while simultaneously consulting with the Board "in reference to proper subjects for the series & proper men to prepare the volumes."[13] Those publications that received the Board's approbation would then be released as a *School Library* edition, with any required emendations.

This model explains the publishers' advertisements for *The School Library*, which often announced editions as forthcoming, "provided they are approved by the Board of Education," and which listed some texts despite Mann's own reservations about them.[14] For example, the publishers' advertisements tout "NEW-ENGLAND HISTORICAL SKETCHES, by N. Hawthorne, *Author of 'Twice Told Tales,' &c.*" as under preparation for the juvenile series despite Mann's well-documented ambivalence toward Hawthorne's writing. The publishers also presented to the Board a list of proposed texts that included a historical volume, "History of the Pilgrims, by a Lady" (the mother of Mann's close friends, the Peabody sisters), which he had declined to advocate personally for fear of appearing partial.[15] The irony, of course, is that, despite its need to appear fastidiously objective in recommendation of texts, when it could not sign desired authors or when it was easier to rely on works from those whose characters were already known, the enterprise relied upon coterie publication practices that characterized much of antebellum print culture.[16]

But while these arrangements alleviated the weight put upon on the Board, Mann could not help feel that, at times, sound business sense might conflict with high-minded educational principle. On one occasion, he was pleased to hear that his friend and fellow reformer, Samuel Gridley Howe, had declined to produce a geography simply because Capen desired it for *The School Library*. Mann confessed that Capen "knows that I look with great anxiety to his success . . . but he must not barter principle for money, nor offer it in the market, nor talk about offering it." Therefore, he applauded Howe's decision to "keep [his] eye on the subject . . . & not compromise the matter by enriching booksellers & impoverishing the cause." It was that base motive, writing for "filthy lucre," as he tells him, that threatened to turn what he called elsewhere the "grandest moral enterprise" ("On District School Libraries," 275) into nothing more than yet another "sordid enterprise" of personal gain masquerading as universal education.[17] Indeed, it was precisely because even the best of booksellers like Capen could, despite their pure intentions, so readily give into mercenary considerations that made the Board's oversight so necessary.

On the whole, however, Mann was pleased with the terms of their arrangement; in superintending *The School Library*, he argued, the Board was rendering the state a service "not only of immeasurable moral and intellectual value," but, with the discount afforded by the agreement, one "capable of being estimated in dollars and cents." He invited detractors to compare the character of his publishers' volumes, both those already issued by them and those on their list of prospective titles, "with a library of the Harpers to learn their cheapness, & it will be seen what the state owes to this Board for its services." Harper & Brothers was a major competitor for school libraries in Massachusetts, but, since their enterprise was, as Mann termed it, "got up under their own impulse of money-making," he believed it to be inferior in both quality of production and rigor of selective principle to his own.[18] It appeared, for example, only in octodecimo (18mo) "pocket" editions, which, as Wesley Harper once described it, were "quite as respectable" but not so "*handsome*" as the admittedly more expensive duodecimo (12mo) format, while *The School Library* was issued in both formats, depending on the series.[19]

Thus, the partnership aimed for the cheapest volumes possible, "bearing in mind," as the publishers put it, "their high intellectual character, and the style of their mechanical execution." Priced at 40 cents and 75 cents each, the volumes were issued in sets of five or ten books at a time to put the library "with in the reach of those Districts, which, from the limited amount of their annual funds, would not otherwise be enabled to procure it," and also to ensure its quality of production. In a dig at Harper & Brothers, which produced its books with startling rapidity, Marsh et al. declared: "It is not the intention of the Publishers to drive these works through the Press with an undue speed, in the hopes of securing the market, by the multiplicity of the publications cast upon the community; they rely for patronage, upon the intrinsic merit of the works."[20] But even at these "reasonable" rates (hardcover books generally ranged from 75 cents to $1.25), the volumes were expensive; at the time, a skilled white male laborer's weekly salary was approximately $6.[21] As the introductory essay's overly sanguine proclamation about modern books—whose "unprecedented cheapness" meant that a "week's labor of a working man, will earn for him, in almost any part of the United States, the price of eight or ten handsome duodecimo volumes"—ironically suggests, books were, in fact, still quite costly ("Introductory Essay," vii).

Given this continued costliness, Mann felt that district school libraries were needed to counteract what he calls, in his *Third Annual Report*, the "inequality with which the means of knowledge are spread," the "few deep, capacious reservoirs, surrounded by broad wastes" characterizing book distribution in Massachusetts (57). As Ronald Zboray has shown, despite publishers' triumphalism about the democratizing power of modern printing, mechanical advances did not significantly improve the general populace's access to books, or necessitate their equal distribution throughout the countryside.[22] In most regions, book acquisition continued to be difficult, and what libraries the state had did little to alleviate this problem. Mann estimated that "but little more than one hundred thousand persons, or one seventh part of the population of the State," had "any right of access" to its few public libraries.[23] Even in metropolitan Boston, where social libraries constituted almost half of all such holdings in the state, only one-tenth of the city's population had any access to them (*Third Annual Report*, 56). But with schoolhouses as "central points" in "minute subdivisions of territory" no larger than two square miles in size under the district plan, school libraries could offer books at "convenient distances, distributed with great uniformity all over the Commonwealth" (94–95).

Since Massachusetts had over 3,000 such districts, the legislature's authorization of $30 for each district in the first year and $10 thereafter meant the possibility of $90,000 raised in a single year, with $30,000 each subsequent year for the purchase of library books. Additionally, in 1842 the legislature offered $15 to each district that would match the amount themselves—an appropriation of another $90,000 for school libraries. This made the state a profitable market for any publisher who could supply its demand. Harper & Brothers, for one, was interested in establishing its *School District Library* (published starting in 1838) there, "taking hold of the enterprise with great spirit," as one of its agents said, in the hopes of seeing its library "scattered, all over the land." The firm had previously negotiated for the Board's sanction, promising to take from their share of the profits "a discount to the trade . . . to make it the interest of all the Booksellers in the Union, to circulate the Library"; although the Board settled on a local firm, still, Harper & Brothers hoped it would "be willing to give some recommendation of our selection" even if "they choose to go on alone."[24]

It was precisely this sort of profitability that could make for headaches when dealing with booksellers. Much has been made of the Mann-Packard controversy already, but, given the stakes involved in the markets fostered by institutions like the Board of Education, such sensational attacks were not at all uncommon.[25] Mann often complained about harassment by "book-makers & sellers, copy-right owners & agents" who self-interestedly railed against the Board whenever it threatened their financial prospects. Indeed, he waggishly proclaimed to have "known a book-maker seek anxiously to learn the opinions of the Board of Education respecting his book, in order to qualify himself to decide upon the expediency of its having been established."[26] Similarly, Michigan's first superintendent of public education, John D. Pierce, wrote to Mann in late 1839, describing his own experiences with the "book-making interest" in the state. After Michigan adopted the district school library model, Pierce was attacked by an "astonishingly sensitive" book-selling faction "sure to be down upon the man who is so unfortunate as not to appease every worthless thing, that it may offer to the public in the form of a school book." In one instance, he was assaulted in an anonymous handbill, which conferred upon him a "shower of abusive epithets," including charges of "ignorance," "partiality," and "intentional misrepresentation." It was written, he surmised, either by an author whose work he had critiqued or by someone "deeply interested in the sale of the book." Michigan, Pierce notes, had organized "about 2000 districts" in the last three years, surely a consideration in the vehemence of the attacks.[27]

Mann's complaints about "book-makers" also extended to his dealings with authors, who seemed always to place financial concerns on par with his sacred cause. But while publishers stood to make huge profits by such enterprises, authors often did not; industry practices conspired to keep them relatively poorly paid. For his part, Mann demanded the best and most celebrated authors for this series, and yet, as Richard Henry Dana Jr. records contemptuously in his journal, he preferred that their compensation be "small," that they content themselves with little more than what "approbation" the Board might offer as recompense. Of course, authorial responses to pay varied by the individual, and were often relative to the labor put into a text. Hawthorne, for instance, confessed to Longfellow that he meant to "turn [his] attention to writing for children" and "the series of works projected by the Board of Education" because, it appeared to him, "there is a very fair chance of profit." Similarly, Sarah P. E. Hale felt "quite repaid" by the earnings for her children's books, and she happily received $142.50 for the two modest-length volumes on the lives of colonial explorers in America she wrote for *The School Library*, claiming the arrangement had "turned out better than [she] expected." One particularly irate author, however, complained to Mann that the $500 premium offered for the outright copyright to his educational treatise "would *not* pay a common laborer's wages for the time expended in preparing myself for it."[28]

Even Catharine Maria Sedgwick, whom Mann greatly admired, was not above financial considerations.[29] When Marsh et al. wrote to inquire whether she would contribute a volume to the series, promising to "pay a premium" to publish it even in the event that it did not receive the Board's sanction, her brother Charles wrote to Mann. Professing that his sister had a schoolbook "designed for girls," *Means and Ends; Or, Self-Training* (1839), he also admitted that she desired the Board's sanction because it would "increase the circulation, & she trusts [the book's] usefulness." But even as he assured Mann of his sister's "sympathy" with and "clear . . . sense of the principle" of his cause, Charles lamented, "I need not tell you what is within the experience of every author that it is difficult to avoid in any contract with a Bookseller a very unequal division of profits & labor." In the letter's postscript, Sedgwick herself agreed with this assessment, telling Mann she did "not wish to publish it in a way to obstruct its introduction with other district libraries."[30] While she was eager for inclusion, in other words, she desired no arrangement that would preclude her from releasing other editions of the book, and thus from maximizing not only its "circulation" and "usefulness," but also her own profits.

One of the region's most celebrated poets, Longfellow had declined to contribute to the library series because it was not, in his estimation, profitable enough. Having conversed with Webb, he informed a friend that a volume for the adult series would have an initial run "of 1500 copies; giving . . . ten percent on the retail price of all published, in semi-annual payments, beginning six months after publication," or, as he put it, "$112.00 & no more." Despite this dismissal (he also calls the pay "very small," and asserts that he had "declined to have anything to do with" the series "on such terms"), ten percent was as good a rate as most writers could expect, and the arrangement had the benefit, as he admits, of carrying "no risk" to the author—more than can be said of many contracts signed at the time.[31] But since a writer of his reputation (and business acumen) might command more advantageous terms, the publishers would have to do better to secure his talent.[32] Longfellow's rejection of what he considered an amateur's salary therefore suggests an incontrovertible economic reality shaping the library; rather than signing only the "most popular and talented authors in this country," Mann might have to settle for the best he could afford ("District School Libraries," 71).

But even as Longfellow denigrated its financial returns, he pointed to a major benefit of writing for the library: the cultural capital to be gained. He informs his friend that, in contributing to the series, an author might have his or her "name carried into every village in New England, & it will grow up with the rising generation."[33] Although this did not entice Longfellow, possibly because he was on his way to becoming a household name, the admiration of the rising generation was a powerful incentive for equally notable writers such as Washington Irving. When approached, Irving offered an abridgment of his *Life and Voyages of Columbus*, remarking upon the opportunities he was willing to pass up in introducing it into the library: "In publishing in your series I lose my chance of making a sale of the work in England, and for this very work, which was written for Murray's Family Library."[34] Similarly, George Bancroft wrote to Mann, confessing "very much" his "desire" to bring his *History of the United States* "within the reach of the Common Schools of Massachusetts by gaining for it a place in the Common School Libraries." So much, in fact, did he relish the prospect that he was "willing to forgo in a great measure" compensation from the work's copyright if that might be a means to his inclusion.[35] Indeed, the potential for the social dissemination of a library volume was great; in 1838, Mann estimated the state had approximately 165,000 schoolchildren (*First Annual Report*, 37). If one considers the families who might also use these libraries, then there was the potential for hundreds of thousands of patrons. *The School Library* would also reach a captive audience, since, for many residents, it would be their *only* access to books; Mann reported that there were at least 100 towns, or a third of the towns in the state, with no other public libraries at all (*Third Annual Report*, 57).

Furthermore, a well-produced school library might find its way into multiple markets, like Harper & Brothers' own New York, or Michigan, Connecticut, Rhode Island, Iowa, and Indiana, all of which began organizing district school libraries in the late 1830s and 1840s.[36] This prospect did not escape the backers of *The School Library*. Remarking upon the "general merit of each volume" in its library, the "Introductory Essay" claims that it "cannot but anticipate . . . a demand coextensive with the void to be filled," that is, "the whole number of school districts in this, and a fair portion of the districts in the neighboring States" (x). The "neighboring state" of New York alone had close to eleven thousand school districts, all of which were to be supplied with libraries under recently passed legislation. The "Introductory Essay" thus crows that New York had allotted a generous apportionment of "*One hundred and ten thousand dollars,* each year" for the purpose (viii; emphasis in original), and, as if transfixed by the possibilities of the enterprise on which the Board had embarked, it reiterates the "munificent appropriation" of "two thirds of a million dollars, within six years" to be paid out for "probably nearly a million and a half volumes" (x). A notice for *The School Library* in *The Christian Examiner* also identifies Ohio, which, along with New York, comprised "about one-fourth of the population of the Union," as yet another lucrative market, with over eight thousand Districts and "the prospect of a similar appropriation for the same object" as New York.[37] Hence, books for Massachusetts schoolchildren represented a potentially national market.

"Respectable" Publishing

As a joint enterprise undertaken by both the Massachusetts Board of Education and the private publishing firm of Marsh, Capen, Lyon, and Webb that attempted to reach consumers beyond the Bay State, *The School Library* walked a fine line between recognition of print as spectacle and commitment to values deemed quintessentially "American," such as economy and self-restraint. In other words, its architects hoped to maintain in some small measure the material pleasures of antebellum reading while transferring the object of these pleasures from cheap and, as many saw it, morally questionable productions to the creations of more "respectable" houses, to use the Board's description of their own publisher (*Second Annual Report*, 20). In so doing, the library's "few good books," as Mann called them ("On District School Libraries," 275), sought to produce a spectacle of morality—a bibliographic respectability—not only as a means to sell copies but also as a way to promote a cohesive and homogenous national identity within the carnival of transatlantic print culture.[38]

Patricia Crain has demonstrated that, from their inception, early American educational texts such as primers and alphabet books were ensconced in the sights and sounds of the marketplace, encouraging literacy through pleasurable looking by scavenging from tavern signs, folk rhymes, street slang, and other popular forms of the day, and by turning the alphabet into an "occasion for display." As hybrid forms born of a "new middle class gentility" and the "rough-and-tumble realm of commerce," early American primers and spellers enacted what Crain calls "festive discipline," a tension or melding between an informational, moralizing ethic and the promise of "sensual and emotional pleasures." "Festive discipline" thus registers both the genre's desire to discipline readers, to induct them into strict bourgeois Christian and republican literacies, and its playful residue of the popular and the low not obscured by "genteel revision" or appropriation.[39]

While no one would ever confuse its decorous, genteel character with the "laughing, raucous, and bawdy mischievousness" of early primers, *The School Library* nonetheless articulates its own kind of "festive discipline," harnessing the "pleasurable looking" of the marketplace to produce ideal consumers, both of the book as object and of the printed word as the foundation for the national identity Mann championed.[40] After all, the design of *The School Library*, as its "Introductory Essay" explains, is to "furnish youth with suitable works for perusal during their leisure hours; works that will interest, as well as instruct them; and of such a character that they will turn to them with pleasure, when it is desirable to unbend from the studies of the schoolroom" (xlvi). Devised to fill children's "leisure hours," the library suggests the totalizing scope of common-school reform, testifies to reformers' Romantic emphasis on the joys of childhood, and reveals their discovery of a superior method for the "introjection" of bourgeois discipline.[41] Consequently, the library's method is to "clothe the subjects discussed, in a popular garb, that they may prove so attractive, as to lure the child onwards, fix his attention, and induce him, subsequently, to seek information from other and more recondite works, which, if put into his hands at the onset, would alarm him, and induce a disgust for that which would appear dry and unintelligible, and, of course, uninteresting" (xlvi–xlvii). This description of "luring" children to books that, at first glance, might normally "alarm" them reads like a caricature of what critics saw as popular literature's pernicious influences. But the final clause makes it clear that in marrying "popular" methods to the principles of educational reform, *The School Library* seeks to make normally "dry" pedagogical texts as pleasurable as other forms of reading, and, in this way, to exert control over its readers, "fixing" or "inducing" in them more appropriate kinds of tastes and behaviors.

In keeping with a "festive discipline" that inculcated self-culture in popular apparel, the library's advertisements promote the materiality of the series' volumes, the textual "garb" meant to attract readers through the spectacle of its production. For instance, they emphasize the series' illustrations, as such images were integral to the success of even the most ordinary antebellum print enterprise, as well as to the "text-image festivals" of early educational books.[42] Therefore, when the *North American Review* lauds the "tasteful" portraits, maps, and engravings it calls "numerous" and "ornamental," its reviewer alludes to a visual abundance that the texts' own publishers were quick to trumpet. One advertisement puffs the library's edition of William Paley's *Natural Theology* (1839), the popular treatise evidencing God's design in nature, as "superior to any ever before offered to the public" because it contains, among other improvements, a "Portrait of the Author" and "*ninety-five* beautiful wood-engravings*" (the advertisement puts the number in italics, as if to emphasize its immensity). Yet another advertisement touts the "numerous copperplate engravings" in the library's edition of Jacob Bigelow's *The Useful Arts* (1840), a history of the mechanical and technical arts, and pegs the number of its woodcuts at a lavish one hundred and eighty. In its review of the library, *The Christian Examiner* best describes the intended effect of all these images when it calls the volumes "verily a treat to the eye."[43]

But even as they suggest the library's abundant visual pleasures, these reviews and advertisements counterbalance claims of material delight with appeals to utility serving to marry the ornamental to the informational. "Whenever the subjects render it necessary," one testifies, the volumes "will be amply illustrated by well-executed wood cuts, and copperplate and steel engravings." In claiming its illustrations are "ample" but always "well-executed," the advertisement asserts that the publishers do not sacrifice quality for the sake of quantity, even when they employ woodcuts, the least expensive of available illustration technologies. Furthermore, it proclaims the publishers' restraint by assuring buyers that these embellishments are included only when "necessary," as dictated by the subjects covered rather than by the whim of the publishers.[44] Even the volumes' more ornamental embellishments had their purpose. The publishers advertised Jared Sparks's three-volume abridgment of his *Lives of Eminent Individuals*, hagiographies of colonial and revolutionary New England's founding fathers, as containing not only portraits of the biographies' historical figures but also "autographs of most of the individuals" discussed in them. In this way, the series incorporates as a selling point yet another popular nineteenth-century fad, autograph collecting, as it makes use of handwritten artifacts that were thought to provide important insights into individual character. In other words, the facsimile signatures served to "authorize" the editions, signifying a conflation of self and text that purportedly offered readers authentic access to the moral "character" of these historical persons through their written "character," while simultaneously allowing the publishers competitive advantage over the unauthorized reprints often circulating in the market.[45] (See figure 1.1.)

In this way, the publishers promote yet another dimension of the library's spectacle, what may be termed the expenditures of moral restraint inherent in its production. One circular, for example, emphasizes the monetary costs involved in creating a product of such high caliber, claiming "no expense will be spared to render the series equal, if not superior, to any published in the world."[46] Yet, at the same time, a review in the *Christian Examiner* calls the price of *The School Library* "exceedingly moderate," when one considers the "labor and learning bestowed upon the improvement of these editions, the beauty and durability of the mechanical execution," and the publishers' own advertisements pronounce it "cheaper than any other series of works that can be procured at home or abroad, bearing in mind their high intellectual character, and the style of their mechanical execution."[47] In making a spectacle of the series, publicizing its price and style, these advertisements suggest an excessiveness to its publishers' displays of economic restraint, noting their refusal to pass costs onto consumers in the form of higher prices even as their expenditures ensure the library's "beauty and durability." Given the

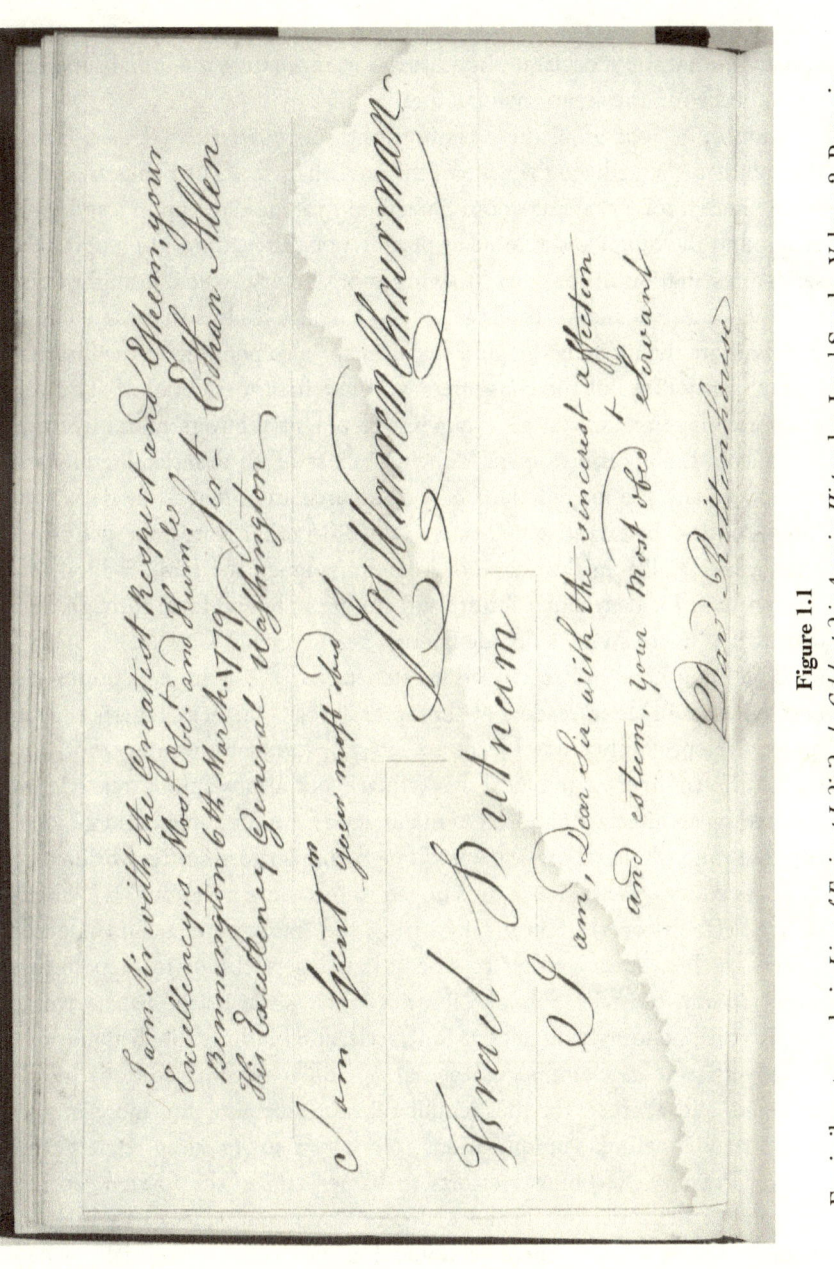

Figure 1.1

Facsimile autographs in *Lives of Eminent Individuals: Celebrated in America History* by Jared Sparks. Volume 2. Page xiv. Boston: Marsh, Lyon, Capen, and Webb, 1839. Courtesy of the Massachusetts Historical Society.

publishers' hyperbolic claims about their expenditures ("no expense will be spared") and the library's affordability ("cheaper" than any other "at home or abroad"), what these declarations advertise is, ultimately, the moral superiority embodied in the series' manufacture.

Indeed, in light of all these features, the *North American Review* claims the volumes "do credit to the taste of the publishers. . . . The books are handsome enough for a drawing-room library, and yet are done up in a style well adapted to the rough and tumble of promiscuous circulation." In judging the series' presentation fit for one's "drawing-room library," where it might strike the eyes of guests and visitors, the reviewer makes it clear that the volumes display more than merely the publishers' "taste," also pointing to the discriminating sensibilities of the consumers who purchase these books.[48] The volumes are, therefore, meant as testaments to potential buyers' moral worth as much as to the publishers' own, "done up in a style" fit to resist, literally and metaphorically, the degradations of a mass circulation that is, by definition, "promiscuous," or excessive and unrestrained. In other words, the publishers offer respectability in the shape of a book, in much the same fashion that Ticknor and Fields would sell taste and culture in bound form through their distinctive "house styles" a decade later.[49] (See figure 1.2.)

The publishers' and reviewers' insistence that the series constituted the best value available to readers at "home or abroad" further suggests that its material respectability was meant to act as a form of advantage not only within the confines of the local marketplace, but also within a transatlantic context; its architects attempted to manufacture a respectable national identity that might hold its own against foreign competitors on the world stage. *The School Library*'s architects thus hoped to introduce a thoroughly "Americanized" (their term) literature by hiring the "most popular and talented writers in this country, either to re-edit existing works, or to prepare new ones" (Mann, "District School Libraries," 71), while its publishers would supply correspondingly distinctive font, style, and bindings. Such alterations, the advertisements claim, signaled that not only were the editions "newly arranged, and adapted for the School Library" but also, and more importantly, they contained "modifications to adapt it to *American* readers" (my italics). Praising the library's efforts to "Americanize" the foreign reprints included in the series, for instance, one reviewer pronounces its edition of *Natural Theology* not a "mere republication" but rather "essentially a new work," a "decided improvement" on the "recent English edition" used as its "foundation," just as the United States itself was thought a refinement of its English antecedent.[50]

Figure 1.2
"Plainly" and "substantially" bound volumes of *The School Library. Adult Series*.
Courtesy of the Massachusetts Historical Society.

Bibliographic Nationalism

Meredith McGill's seminal study charting the development of a distinct national literature through the wide dissemination of cheap, often unauthorized reprints, what she calls an antebellum American "culture of reprinting" that claimed to foster democratic values through "*republic*ation," is a useful reference point for understanding the foreign texts included in *The School Library*. As McGill observes, the traditional, author-centered "nationalist framework" of American literary criticism has tended to dismiss reprints in its search for "signs of an original, national difference" in literary productions. This emphasis, however, obscures the centrality of publishers, publishing formats, and distribution methods to antebellum literature, and too often overlooks "the ways in which foreign literature is repackaged and redeployed" by the practice of reprinting. To a degree, then, *The School Library* should be understood as cultivating national identity through similar practices, appropriating popular English texts long circulating in America. In particular, an edition such as Sarah J. Hale's *Things by Their Right Names* demonstrates that foreign reprints were "not passive vehicles for the dissemination of European culture," but rather were "sophisticated instrument[s] for projecting an image of a nation that is at once colonial and imperial."[51]

The volume's title page suggests these dual impulses. In one sense, Hale assumes the mantle of her English foremother's literary reputation, depending upon Barbauld's international celebrity as both an author and an editor to enhance her own reputation as a woman of letters at home.[52] She makes such a gesture in her edition's preface: "There is no need of commending this Volume to the attention of the reader, or the approbation of the public. The name of Mrs. Barbauld will be a sufficient guarantee of the worth of the selection."[53] But if Barbauld's name is "sufficient" to ensure the "worth" of her editor's selections, in the act of declaring this, the preface nonetheless "commends" the worth of "*this* Volume" (my italics), thereby calling the "attention of the reader" to the material text edited by Hale (in contrast to the innumerable other editions of Barbauld's work available in the United States). Indeed, the title page privileges Hale's editorial role and suggests the edition's distinction from other volumes on the basis of its literary nationalism. Even as Hale's editing depends on Barbauld's reputation, in other words, the title page simultaneously positions Hale as the ultimate arbiter of Barbauld's worth on this side of the Atlantic. It indicates that these writings have been "Selected and Arranged," adapted for American readers by Hale, whom the title also takes pains to point out is a resident expert of sorts on the matter, having penned "Sketches of American Character." (See figure 1.3.)

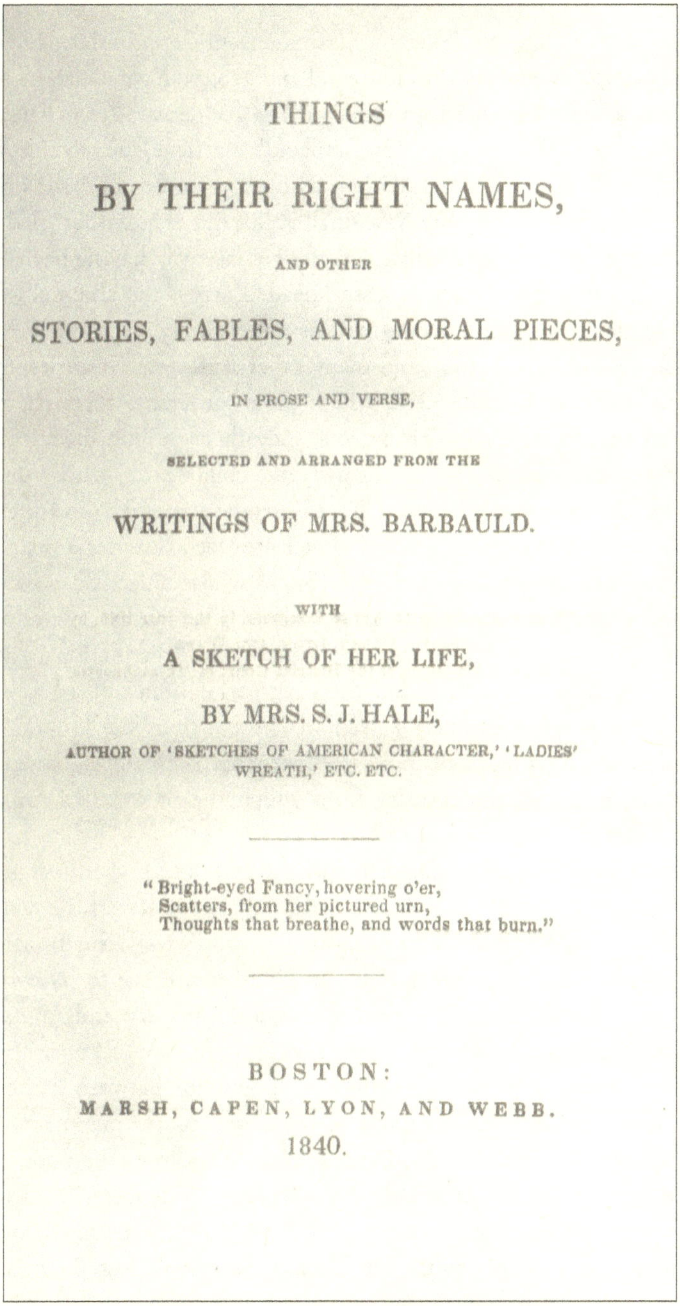

THINGS

BY THEIR RIGHT NAMES,

AND OTHER

STORIES, FABLES, AND MORAL PIECES,

IN PROSE AND VERSE,

SELECTED AND ARRANGED FROM THE

WRITINGS OF MRS. BARBAULD.

WITH

A SKETCH OF HER LIFE,

BY MRS. S. J. HALE,

AUTHOR OF 'SKETCHES OF AMERICAN CHARACTER,' 'LADIES' WREATH,' ETC. ETC.

"Bright-eyed Fancy, hovering o'er,
Scatters, from her pictured urn,
Thoughts that breathe, and words that burn."

BOSTON:
MARSH, CAPEN, LYON, AND WEBB.
1840.

Figure 1.3
Title Page for Sarah J. Hale's *Things by Their Right Names, and Other Stories, Fables, and Moral Pieces*. Page 1. Boston: Marsh, Capen, Lyon, and Webb, 1840. Courtesy of Special Collections, Monroe C. Gutman Library, Harvard Graduate School of Education.

Similarly, Hale's new "Sketch of Barbauld's life" appropriates biographical details to provide readers with temporal and geographical contrasts on which to found a sense of American national identity derived from England. For instance, when Hale remarks upon Barbauld's marriage, she recounts the story of Barbauld's husband's grandfather, who experienced religious oppression because he was a Protestant. As a small child, the grandfather "fled to England during the persecutions of Louis the Fourteenth," having been "enclosed in a cask, and put on board a vessel" headed across the channel (*Things by Their Right Names,* 11). Recounting this removal, Hale opines: "People were not then allowed, in France, and many other European countries, to choose the mode of worshipping God, which their conscience dictated; and even children were taken from their parents, and otherwise punished, if they were thought to be heretics. We, in our own free country, can hardly understand how such things were allowed" (11). In juxtaposing "then" and there (eighteenth-century "France, and many other European countries") with here and now (the "free country" of the United States whose citizens can barely comprehend a time when such abuses "were allowed"), Hale articulates what was, by the mid-nineteenth century, a hoary rhetorical distinction between the feudal prejudices of Europe and the progressive values of a "New World" that cherishes religious liberty. Even so, she positions the United States as extension and apotheosis of those freedoms that Barbauld's grandfather had sought in England, the country from which the nation had since gained independence.

But the cultural contrasts posited by the book's textual editors go beyond conventional formulations to assertions about the "matter of the text," in this instance how the edition's reprinting of Barbauld's work functions to signal its "Americanness" to readers. Self-consciously pointing to its own textual materiality as a distinguishing feature between European and American cultures, the edition includes the story "The Manufacture of Paper," from Barbauld's *Evenings at Home.* It describes a conversation between Father and his son, Henry, about a "delicate and beautiful substance" manufactured from "the meanest and most disgusting materials," rags from the poor, "carefully picked from dunghills, or bought from servants by Jews" (71). In what one might term a moment of "bibliographic nationalism," the sketch commences with a peculiar footnote by the series' editor, Joseph W. Ingraham, informing readers about the differences in the two cultures' paper-production practices: "The manner of procuring the rags for the manufacture of paper, described in this dialogue, is not the same in America as in Europe. Here, in America, we have no persons so very poor as to be obliged to wear old rags for clothing. Nor are there any Jews, who go about to pick up rags to sell. We should be thankful, that we live in a country where none need be so very poor" (71). Articulating a self-delusion not uncommon to nineteenth-century American expressions of patriotism, Ingraham thus claims that the United States, as embodied in its paper-making industries, had grown beyond the kinds of economic and racial exploitation that still characterize European society, that its paper is not "so very poor" as Europe's precisely because superior cultural practices are reflected in that paper's production.

Similarly, in an editor's note at the end of the sketch, Ingraham informs the reader that "almost an entire revolution has taken place" in paper making since the initial publication of Barbauld's story (76). The "revolution" he evokes is not just technological, involving the mechanization of paper making in the first few decades of the nineteenth century, but also sociopolitical; it indicates the country's break from Europe, embodied in its move away from the traditional source of paper fiber, linen rags, to a more "American" fiber source, cotton, processed through modern innovations envisioned as progress, or an American "revolution" in the old ways. After the invention of the cotton gin in 1793, cotton slowly began to replace linen in the West as the most common source of paper fiber, and, by the 1840s, it accounted for 65 percent of the fiber content in books.[54] While Ingraham thus denies the existence of poverty and exploitation in America and elevates American manufactures as a reflection of superior national character, Ingraham overlooks the fact that the paper and book industries thrived in large part thanks to the fruit of southern slave labor and the products of that peculiarly American institution, chattel race slavery. This omission subversively points to what is another, if unintended, feature of American culture and character: an often unfounded exceptionalism that, like the texts it appropriated and the transatlantic publishing practices it reproduced, had little to separate it from Europe beyond a gnawing national anxiety of influence.

But even as Ingraham's similarly problematic and anti-Semitic comments about European Jews—"Here, in America . . . nor are there any Jews, who go about to pick up rags"—suggest the nativism inherent in his praise of U.S. paper making, the practice of importing, reprinting, disseminating, and consuming texts by English authors about English life constitutes a kind of "Anglophilia" that, at first glance, appears at odds with a sensibility predicated on America's separation from Europe. Yet Elisa Tamarkin has argued that U.S. nationalism "works every bit as seriously at bringing some aspects of the outside in, as it does at keeping others out," and that, consequently, "Americans adore England as part of their national character."[55] Anglophilia and anti-Semitism, therefore, are not contradictory impulses, but acts of "bringing in" and "keeping out" consonant with the promotion of Anglo-American identity derived from both white racial and English cultural roots even as it comes to constitute a unique national character. The publication of books such as *Things by Their Right Names,* whose title purports to distinguish between nations even as its appropriation of Barbauld's similarly titled story aligns the two cultures, can be read as part of a practice by which, as Tamarkin describes it, Americans evinced nostalgia for the stability of English cultural forms amidst the threat of democratic political and social diversity, and as the basis of a new patriotism that grew as England's own power over America diminished.[56] In this moment, then, the editor's anti-Semitism mediates the relationship between Anglophilia and nativism; the Jew becomes a symbol of an ethnically and racially diverse Europe whose predatory social practices the United States rejects. As an expression of nativist angst at the waves of unwanted European immigrants flooding the United States in the antebellum decades, the footnote thus construes a homogenous Anglo-American citizenry as a moral imperative necessary for the production of an egalitarian society, one unaffiliated with Europe's diverse peoples and fractured identities, as well as the exploitative practices resulting from exchange between races.

A fierce advocate for precisely this sort of cohesive national identity, Mann himself often complained about the dangers of schoolbooks appearing in all "sizes, types, [and] mechanical execution," his reasons for seeking uniformity going "deeper" than problems with "workmanship" ("District School Libraries," 68) to ideological fears about the enervating effects of cultural pluralism. Taking as its premise what it calls the "evil of diversity" aggravated by the wide assortment of books in use from district to district, Mann's discussion of "Books" in his *Fourth Annual Report* suggests that uniformity is "so important" precisely because without it "a school loses its collective character, and becomes a promiscuous company of individuals" (*Fourth Annual Report,* 63, 61). Hence Mann hopes his district school library will spread moral conformity to the heterogeneous masses beyond the schoolroom proper, since these individuals would otherwise have an atomizing and alienating influence on the new nation, rending its moral fabric at a most precarious moment in its existence. The description of uniformly produced schoolbooks encouraging a "collective character" in readers further explains his demand for plain and substantial library volumes, designed as they were not simply to resist but also to transform the "promiscuous circulation" of mass literary dissemination. Unlike other institutions that tended, as Mann says in an editorial, to reflect the growing "spirit of party" infecting the nation, the common school and its organs such as the district school library are an "antidote" to the fractious diversity of American life. Ultimately, only these institutions are "capacious enough to receive and cherish in [their] parental bosom every child that comes into the world."[57] (See figure 1.4.)

The imperial dimensions of *The School Library*, as it promoted moral and cultural homogeny by seeking to assimilate into its bosom every child, is registered in its *Juvenile Series'* frontispiece. Appearing below the series title, the engraving depicts three young boys lounging beneath a tree, each absorbed in a book. In this manner, the image performs the advertisements' and the introductory essay's insistence that the work of the library is beyond the classroom, being composed of "*reading*, and not *school*" books for those times when it is "desirable" for children to "unbend" from the schoolhouse ("Introductory Essay," xlvi). But "unbend" is precisely what the books are designed not to allow the boys to do, in so far as such a term implies escape from the lessons of the classroom. Rather, the engraving suggests *The School Library*'s domesticating impulse, its hope to mold "the world" outside the classroom in accordance with the ideals of bourgeois literacy.[58] Equally significant is the depiction of the boys' features, their cherubic characters revealing themselves in the iconography of pudgy, half-robed forms common since the Renaissance. In this context, the frontispiece embodies not only the power of reading to mold character for good or ill, but also *The School Library*'s ability to turn the nation's diverse and potentially disruptive masses into the uniform mold of the virtuous little angel. More important still is the racial inflection of this transformation, since, as the engraving suggests, the Americans for whom the library is produced will be transformed into a reflection of whiteness, constructed as a universal standard of moral and intellectual worth. (See figure 1.5.)

In delineating *The School Library*'s racial project, I do not mean to obscure the complexities of Mann's politics, either his commitment to causes such as abolition (which he would champion in full force when elected to the U.S. House of Representatives in 1848), or his moral fortitude in resisting practices such as school segregation while Secretary of Education. For instance, when a young African-American woman named Chloe Lee enrolled in the West Newton Normal School in 1847 but then could not find any one among the community willing to provide a black student with room and board, Mann and his wife took her into their own home.[59] Rather, *Things by Their Right Names*, and series to which it belongs, reveals the way in which Mann's efforts to standardize education for local and national markets and to

Figure 1.4
"Plainly" and "substantially" bound volumes of *The School Library. Juvenile Series.*
Courtesy of Special Collections, Monroe C. Gutman Library, Harvard Graduate School of Education.

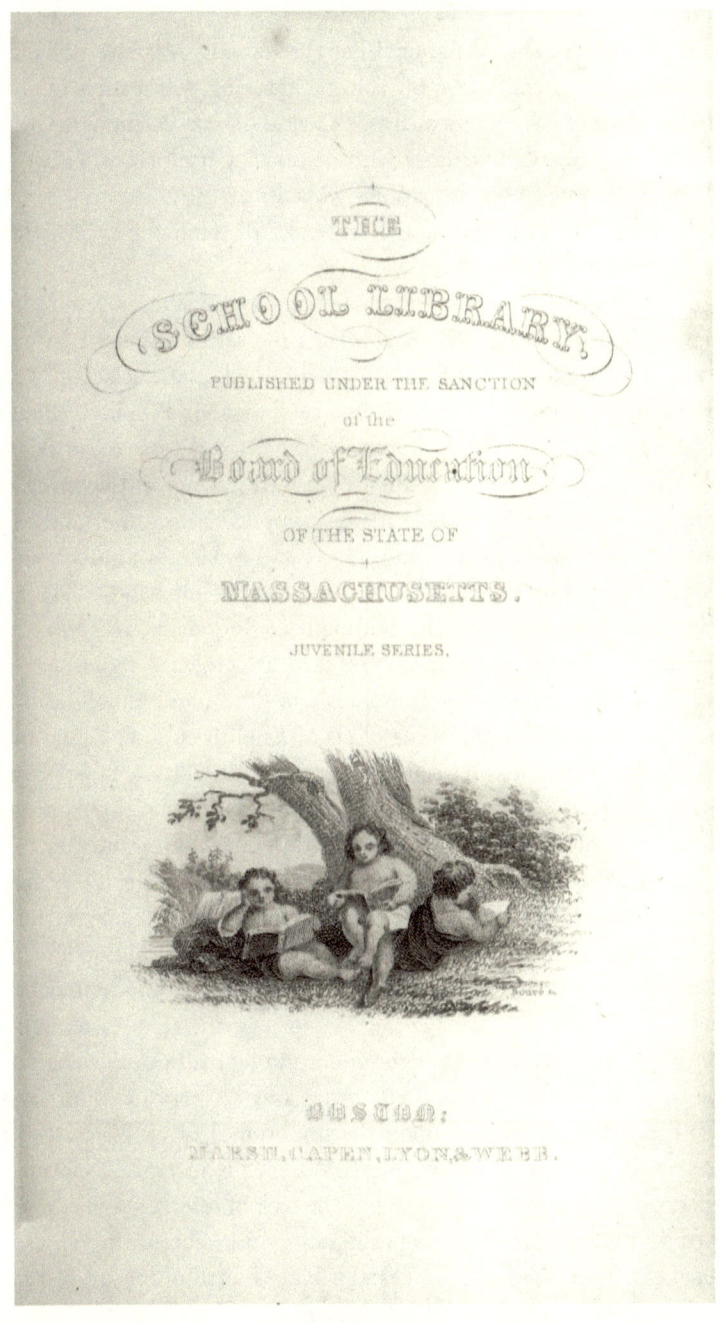

Figure 1.5
Frontispiece for *The School Library. Juvenile Series*, in Sarah J. Hale's *Things by their Right Names*. Boston: Marsh, Capen, Lyon, and Webb, 1840. Courtesy of Special Collections, Monroe C. Gutman Library, Harvard Graduate School of Education.

cultivate a sense of shared national heritage among a diverse populace produces a troubling racialization of "culture" ensuring that readers of all stripes "learn to be white." Simultaneously, *The School Library* encourages the conflation of supposedly white culture with democracy itself since, in its material production, it aimed both to capture what its architects saw as the nation's egalitarian spirit and to encourage its books' dissemination throughout the ranks of American society.[60]

One of Barbauld's sketches, titled "On Manufactures," reproduced in *Things by Their Right Names*, encapsulates the series' impulses. In it, Henry asks his father the meaning of the aforementioned term, declaring: "I remember, the other day, at dinner, a gentleman said, that Mr. Pica had *manufactured* a large volume, in less than a fortnight" (*Things by their Right Names*, 40; emphasis in original). Henry's father replies: "It was meant to convey a satirical remark on his book, because it was compiled from other authors, from whom he had taken a page in one place, and a page in another; so that it was not produced by the labor of his brain, but of his hands" (41). Selected by Hale and presented without comment by Ingraham in *Things by Their Right Names*, this exchange might be read as a meta-commentary on *The School Library*'s efforts to self-consciously, willfully, and literally produce an "American" identity out of the materials of English culture. While Barbauld satirically lampoons the piratical habits of English editors, Hale's reprinting of Barbauld's stories redeploys such moments for nationalist purposes. In the process, her editions suggest that the creation of American literary culture is not so much the unique production of authors' "brains," or their "genius" as Father calls it earlier in the story, as of the skilled "hands" of democratic publishers and editors who compile texts for the sake of an Anglophone nation.

Precisely because a text's material production was thought not only to reflect the moral worth of its contents and its purchasers' taste, but also to "*create* one's character, inculcating or undermining culture and virtue in accordance with [its] moral and aesthetic properties," American editors and publishers commonly declaimed upon the importance of well-produced books, even as they engaged in reprinting.[61] When, for instance, Nahum Capen complained to Congress in 1844 about the lack of international copyright, he warned that the careless reprints proliferating in its absence stood to degrade national character. Without the "responsible ownership" encouraged by copyright, books were "reprinted on poor paper, small type, and put into binding that rather serves to hide their blurred pages, than to protect fair ones; and thus millions of volumes of standard works are produced and sold, which serve but to weaken the eyes of the people, or to refill the vat of the papermaker."⁶² In a business whose products both reflected and determined the state of American character, a book's materiality therefore could affect not only a citizen's intellectual penetration, his or her ability to "see" what the book is about, but also, and quite literally, a citizen's physical health as well.

If the Board and its publisher hoped *The School Library* might combat the enervating influences of poorly produced literature, conversely, Mann also confronted the perils of lavish productions. In his *Third Report*, Mann describes the typical contents of household libraries, suggesting that danger in reading rests less with the laborer who could afford few books beyond a family Bible, than with those of more abundant means. While one might find "really useful and instructive books" in some wealthy households, in too many others, "where wealth is, unfortunately, united with a love of display," one undoubtedly found questionable material, such as "elegantly-bound Annuals, and novels of a recent emission" (120–21). Mann's feelings on fiction are well documented—he called it a medium for "unchastened imaginations and perverted morals" ("On District School Libraries," 295)—but I am interested in the way he characterizes the materiality of "Annuals," those sumptuously produced holiday gift-books exchanged as tokens between friends or loved ones. Rather than chastising annuals for their fictional contents, however, he excoriates them for elegant bindings and costly appearances. Conflating this elegance with ephemerality, he then classes annuals with novels whose primary sin is their "recent emission," the fact that they are not enduring. Indeed, the problem with annuals was that the genre itself was annual rather than perennial. Their contents changing from year to year, annuals thus enshrined novelty in precious packaging rather than protecting time-tested works of literature. That they functioned within an economy of sentimental exchange obscuring their commercial nature only made matters worse. Although thought uplifting in function, annuals served little purpose, Mann suggests, beyond sensual gratification, their expense testifying merely to their purchaser's or owner's lavish tastes. With retail prices ranging from $3 to $15, they were as much signs of affluence as of affection; one historian characterizes their cost as a "constant reminder of their exclusive character. Not many a brother, husband, or lover could afford to pay at least $3 for a little book."⁶³

At least one of *The School Library*'s contributors shared these concerns about luxury and reading. Published as the juvenile series' first volume, Emma Embury's *Pictures of Early Life* (1839) is, like Barbauld's work, a "domestic literacy narrative," a collection of stories about mothers teaching their children to read, in which literacy is understood as a "set of ideologically charged social practices" enabling children to decode texts in such a way as to reinforce proper values and behaviors.[64] In "A Day's Pleasure" (the second story in the collection), a girl named Mary Herbert eagerly visits her mother's affluent friend and her two daughters, Sarah and Elizabeth Ellison, only to learn an important lesson about the disappointments of wealth and privilege. Embury signals Mary's developing literacy in not only her taste for reading—one of the first things she asks the girls to see is their books—but also in her ability to read books by their covers, correctly discerning the moral and social significance of texts in their material appearances. As if Embury were channeling Mann's disdain for the private libraries of the wealthy, Mary finds in the rich girls' drawing room a "marble table covered with annuals and prints," which, to her great dismay, are "all so costly and magnificent, that she feared to touch them."[65] In this way, Mary, whose middle-class upbringing offers the "*comforts*, but very few of the *luxuries*, of life" (33; emphasis in original), and whose chaste sensibilities thus match her family's moderate means, recoils from a "display of wealth" (33) so similar to that "love of display" Mann deplores in the annuals littering the libraries of wealthy households.

Making explicit what he only hints at in his *Third Report*, the description of the Ellisons' annuals calls attention to opulence considered un-American; the story associates such extremes of wealth with a foreign social order unsuited to the more equitable distribution characterizing life in the United States. When Mary first arrives at Mrs. Ellison's estate, for example, she compares the family's "luxury" to a "scene of enchantment" right out of the Orient, involuntarily juxtaposing their mansion's splendor with "the palace raised by Aladdin's lamp" (33). Like Ingraham in "The Manufacture of Paper," the story invokes a contrast between Europe and America, here rooted in the families' different material circumstances. Mrs. Herbert and Mrs. Ellison grew up together, but "their course through life had been so different" that they now only "rarely exchanged visits" (33), and their daughters follow similarly divergent paths. Their family's riches increasing "almost daily" (33), Sarah and Elizabeth receive a continental education; "brought up, from infancy, by a Swiss nurse," educated "under a French governess," and molded into "perfect miniatures of women of fashion," even their "dress, their manners, their very accent were foreign," so much so that "no one would have ever suspected them of being American children" (34). While they express "contempt" (35) for Mary's traveling dress, Embury clearly positions their appearance as inferior to the protagonist's garb, despite their scorn: their "silk dresses, embroidered pantalettes seemed quite disgraced by her neat muslin dress and plain apron; and [Mary] wished herself home again" (34). Although Mary feels embarrassment at the sight of her clothing, being "quite mortified" to see it reflected in a "full length dressing-glass" next to her "fashionable little friends" (34), the phrase also condemns the Ellison girls' moral character, suggesting their inferiority next to Mary's more homely, and thus American, virtues.

A variation on the "plain" and "substantial" bindings of *The School Library* itself, the contrast between Mary's "neat" and "plain" attire and the Ellison girls' excesses is also manifest in the two families' divergent pedagogical practices, embodied in their selection of schoolbooks. After leaving the annual-strewn table, Mary asks to see their books, and

> immediately a quantity of richly bound volumes, containing Conversations on Botany, Dialogues on Political Economy, Elements of Geography, Diversions in Chemistry, etc. were put into her hands. Mary had been carefully instructed by her mother in all those branches, which a child of twelve years of age might be supposed capable of advantageously acquiring; but her new friends, although of an equal age, had been subjected to the hotbed process of a more fashionable education, and a smattering of every kind of knowledge had been made to serve the purposes of more useful information. Mary was abashed at her own inferiority; and after an ineffectual attempt to understand their philosophical books, relinquished all hope of deriving amusement from their library. (35)

As with the girls' clothes, Embury attacks the "fashionable" education these books represent. When Mary rejects the volumes, relinquishing "all hope" of finding "amusement" in them, she enacts what *The School Library*'s architects had warned was the child's response to dry and incomprehensible texts not designed for his or her use. While Mary's own studies are no less varied, ranging from geography to arithmetic to lessons in domestic economy (27), what distinguishes her education is her mother's method: Mrs. Herbert "carefully" instructs her daughter in only the most "useful information" necessary to her "moral education" (28). Unlike Mrs. Herbert's judicious selection of reading material, adapted to her twelve-year-old daughter's moral development, Mrs. Ellison's "smattering" is the product of an indiscriminate diffusion of knowledge that Embury fears might be as damaging as no diffusion at all. In contrasting the two familes' practices, therefore, Embury collapses the materiality of the girls' "richly bound volumes" with their mother's lax pedagogical principles, their library embodying a material and moral excess that inculcates extravagance in the girls rather than self-discipline. Ultimately, Embury positions the library as an un-American one, suggesting that it serves only to encourage social divisions (producing in Mary, for example, a mistaken sense of her own "inferiority" compared with the Ellison girls) rather than the sort of homogenous cultural identity the nation badly needed to assert its superiority on the world stage. What the Ellison girls require, in other words, is not a "hotbed" of "fashionable" texts or pedagogies imported from abroad, but rather the thoroughly "American" values embodied in the well-adapted and yet sensibly produced volumes of *The School Library* itself, including Embury's own text, since it first appeared in that series.

Conclusion: "Grandest Moral Enterprise"

In a journal entry for 14 September 1841, Horace Mann records a conversation with two gentlemen of Lowell, superintendents of some "of the larger establishments in that city," as he drummed up support for his proposed educational reforms. "My object," he tells them, "is to show that education has a market value; that it is so far an article of merchandise, that it may be turned to a pecuniary account; it may be minted and will yield a larger amount of statutable coin than common bullion. It has a pecuniary value, a price current." Selling skeptical citizens on the practical benefits of reform, Mann thus envisions "intellectual and moral education" commodified like "an article of merchandise" through such literary efforts as *The School Library*. In this way, Mann hopes to convince them that the "respectability" this enterprise offers in exchange for their hard-earned dollars might then produce its own "returns of silver and gold," rendering their material circumstances "superior" to those less educated.[66] An editorial in the *Common School Journal* describes *The School Library* explicitly in these terms, calling its books "little treasuries of knowledge and wisdom" whose expense to purchase must "sink . . . when compared with the *pecuniary* advantage, to say nothing of the higher considerations of knowledge and virtue, that must and will be derived from the investment!"[67]

Early on, publishers also realized that education had a "market value," to use Mann's terms, and could be turned to "pecuniary account," translating into "silver and gold" for those competent enough to produce and distribute it. Unfortunately, Marsh, Capen, Lyon, and Webb would not reap the "returns" of their own "investment": the recession following the Panic of 1837, and its lingering economic instabilities lasting into the early 1840s, ensured their financial collapse, as it had so many other small firms in those uncertain times. Although Webb had vowed to Sarah P. E. Hale in early 1841 that, despite an unexpected "interruption in our business," the firm would "proceed again with renewed vigor," Hale was not convinced; she confessed to her brother that "poor" Webb "did not seem very sanguine." They had, of course, experienced previous "interruptions" in the form of incessant partisan political assaults, including a failed vote by the legislature's Democrats to abolish the Board of Education, and a halt in the sanctioning of books under the Democratic governor Marcus Morton in 1840. But, unlike the ebb and flow of antebellum politics, the firm could not escape the recent financial "hot water," as Hale called it, that had put them "pretty much at a stand." By February 1842, the firm had collapsed, managing to publish only 38 volumes of the series before bankruptcy halted further production. Mann told his friend, George Combe, that "sympathy for them is useless. They were dead, defunct, decomposed long ago," and this despite a $1000 he had lent to them, much of it "*quasi*-stolen," as he described it, because they had borrowed "without any prospect or possibility to pay."[68]

In late 1842, a squabble between Nahum Capen and Thomas Webb over the Board's sanction further hindered the library, and, although it was neither the first nor the last controversy the series would see, the dispute suggests that publishers' school libraries were fast becoming very competitive business.[69] After their firm dissolved, Capen negotiated the rights to continue publishing Mann's *Common School Journal*, while Webb retained the right to act as agent for *The School Library*. However, Capen's new firm began advertising a "New Plan for the Supply of District Libraries" detailing five series published under its own imprint. Because he promoted this plan in his "Advertiser" for the *Common School Journal*, there was confusion in the mind of some readers as to whether he had the approbation of the Board in producing them.[70] Webb launched an attack in the local papers, accusing him of falsely pretending to the sanction and insinuating that his own firm alone held the right to produce books for the state's district school libraries.[71] The situation appears to have gotten so bad that the Board distanced itself from it in its *Sixth Annual Report*, reaffirming their sanction of "*the two series* . . . in the hands of Thomas H. Webb and Co.," while simultaneously clarifying that they did "not deny the right or the ability of other gentlemen to make other, and better selections" and "gladly would rather encourage than retard the sale of any libraries" which might help the young.[72]

Harper & Brothers ultimately bought the copyright to most of the library's volumes in 1846 and, integrating the series into their already-voluminous catalogue, sold it under a new title, *The Massachusetts School Library*. As a bigger, better-capitalized firm than their Boston competitor, they had been able to weather the nation's economic downturn, and they had established a particularly strong presence in New York state, with its almost 11,000 school districts, for which they received the sole commission of the State Secretary to provide library books. As a private enterprise, Harper's *School District Library* also was not as liable to the frequent political attacks and delays experienced by its New England counterpart (such as when Mann's library was assaulted for its "whiggism" by Democratic localists wanting to abolish the Board, despite the reality of strong public and cross-denominational support for many of its positions). Together with the newly acquired *Massachusetts School Library*, then, such school library series cemented Harper's growing influence in the antebellum market, and bolstered its rise to national prominence.[73]

Just as the *Massachusetts School Library* helped consolidate Harper's cultural and financial capital, so too did its new publisher provide its authors with increased exposure and stable income. In October 1846, Thomas Webb wrote to Sarah P. E. Hale to inform her of the sale and transfer of her editions, telling her that, while "Authors & Editors have not reaped the benefit they should" from the enterprise owing to the numerous "obstacles" preventing it from proceeding "in the manner originally contemplated," the works "will now be published, and large sales effected, so that you will hereafter without doubt receive considerable in the way of premium from the Works."[74] While Webb positions the transfer as long-deferred reward finally realized, *Godey's Lady's Book* had prophesied similarly about the bright prospects of *The School Library* in 1840: "To keep economy always in view, and yet to hold out sufficient inducements to employ the pen of some of the most eminent of our literati, male and female, is an undertaking which cannot fail of being duly appreciated."[75] While *Godey's* seemed certain that the library's democratic and literary nationalist aspirations would attract appreciation, the question of whether this would take the form of "considerable" compensation for "Authors & Editors," as Webb puts it, was another matter. With the transfer of the library to its new publisher, however, it finally would.[76]

Although short-lived, the library's history provides a glimpse at just how serious the business of educational publishing could get, especially when a market like Massachusetts was at stake. But even as its history reminds us that there was never a heyday when educational principle trumped profit, it also points to the way such private–public enterprises were crucial to the rise of professional authorship; while others have suggested the way pedagogical activities such as literacy training were catalysts for the growth of the novel and the legitimization of antebellum women writers, state-sanctioned enterprises like *The School Library* were important because they offered moral and ethical justifications for writing, and the lucrative markets to support it.⁷⁷ As a state-sanctioned but privately published venture both produced and marketed in terms of sociability—as when its proponents pitched it to "friends of education" in America—it also anticipates more modern public–private enterprises such as the educational textbook industry.⁷⁸ But if this hybridity opened such endeavors, in the nineteenth century no less than today, to accusations of cynical political self-interest, on the one hand, or cynical business self-interest, on the other, those involved in the enterprises internalized the moral logic that the series and their advertisements articulate, justifying participation in an industry in which success was most often illusive and fleeting. In other words, such moral language justified the inherent risks of the educational literature business as worth taking, on the part of both producers with no guarantee that consumers would buy their product and subscribers with no way of knowing whether the products they paid for would come to fruition. In the words of William Penn, from the series' introduction: "For learning be liberal. Spare no cost; *for by such parsimony all is lost that is saved*" ("Introductory Essay," xviii; emphasis in original). Even those aspiring contributors whose works did not find their way into the library, such as Hawthorne, came to internalize its logic of bibliographic respectability, seeking the moral, cultural, and financial "gold" of "Americanized" children's literature. Indeed, in the fledgling medium of children's fiction validated by ventures such as *The School Library*, enterprising literary pedagogues saw a promising future; wreathed in "tender shoots and dewy buds, instead of such withered and dusty leaves as other people crown themselves with," they hoped to enjoy both a "very pleasant and peculiar kind of reputation" and put "money in [their] purses" (*CE*, 15:266–67).

CHAPTER 2

"Disorders of the Circulating Medium"

Hawthorne's Early Children's Literature

IN A PASSAGE that could have been lifted from the sternest of nineteenth-century diatribes against fiction, Oberon, the aspiring writer in Hawthorne's short sketch "Devil in Manuscript" (1835), complains that he has become "ambitious of a bubble, and careless of solid reputation," surrounded by "shadows, which bewilder me, by aping the realities of life," and cloistered in a "strange sort of solitude—a solitude in the midst of men." But while he threatens to burn his manuscripts to restore some semblance of normalcy to his life, it is clear that his feelings arise less from the dangers inherent to the genre of fiction than from what he perceives to be his inexplicable neglect by publishers. He admits to his colleague, "the sacrifice [of burning his manuscripts] is less than you may suppose; since nobody will publish them," to which this friend replies knowingly, "That does make a difference." In actuality, then, the sense of detachment Oberon bemoans originates in his rejection by "some seventeen booksellers," one of whom already "has five novels already under examination," a "strange . . . solitude" for Oberon indeed given that these men, and the audiences to which they cater, obviously share a taste for fiction (*CE*, 11:172).

When his friend then retorts that the "unpublished literature of America" must form a "voluminous mass," and when Oberon characterizes these unpublished manuscripts as "Alexandrian" (172), the sketch articulates anxieties aligning Hawthorne with Horace Mann, who, in remonstrating against the culture's "Alexandrian library," voices his apprehensions of a culture inundated with printed texts. To this formulation, however, Hawthorne adds, startlingly, that those texts printed are but the tip of the iceberg, a mere fraction of the manuscripts awaiting publication—or as Washington Irving had characterized it, a vast "sea of literature" produced in a modern world that has "made every one a writer."[1] It is tempting, in other words, to read the exchange between Oberon and his friend as Hawthorne's own response to the "bibliomania" sweeping the United States in the first half of the nineteenth century.[2] Depicting the anxieties of a writer still unsure of his place in the market, the sketch posits the sheer number of texts, both those in circulation and those aspiring to it, as a threat to his chances for literary success: the phenomena that marked the success of the antebellum author's profession—the widespread production, distribution, and consumption of literary texts—paradoxically threatened to alienate Hawthorne from consumers, inhibiting his quest for an audience. Given these circumstances, not the least of which is the competition he faced from other would-be writers also in search of recognition, how in the world might a young author like Hawthorne build a "solid reputation" for himself?

Amidst his complaints, Oberon offers a clue, even if, in 1835, Hawthorne had not yet realized its full import. Rebuffed by seventeen publishers, Oberon tells his friend: "It would make you stare to read their answers . . . one man publishes nothing but school-books" (172). While he levies this charge dismissively—and thus anticipates Hawthorne's oft-cited remark about the "drudgery" of juvenile writing—it simultaneously suggests the significance of "school-books" to the antebellum publishing industry and points to children's literature as a fast-growing market that Hawthorne himself would hasten to join by decade's end.[3] Indeed, it was at this time of heightened anxiety about the literary market—amid growing concerns about his reputation and financial security, not to mention his engagement to Sophia Peabody in 1839—that Hawthorne turned to children's literature as a potential remedy for his troubles. One useful way to read his early career is to view it as a series of frustrated efforts to transform himself from a poorly paid, anonymous magazine scribbler into a full-fledged professional author through writings increasingly directed at children. Didactic children's writing, "school-books" more broadly considered, represented a chance to exercise the bewitching power of fiction while exerting an influence more positive than the "devil" inhabiting Oberon's manuscripts. It was a chance for Hawthorne not only to prove himself by committing to a great moral undertaking but also to attract an enthusiastic audience of reformers, parents, and children willing to support such books. What he initially saw in children's literature was a medium in which he might stand out, using it to reshape, at as early an age as possible, the literary tastes he believed were leading adult readers to look elsewhere for their amusement. In his children's writings, therefore, he sought to create exemplary citizens by producing ideal consumers, instilling in them habits that might lead them to prefer his books over the abundance of other texts in the unregulated marketplace.

While Hawthorne was a prolific children's author—dedicating himself to juvenile literature from 1839 to 1844 and returning to it in 1851, penning in the process several book collections as well as magazine sketches—comparatively little critical attention has been directed to this part of his career. Traditionally, literary scholars have dismissed Hawthorne's forays into children's writing as an anomaly, an embarrassing detour in the oeuvre of an otherwise "serious" artist. For instance, one of the introductions in the *Centenary Edition* of Hawthorne's writings argues that his children's sketches are examples of "the lovingly sentimental hackwork that from the outset he was willing to undertake in order to make his way as a writer."[4] A growing number of critics, however, have resisted the *a priori* conflation of juvenile literature with artistic debasement, countering with an image of this writing not only as an important nineteenth-century concern but also as a genre in which both Hawthorne and his wife, Sophia, firmly believed.[5] In what is still one of the only book-length treatments of this subject, for example, Laura Laffrado argues that Hawthorne in his children's writings sought a new artistic direction for his career, a genre in which he could write confidently, and at the same time a means of "escape" from the confines of his everyday life—from his personal history, the Boston customhouse, and his weary bachelorhood, and even, I would add, from what he saw as the daunting challenge of competing for an unsympathetic adult readership in a culture overwhelmed with texts.[6]

While Laffrado's argument has merit, the term "escape" can be misleading because Hawthorne's children's writings so insistently register his investment in contemporary circumstances. In addition to joining the crusade for the creation of a new, thoroughly "American" juvenile literature, Hawthorne's early contributions to this genre reveal an obsessive interest in images of circulation and exchange—of money, texts, viruses—that betrays his anxieties about the market's direction and his own standing in an increasingly competitive and mass-market print culture. At the same time, they demonstrate his belief in the medium as a chance to educate his readers, to model for an impressionable young audience not yet complicit in the "vices" of the adult market the kind of sympathetic, loving, and disciplined relationship between writer and reader that might bind them to him and, thus, ensure his literary future. For Hawthorne, love was not only a transcendental truth and a nurturing means of education but also a competitive market force, encouraging sales of good books by producing the right kinds of readers to purchase them. In other words, Hawthorne's early children's writings record his desire to regulate literary tastes as well as morality—indeed, literary tastes *as* morality—by raising his youthful audiences into a reading public that would buy his adult books.

"Benumbed Fingers"

As "The Devil in Manuscript" suggests, Hawthorne's first experiences in the literary market were disappointing. From very early on, he had to confront the disheartening fact that the profits from his works did not meet expectations. The dilemma was not, as many scholars long assumed, that he found himself in a culture inhospitable to fiction, but rather that his culture was perhaps *too* receptive to it—so receptive, in fact, that the average scribbler had little chance to make a living amid the flood of texts offered for consumption.[7] His financial troubles were bad enough for Elizabeth Peabody to remark to Horace Mann, "Authorship does not seem to offer a means of living—He has not thriven with the booksellers," further attributing his failures to a lack of "genius for negotiation" with publishers (*Letters*, 199, 200). It was true that Hawthorne had no relish for publishers or editors; he suspected them all, in fact, of cheating him continually, either paying too little for his work, delaying promised payments, or faltering on proposed projects.

Perhaps no one person typified these suspect publishing figures better than Hawthorne's onetime editor Samuel Goodrich, whose firm, the American Stationers Company, issued his first collection, *Twice-Told Tales*, in 1837. Goodrich had offered Hawthorne one of his first windows into the literary world outside of the Salem papers, publishing his stories in the holiday gift book *The Token* while exploiting his labor for other projects as well.[8] For instance, in early 1836 Hawthorne became the editor of Goodrich's *American Magazine of Useful and Entertaining Knowledge*, only to complain bitterly in a 15 February letter to his sister Louisa of Goodrich's continual false promises: "[N]ot a damned cent have I had. . . . I came here trusting to Goodrich's positive promise to pay me 46 dollars as soon as I arrived; and he has kept promising from one day to another; till I do not see that he means to pay me at all" (*CE*, 15:236).⁹ With the help of his sister Elizabeth, Hawthorne also ghostwrote a juvenile textbook, *Peter Parley's Universal History* (1837), as part of Goodrich's wildly successful *Peter Parley* series of children's books. Lamenting to Elizabeth on 12 May 1836 the "very grievous vexations" he had suffered at Goodrich's hands, he called the pay the two were to receive for their services "poor compensation" given the scope and length of the manuscript: "Our pay, as Historians of the Universe, will be 100 dollars the whole of which you may have" (*CE*, 15:247).¹⁰

But even if we accept the idea that trouble with individual editors like Goodrich contributed largely to Hawthorne's predicament, a crucial reason he did not "thrive" in the literature business lay more broadly in the fundamental nature of the antebellum publishing industry itself. As Meredith McGill has argued, while his works circulated widely among regional magazines and enjoyed a fair degree of popularity, there was little corresponding remuneration to identify them as successful in his eyes—particularly as various industry practices and innovations conspired to keep magazine writers like Hawthorne poorly paid.¹¹ These included the practice of anonymous publication, which reduced fees any contributor could demand of magazines based on name recognition, while at the same time promoting constant piracy of articles and stories between magazines. The lack of any international copyright certainly did not help matters, often leading to inexpensive pirated editions of English works rather than the cultivation of American talent. Moreover, new publishing technologies resulting in a flood of cheap massmarket texts allowed publishers to enrich themselves while authors remained poor.¹²

Rather than faulting the state of the publishing industry, however, Hawthorne seems to have attributed much of his frustration to the reading public. In a letter to Longfellow on 4 June 1837, shortly after the publication of *Twice-Told Tales*, Hawthorne blamed the public's indifference for his literary failures:

> They would have been better, I trust, if written under more favorable circumstances. I have had no external excitement—no consciousness that the public would like what I wrote, nor much hope nor a very passionate desire that they should do so. . . . [I]f my writings had made any decided impression, I should probably have been stimulated to greater exertions; but there has been no warmth of approbation, so that I have always written with benumbed fingers. (*CE*, 15:252)

While McGill contends that Hawthorne developed a "fiction of readerly neglect" or obscurity after his later successes as a means to control his literary image and renegotiate his relation to the reading public, we can see such a strategy earlier, in this letter to Longfellow, which attempts to justify his disappointing career to a more successful colleague.[13] Despite the claim that he does not have "a very passionate desire" that the public should admire what he wrote, Hawthorne's assertion that he would have been "stimulated to greater exertions" had his efforts only made a "decided impression" with his readers clearly indicates otherwise. And in light of local reviews of his work that were, in fact, often complimentary, perhaps the sympathetic "warmth" Hawthorne desired was in large part the monetary gain and financial stability bestowed on someone like Longfellow by a wider public.

"Disorders of the Circulating Medium"

Given these sentiments about the indifference of his adult reading public, it is not surprising that, in the earliest record of Hawthorne's intention to write a children's book, Elizabeth Peabody notes what she describes as his desire to "control" the direction of American society at its *"fountain of youth."* Soliciting employment for Hawthorne as a potential contributor to Mann's *School Library*, Peabody thus presents the "great moral enterprise" of children's literature as an effort to combat the literary market's excesses (*Letters*, 200). By evoking America's *"fountain of youth,"* she also tries to help him into a potentially lucrative position by way of Mann's own moral crusade—the systematized education of America's young through school reform, in which the creation and distribution of a new children's literature would play a large part, acting as a "purer current of thought at the fountain" and helping to "wash the channels clean" (Mann, "On District School Libraries," 301). Unfortunately, Mann had severe reservations about fiction. He repeatedly attacked the genre as "vain and pernicious reading," as "'light reading,' 'trashy works,' 'ephemeral,' or 'bubble literature.'"[14] Arguing that it promoted mere amusement at the cost of instruction, duty to others, and a proper sense of reality, he went so far as to claim that "ninety-nine parts in every hundred of all the novels and romances extant, are as false to truth and nature, to all verisimilitude to history and to the affairs of men, as though they had been written . . . by lunatics themselves" (295). It should come as no surprise, then, that Mann was less than enthusiastic about Peabody's recommendation. Although he read *Twice-Told Tales* and admitted that they were "written beautifully—'*fine*' is the true word," unfortunately he wanted "something nearer home to duty and business."¹⁵ In truth, he found little moral significance in Hawthorne's writing, believing his own project demanded "something graver and sterner" than what Hawthorne seemed capable of, and doubting whether Hawthorne was "competent" of such a task. The slight was not personal; he dismissed "the great mass of our popular literature as a popular curse," calling it "all outside humanity."¹⁶

It was an abortive collaboration with Longfellow, however, that led Hawthorne to articulate the organizational principle for his inaugural children's book, *Grandfather's Chair* (1841), the first in a three-volume series interwoven with a "slender thread" of authorial anxiety (*CE*, 15:266) as it aimed to mold the sympathies of America's youth and shape them into a receptive audience.¹⁷ In March of 1838, the two began corresponding about an idea for a collection of modernized fairy tales they intended to call "The Boys' Wonder-Horn."¹⁸ While Longfellow quickly lost interest, Hawthorne imagined a volume structured with a "slender thread of story running through the book, as a connecting medium for the other stories" (*CE*, 15:266). Ultimately, this idea would manifest itself in a frame narrative about a kindly old grandfather who relates the distinguished history of a fireside chair to a group of amiable grandchildren named Laurence, Clara, Charley, and Alice. But just as this "slender thread" of narrative would link Grandfather and his grandchildren with the collection's historical sketches, the book itself represents a kind of "connecting medium" in Hawthorne's own career, a project through which he hoped to unite literary effort with the ever-elusive financial success he longed for.

This sense of urgency was not ill founded. By the time Hawthorne began his children's book, it was late autumn of 1840, shortly after he resigned his political appointment as a coal inspector in the Boston customhouse—a rather mind-numbing and embittering experience that he believed had "broken" him as a literary man.¹⁹ Hawthorne's literary spirits were low as he renewed his attempt at professional authorship, and his letters to fiancée Sophia in the weeks before the book's publication betray his anxiety about its reception among consumers. On 27 November 1840, he poked fun at himself for what he was sure would be its failure, asking Sophia "whether [she had] drawn those caricatures—especially the one of [her] husband, staggering, and puffing, and toiling onward to the gate of [Brook] farm, burthened with the unsaleable remnant of Grandfather's Chair." "Dear us," he continued, "what a ponderous, leaden load it will be!" (*CE*, 15:505). Appearing after his political appointment, and shortly before an even briefer stint at Brook

Farm, the *Grandfather's Chair* series aimed at the financial stability necessary to marry Sophia at last. While Hawthorne would take on various jobs during his engagement, none of them was satisfactory, either paying too little or leaving no time for writing. Thus, this "leaden load" weighed heavily, as much a "burden" on his manhood as an indictment of his abilities as a writer, particularly as it came in the shadow of an earlier, failed courtship with the social-climbing Mary Silsbee, who, as the story goes, once told Hawthorne that she would marry him only when he had an income of at least $3,000, an amount, at the time, he never expected to secure.[20]

Of course, part of Hawthorne's concern for the book's reception stemmed from his insistence on using fiction as his educational medium, a risk given the anti-fiction sentiments of many antebellum parents and educators (even if everyone *did* read it). If Horace Mann's response to Elizabeth Peabody's recommendation can be taken as any indication of the hurdles *Grandfather's Chair* might encounter, then Hawthorne had some cause to worry. While many reviewers praised his earlier tales, there were those who simultaneously felt the need to qualify their remarks with denunciations of fiction more generally. One such reviewer, Andrew Preston Peabody, begins his review of *Twice-Told Tales* with an exposition upon the perils of fiction: "The mental and moral influence of the most faultless novels and tales of the fashion now current is at least questionable. There is reason to apprehend that no mind could feed much upon them, without finding its notions of life unsettled, and the balance of its moral judgment disturbed." His qualms about the genre were much like Mann's; whereas Mann found it false to life and duty, Peabody believed fictions created "where there is a creation already": "They usurp the realm of fact, and change its order into anarchy. They disturb and displace the fabric of things as they are, and build up their ideal world in the very same space, which the actual world occupies."[21] If fiction might be this harmful to adult readers, unbalancing their moral judgments and distorting their sense of reality, then how much more damage might it inflict on the impressionable minds of young children?

Not surprisingly, Hawthorne hoped to pre-empt any criticism by developing a pedagogy of storytelling that not only addressed the shortcomings of more traditional schooling methods but also emphasized the educational powers of fiction. *Grandfather's Chair*, in fact, begins with Grandfather agreeing to relate the story of the "strange looking old chair" in which he sits, but only on such terms as he sees fit. When his granddaughter Alice asks him to "tell [her] a story to make [her] go to sleep," far from accepting storytelling as an idle medium meant simply to pass the time, Grandfather jokingly retorts, "That is not what story-tellers like." Instead, he sees her request as an opportunity to educate his grandchildren, suggesting to them that his tale might offer lessons otherwise unavailable through usual pedagogical methods. Turning to Laurence, who at 12 years old is the eldest of the grandchildren, Grandfather proposes to "teach him something about the history and distinguished people of his country, which he has never read in any of his school books" (*CE,* 6:10, 11).

Hawthorne's preface to the book, furthermore, anticipates his critics' concerns by implying that, far from being a pernicious purveyor of falsehoods, fiction could act as a powerful educational tool in the service of truth. His narrative, he tells us, has at all times "endeavored to keep a distinct and unbroken thread of authentic history." Even as this insistence disrupts any sense of history as something unchanging or objective, the preface takes great pains to differentiate the genre of "fiction" from a notion of the "fictitious" as something false or untrue: "Setting aside Grandfather and his auditors, and excepting the adventures of the chair . . . nothing in the ensuing pages can be termed fictitious. The author, it is true, has sometimes assumed the license of filling up the outline of history with details, for which he has none but imaginative authority, but which, he hopes, do not violate nor give false coloring to the truth" (*CE,* 6:5, 6). In stressing history's narrative qualities, Hawthorne tries to remove the stigma from the term "fiction" by depicting it as a supplement to, and not a replacement for, existing facts and principles. In his view, historical fiction assumes narrative liberties only to fill in missing details and exemplify values already determined by the general "outline" of events. After all, in assuming such imaginative liberties, he was only following the precedent set by the popular romantic histories of such contemporaries as George Bancroft and William Prescott.[22]

But if educational reformers like Mann criticized fiction for its harmful influences, they also attacked the teaching of traditional histories to children precisely because the narratives articulated were, among other things, catalogs of violence illustrating values as repulsive to them as the plot of any novel or romance. For example, in his *Third Annual Report,* Mann contends that many histories record little else but "the destruction of human life, and the activity of those misguided energies of men, which have hitherto almost baffled the beneficent intentions of Nature for human happiness." So filled with "Descriptions of battles, sackings of cities, and the captivity of nations," and so empty of any useful virtue are these narratives, he concludes, that the "inference which children would legitimately draw," should they be given these books to read in school, "would be, that the tribes and nations of men had been created, only for mutual slaughter, and that they deserved the homage of posterity, for the terrible fidelity with which their mission had been fulfilled."[23]

Grandfather's Chair would be quite a different kind of endeavor. Sarah Wadsworth has claimed that Hawthorne's children's books from this period were unoriginal efforts in the vein of *Peter Parley* rather than such revolutionary texts as the one he would produce later in *A Wonder-Book for Girls and Boys* (1852).[24] Yet with the publication of *Grandfather's Chair*, Hawthorne would in fact participate in a "revolution" of sorts already taking place in American juvenile literature, though it would not be the first flowering of myth and fantasy that Wadsworth posits as groundbreaking in the trajectory of this literature. Rather, he would participate in a project "nearer home to duty and business," to use Mann's phrase, that accompanied the consolidation of bourgeois power in antebellum American culture. In other words, his book would take part in a valorization of the home and domestic sphere that was the work of reforms sweeping children's literature in the 1830s, and beyond.[25]

In the preface to *Grandfather's Chair*, Hawthorne assures his critics that his stories work in the service of the bourgeois domesticity so dear to them. He defends his choice of form through the language of hearth and home, declaring:

> There is certainly no method, by which the shadowy outlines of departed men and women can be made to assume the hues of life more effectually, than by connecting their images with the substantial and homely reality of a fireside chair. It causes us to feel at once, that these characters of history had a private and familiar existence, and were not wholly contained within that cold array of outward action, which we are compelled to receive as the adequate representation of their lives. (*CE*, 6:5–6)

In a sense, Hawthorne brings the role of historians as storytellers into focus by questioning the criteria they use to create their histories. As he tries to replace a "shadowy," older model of history founded upon "cold . . . outward action" with a new domestic-centered one represented by the "substantial and homely reality of a fireside chair," Hawthorne explores, as Gillian Brown puts it, "the literary techniques by which national stories achieve and maintain their power," and teaches that, as Laura Laffrado argues, "stories are involved in a world of power, are written or told for certain interests against other interests."[26] Thus, in stressing the "private and familiar existence" of historical figures, he writes not only in the hopes of creating a nurturing environment for children but also with the moral and social values of educators like Mann in mind.

Even as he curried acceptance from educators, Hawthorne still worried that the book would not find an audience willing to buy it. Writing to Sophia on 13 January 1841 before the publication of *Famous Old People* (1841), the second volume in the series, Hawthorne expressed this concern: "Grandfather is very anxious to know what has become of his chair, and the Famous Old People who sat in it. I tell him that it will probably arrive in the course of to-day; and that he need not be so impatient; for the public will be very well content to wait, even were it till Doomsday. He acquiesces, but scolds, nevertheless" (*CE*, 15:512–13). As several sketches in the series deal with similar issues of undeserved scorn, unearned abuse, misunderstood or unappreciated genius, and painful exile, it is not hard to read them as allegories for the fears of exclusion and failure that Hawthorne harbored at the time, as well as his frustrations over the indifference of a reading public "content to wait" until "Doomsday" for his work.

It is not surprising, then, that the sketches in *Famous Old People* register as much about problems of the antebellum literary marketplace as they do about events long past in American history. At one point in the narrative, describing the chair's adventures in the New England Province House beginning in 1730 with the appointment of Governor Belcher, Grandfather mentions that all the government's attention "was principally taken up in endeavoring to settle the currency," which had been in a state of disarray since metal coins were replaced by "bills of paper or parchment," the value of which "kept continually sinking, because the real hard money could not be obtained for them." Grandfather concludes, "These disorders of the circulating medium were a source of endless plague and perplexity to the rulers and legislators, not only in Governor Belcher's days, but for many years before and afterwards" (*CE*, 6:111–12). Looming behind these comments no doubt is Hawthorne's acute sense of an ailment afflicting the United States "many years . . . afterwards" during the Panic of 1837, when a "disorder" of the "circulating medium"—namely, a sharp devaluation in paper monies as banks began to suspend specie payment—became a "source of endless plague and perplexity" to all Americans.

In bewailing the state of the nation's currency, Hawthorne likely had in mind the diminishing worth of his own books and the profits he had hoped to earn from them. Indeed, the reductions in sales, profits, and even prices for his publications during this period eerily reflected the devaluating "disorder" he saw afflicting America's paper monies because, as he says, "real hard money" could not be obtained for them. By the time his children's volumes appeared in 1841, the financial panic had already killed the profits from *Twice-Told Tales* (1837). As the book's sales slowed to a trickle after a fairly decent start, Hawthorne saw the end of any financial return when its publisher, the American Stationers' Company, went bankrupt after the start of the Panic.[27] The profits for *Grandfather's Chair* also saw a sharp drop as booksellers like Elizabeth Peabody, who had opened her West Street Bookstore and served as publisher for the first edition of Hawthorne's new juvenile writings, eventually tried to unburden themselves of excess inventory by selling stock at reduced cost.[28]

Unfortunately, Hawthorne, anxious to prevent his literary efforts from becoming complete losses, contributed to his book's devaluation by urging Peabody to sell the remaining copies as quickly as possible. On 23 June 1841, he wrote a terse and self-deprecatory letter to her, signaling concern over his financial failures during the depression and indicating his intention to negotiate with the Munroe publishing firm for the remaining copies of his troubled first volume: "Mr. Hawthorne particularly desires that the bargain with Mr. Munroe, in respect to the remaining copies of Grandfather's Chair &c. may be concluded on such terms as Miss Peabody thinks best, without further reference to himself. Being wholly ignorant of the value of the books, he could do no other than consent to any arrangement that she might propose" (*CE*, 15:547). Hawthorne's irritation at his (and perhaps Peabody's) inability to find the formula by which good writing might exact corresponding profit erupts when he bitterly proclaims himself "wholly ignorant of the value of the books." In February of 1842, when the books still had not sold through their first printing, and Munroe had declined to pick up the extra volumes, he would recommend to Peabody that "they should be got rid of on *any* terms" (*CE*, 15:609; emphasis in original).

But ultimately Hawthorne believed that the roots of his problem were deeper than mere publishers or booksellers. On 16 March 1843, he complained to Sophia: "I do wonder—and always shall wonder, until the matter be reformed—why Providence keeps us so short of cash. . . . The world deserves to come to a speedy end, if it were for nothing else save to break down this abominable system of credit—of keeping possession of other people's property—which renders it impossible for a man to be just and honest, even if so inclined" (*CE*, 15:678–79).[29] Hawthorne's complaints about the credit system and concerns over the state of the paper currency clearly align him, at least in part, with more radical members of the Democratic Party, the "hard" Democrats, so-called because they saw the solution to the nation's credit and banking problems in reversion to a self-regulating all-metallic currency.³⁰ The influences of this assumption find their way into Hawthorne's desire for a literature of intrinsic moral worth, one that would by its very nature help combat the excess of a print culture that he believed was hindering his own books' sales. For if the unchecked circulation of a questionable paper currency lent itself to widespread economic problems, as many Americans thought, then why shouldn't the unchecked circulation of print texts of questionable moral worth have a similarly negative effect on the literary market?

Hawthorne's anxieties to this effect manifest themselves in the collection's obsessive interest in circulation, its stories ranging in their concerns from the marriage market, to disease, to money-minting, to the passing of Grandfather's chair from one famous historical figure to another. When Grandfather relates an anecdote about the "first newspaper ever printed in America," the *Boston News Letter*, Hawthorne reveals his preoccupation with the overabundance of texts in antebellum print culture. Suggesting Hawthorne's desire to teach his readers what he believes is an important truth about the literary market, Grandfather's account begins in the classroom, with the New England Puritan schoolmaster Ezekiel Cheever taking a strange printed sheet out of his pocket one day in 1704, much to the wonderment of his students. No sooner does Grandfather embark on the story, however, than he finds himself interrupted by the "entrance of three newspapers, which were all published that same evening, and every evening of the year." This interruption abruptly terminates his narration and leads him to brood on life in an age dominated by mass-produced texts: "[He] could not help thinking how our forefathers would have wondered, had they foreseen the innumerable host of newspapers that now fly forth, from all quarters and in all directions, throughout the land. What a dull, incurious people must they have been, when one little weekly sheet sufficed for a whole continent!" (*CE*, 6:90, 91).

Laffrado reads this moment as an "inability to imagine New England before industrialization and urbanization brought about a modern society dominated by commerce and mass production."³¹ But what seems to drive Hawthorne's irony in this moment is precisely his nostalgia for the apparent simplicity of American life a couple of decades earlier, before the mass-produced media of the 1820s and 1830s, and before overwhelming print competition (when "one little weekly sheet sufficed for a whole continent"). Indeed, Grandfather is in the very act of envisioning Master Cheever and his class reading their sole paper when the arrival of his own newspapers interrupts—bringing his story to an abrupt close, and suggesting that, in antebellum

America, unlike the world of the early eighteenth century, one's storytelling is always made to vie with the arrival of other texts.

Grandfather's Love

If the more radical voices in the Democratic Party were correct in advocating a self-regulating currency of intrinsic worth as the answer to the nation's economic woes, then why should Hawthorne not turn to a literature of self-discipline as a fix for the ills of the literary economy? Believing, as many nineteenth-century Americans did, that the economic evils of society were moral in their origins, and locating them in some failure or excess at the level of the individual, Hawthorne not surprisingly sought the solution to his dilemma in the creation of a children's literature espousing self-discipline—brainchild of a rising bourgeois ideology, by-product of the Unitarian "self-culture" movement, and linchpin of liberal nineteenth-century American educational reform. Still cautious over past failures in reaching an audience, Hawthorne attempted to capitalize on the notions of self-discipline that many Americans thought crucial to education, turning it toward regulating readers' consumption of literary texts. Just as Grandfather attempts to shape his grandchildren, Hawthorne attempted to shape readers' habits through storytelling, encouraging in them the self-discipline necessary to ensure they chose, purchased, and circulated *his* texts over others.

Unsurprisingly, education and discipline are the central concerns of "The Old-Fashioned School," the sketch about Cheever and Puritan pedagogical practices. Endeavoring to "give his auditors an idea of how matters were managed in schools, above a hundred years ago," Hawthorne provides us with an image of a stern, dour teacher whose "old-fashioned" pedagogy centers on corporal punishment. Hawthorne's assertion that the scene might be "an interesting subject to [his] readers" supports Richard Brodhead's contention that American culture in the 1830s and 1840s evinced a heightened interest in depictions of physical punishment. Indeed, when Grandfather introduces Cheever as a "venerable school-master . . . like an ancient Puritan" who sits on the "look-out" for any sign of misbehavior, the most prominent aspect of his description is "a rod of birch . . . hanging over the fire-place, and a heavy ferule . . . on the master's desk"—standing in constant reminder of the punishment awaiting any student who falters (*CE*, 6:81, 82).[32]

In contrast, Hawthorne valorizes a disciplinary ethos of education in which storytelling, as Nina Baym notes, becomes "a process marked by mutual affection and respect as well as by a clear understanding of the appropriate behavior for teller and listener."³³ Implicit in Grandfather's ironic appraisal of "those good old times" when "a school master's blows were well laid on" (*CE*, 6:84) is Hawthorne's disapproval of an outdated pedagogy whose main purpose was to bridle the sin and depravity that Calvinists believed characterized human nature. Thus, while Grandfather's sketch stigmatizes the older New England culture that Cheever represents, the book's frame narrative registers the humaneness of Grandfather's (and Hawthorne's) storytelling as an educational method.³⁴ When little Alice begins to cry in response to the image of Cheever as godlike judge doling out punishment to transgressors, she acts, of course, as a moral barometer and guide for reader reaction; throughout *Grandfather's Chair* she not only initiates many stories while encouraging her siblings to listen, but also "speak[s] for all" in her emotional responses (*CE*, 6:74). And Grandfather's response to her tears reveals a further layer of authorial control: offering comfort with the words "do not cry, sweet Alice[,] for they have ceased to feel the pain, a long time since," Grandfather is careful to soothe her cries, even as he must manipulate her (and, by extension, the readers') emotions in order to reveal his own benevolence.³⁵

Dwelling (with some relish) on the cruelty of corporal punishment in order to discredit rival cultural formations, mid-nineteenth-century educational writings helped to construct a subtle phenomenon that Brodhead calls "disciplinary intimacy," or simply discipline through love. As counterpart to what reformers hoped to portray as the inhumanity of an old order, this rising bourgeois system sought to embody its notions of loving discipline in representations of family and home. As a model of behavioral regulation, disciplinary intimacy relied on personalized authority figures (often in the form of mothers, fathers, or other family relations) and extremely sentimentalized images of relationship. To help regulate the actions of a child-subject, this system also required a conscious intensification of the emotional bond between parental figure and child in order to awaken feelings of love in the child and fix them on the parent. Disciplinary intimacy thus used love to cultivate self-discipline, a process that "initiates the child into a world of other-directedness" and begins the "socialization of identity that is this system's real concern."³⁶

In keeping with Hawthorne's desire to control his readers' literary tastes on these terms, the next story in *Famous Old People*, "The Rejected Blessing," espouses a notion of love as a means to self-discipline. It begins when Grandfather describes the Boston smallpox epidemic of the early eighteenth century—yet another "disorder of the circulating medium" in need of regulation—and Cotton Mather's attempts to introduce an inoculation for it. In the process, Grandfather reduces the crisis to a tale of a father's love for his son. The story turns on the moment when Mather, sitting one night in his study and pondering the recent outbreak, acknowledges with a pang that he has children of his own who are "exposed to the danger"; Mather then hears "the voice of his youngest son, for whom his heart [is] moved with apprehension," and, almost instantaneously, he turns his attention to a nearby book, discovering news of an inoculation sitting before his very eyes. When he resolves to act on this information despite communal opposition to what his contemporaries perceive as interference in the will of Providence, it is love for his son that motivates him. If Mather's discovery of an inoculation is due, in his Puritan understanding, to "a merciful Providence that brought this book under [his] eye," then, in the narrative's own logic, it is a miracle occasioned by his own love for his son (*CE*, 6:100, 101).

Much as Mather's love for his child spurs him to contain the circulation of smallpox among Boston's residents, Grandfather's love for his grandchildren regulates the kind of stories he tells, restraining the circulation of inappropriate or immoral subjects among them and among the readers they represent. The primary moment for this kind of discipline comes at the end of the tale, when Grandfather tells the children:

> And now, if you wish to learn more about Cotton Mather, you must read his biography, written by Mr. Peabody, of Springfield. You will find it very entertaining and instructive; but perhaps the writer is somewhat too harsh in his judgment of this singular man. He estimates him fairly, indeed, and understands him well; but he unriddles his character rather by acuteness than by sympathy. Now, his life should have been written by one, who, knowing all his faults, would nevertheless love him. (*CE*, 6:105)

While prizing the book's intent both to delight and to instruct its readers, Grandfather finds Peabody's method misguided in its "somewhat too harsh" treatment of Mather.[37] And he proposes new criteria for storytelling, suggesting that a narrative should unfold by "sympathy" and "love" for its subject, in full knowledge of his or her faults, rather than by "acuteness," that it should be governed by a kind of disciplinary intimacy. By revising Mather's legacy as the "chief agent of the [witchcraft] mischief" into a legacy as the savior of Boston during the smallpox epidemic, therefore, Hawthorne enacts for his readers the very lesson in loving self-discipline that Grandfather tries to impart to his audience (*CE*, 6:94).

Of course, more is at stake for Hawthorne than Mather's reputation; one can easily read the sketch as an allegory for his own plight as a professional author. Like Mather, he himself, he felt, was a man ahead of his time with abilities grossly under-appreciated by his contemporaries.[38] He, too, believed he could offer the populace an "inoculation" for the "disorder" of the "circulating medium" that plagued them—in this case presenting them with a collection of moral, lovingly told stories to protect against the "disease" of trashy fictions circulating throughout the market. Toward the end of the sketch, Grandfather informs his listeners of the "strange thing in human experience" by which "Men, who attempt to do the world more good, than the world is able entirely to comprehend, are almost invariably held in bad odour" (*CE*, 6:104). One cannot help but notice in Grandfather's moral a hint of Hawthorne's own self-righteousness as a writer attempting to do good for a reading public that he felt constantly under-appreciated him.

In particular, much of Hawthorne's interest rests in cultivating, through Grandfather's lessons in love and self-discipline, a young *male* readership for the kind of fiction he hopes to write. In an 1838 letter to her sister Elizabeth, Sophia Peabody mentions a casual conversation with him in which he expressed a wish for "intercourse with some beautiful children—beautiful little girls; he did not care for boys."[39] We find reason for such ambivalence in his portrayal of Charley, in whom we see Hawthorne's professional fears about the apathetic nature of many boyish readers.[40] While Hawthorne pictured the sympathetic reader as feminine, he was (as a male author) uncomfortable with the possibility of a too-feminized audience—but this put him in the paradoxical state of needing to court those male readers whose interests he presumed were more difficult to engage. Laurence, the oldest boy and the young scholar for whose benefit Grandfather tells many of his stories, and Charley, the troublesome younger brother, are at different ends of the spectrum, one exemplifying Hawthorne's ideal and the other attitudes he clearly considers inappropriate. Laurence, much like his sisters (representing the vast numbers of women already reading similar sentimental and domestic fictions), is an attentive and sympathetic listener, a "bright scholar, in whom an early thoughtfulness and sensibility began to show themselves," and the mold into which Hawthorne hopes to reshape his boyish audience. Charley, on the other hand, is an "inattentive auditor"—so easily bored and distracted that Grandfather often wonders whether it is worth the time to tell him stories. He embodies the kind of uninterested reader whom Hawthorne desperately wished to attract, hoping to educate and discipline him through his narratives. A "bold, brisk, restless little fellow of nine" who can "be quiet for at least ten minutes, should the story last so long," Charley gravitates toward tales of action and adventure, of brash and belligerent military exploits, when he deigns to listen at all (*CE*, 6:11, 21, 11).

Boys like Charley concern Hawthorne because they presage the adult tastes from which he had sought retreat in children's literature. For example: One evening when Grandfather hears a great "tumult and uproar, passing through the streets," Laurence informs us that it "is a procession of the boys of Boston, in honor of Old Tippecanoe" and that "Charley has run away to join them"—a reference to William Harrison's victory in the presidential election of 1840 and the defeat of Hawthorne's own Democratic Party. Upon receipt of this news, Grandfather responds: "Boys are the same in every generation—always aping their fathers—always taking a mimic interest in grown men's affairs. No doubt, the scholars of old Master Cheever used to talk politics, and mingle themselves with the turmoil of whatever was going forward." These remarks suggest Hawthorne's worried anticipation that the children's market would grow to resemble the adult he sought to reform. In Charley, with his rush to join the rowdy Whig parade, we see the combination of "low," mass-marketed literature and popular, partisan politics that Hawthorne most fears, and it is the prospect of such tastes infiltrating the juvenile market that spurs him toward the storytelling represented by Grandfather's efforts: "This triumphal procession, as shewing the interest which schoolboys take in public affairs, suggested to Grandfather a method of interweaving the history of the province with the narrative of the chair" (*CE*, 6:86–87).

The problem, for Hawthorne, is that while Charley's engagement seems like youthful frolic—the narrator describes the parade as "music of drum, fife, and bugle, intermixed with shouts, seemingly of boyish voices, and the clatter and tramp of innumerable feet upon the pavement" (86)—such pastimes threaten to transform, as such boys grow up, into excessive and violent indulgence that subverts the domestic order antebellum Americans so valued (and the series so forcefully espouses). The unruly masses of "The Hutchinson Mob," a sketch in the series' third volume, *The Liberty Tree* (1841), suggest Hawthorne's ambivalence to the "mobs" he believed liberal society empowered.[41] Like an exaggerated version of Charley's parade, a rabble of "idle" mischief-makers, among which, the narrator knowingly tells us, "Doubtless, [were] some school-boys" (154), amasses in King Street on the night of 26 August 1765, "aroused" to such "fierce and dangerous spirit" (153) after the Stamp Act that they assault Lieutenant Governor Thomas Hutchinson in his home. But while Charley's antics only interrupt Grandfather's reveries, this mob defiles the "domestic quiet" (156) of the entire

Hutchinson household, disturbing an affectionate exchange between father and daughter, forcing their narrow escape, systematically destroying "marble hearths and mantel pieces" (158), and callously leaving the family "homeless in the street" (159). In depicting this riot, Hawthorne leaves little doubt as to where his sympathies lie; with "an evil aspect" made "more terrible by the flickering blaze of the bonfire" around which it had gathered (154), this infernal mob is "so utterly lawless as to assault [Hutchinson] in his peaceful home" (157), violating the sanctity of a domestic space Hawthorne believes should transcend partisan rancor. In their blatant disregard for Hutchinson's "enjoyment of his home" (155), furthermore, the rioters are "guilty of outrageous violence" transforming free and spirited political protest into a "most unjustifiable act" (159). Relating this sordid history to his grandchildren, Grandfather can only offer this consolation: "Afterwards, the people grew more calm, and were more influenced by the counsel of those wise and good men who conducted them safely and gloriously through the Revolution" (159).

Positioning himself as another "wise and good" man offering "counsel" to the young in tumultuous times (a print, if not a social, revolution), Hawthorne identifies not with political hacks like Harrison, whose parades serve only to lure boys (and boyish men) to partisan battle, but with a very different kind of statesman, whose transcendent influence prefigures the harmonious republic of print he hoped to produce. In the interstitial between *The Liberty Tree*'s "Boston Tea Party" and "Tory's Farewell," Hawthorne introduces General Washington to readers as the one-time occupant of Grandfather's chair, offering in the process rhapsodies of praise and reverence for the "father of his country" (185). Chief among Washington's many "invaluable characteristics" is, interestingly, the ability to transform the "rough mob of country-people" through his "faculty of bringing order out of confusion. All business, with which he had any concern, seemed to regulate itself, as if by magic. The influence of his mind was like light, gleaming through an unshaped world" (187–88). In this description of Washington's influence, Hawthorne articulates a fantasy by which he himself uses his own miraculous intellectual powers to transform, through the "magic" of storytelling, a motley rabble of young male readers into self-regulating members of the same national family. Indeed, he implores the reader in *The Liberty Tree*'s preface: "Will *he* not come, this once more, to our fireside, and be received as an own grandchild, and as brother, sister, or cousin to Laurence, Clara, Charley, and little Alice?" (143, emphasis added). In using the pronoun "he" while inviting both "brother" and "sister" to his fireside, Hawthorne reveals a continuing preoccupation with boys like Charley whose attentions may have wandered between the books' installments.

In this way, Hawthorne attempts to "domesticate" the rambunctious little Charleys of the world, using Grandfather's lovingly told tales to transform them into veritable Laurences who allow love for others to regulate their actions. An article in the *American Annals of Education* similarly suggests that "parents, grandparents, and neighbors" might adopt narrative conventions such as "Tales of a Grandfather," and "Simple Stories of a Mother's Love" to manipulate children's sense of familial affection and geographical attachment.[42] Just as the *Annals* envisions history taught through affectionate family stories, therefore, so too does Hawthorne understand what Gillian Brown has described as the imaginative, affective dimensions of nationalism, of love's capacity to bind young auditors' attention to stories of American life. As such, "Grandfather's Dream" at the end of *The Liberty Tree* records a moral fable in which Grandfather converses with his chair, that venerable piece of furniture which, after two centuries of American life and "familiar intercourse with men who were esteemed the wisest of their day," had obtained peculiar insight into "the riddle of life" (209). Implored to tell "us poor mortals" the secret to this perplexing mystery, the chair responds with the rather "oracular enunciation" that "JUSTICE, TRUTH, and LOVE, are the chief ingredients of every happy life" (209). When Grandfather then replies, "This is no secret. Every human being is born with the instinctive knowledge of it," their exchange participates in the discourse of liberal, bourgeois morality that champions love's transcendent properties. As Grandfather's heavy-handed moralizing attests, Hawthorne's fiction thus aimed to cultivate in American children a self-regulating conscience guided by seemingly universal notions such as truth, justice, and love.[43]

Still, this is no easy task. If the series ends with this "dream" of loving domestication, it begins with a more sobering reality. Grandfather's first story, "The Lady Arbella," is a sentimental tale about the chair's first owner, who was transplanted to an inhospitable New World only to wither away like a "pale English flower in the shadow of the forest," her gentle and timid spirit incompatible with the rough and hardy soil of Puritan New England. Laurence and Clara listen "attentively, . . . affected by this true story of the gentle lady, who had come so far to die so soon," and little Alice, whom Grandfather expected would be sleeping by this point, listens with her "blue eyes . . . wide open," tears forming in them "like dew upon a delicate blue flower." But while the three children enact appropriate affective responses to the story, Charley is nowhere to be found, having "almost at the commencement of the foregoing narrative . . . galloped away, with a prodigious clatter, upon Grandfather's stick." Believing that storytelling requires a degree of sympathy on the part of the listener, a level of consideration that Charley is not willing to entertain, Hawthorne finds his behavior inexcusable. Irked that Charley would prefer childish gambols to Grandfather's stories, Hawthorne intrudes his own voice into the narrative, complaining, "So large a boy should have been ashamed to ride upon a stick" (17–18).

Loving "Sam" Johnson

The *Grandfather's Chair* series was not the only chance Hawthorne would have to expound upon this notion of love between storyteller and audience. In mid-1841, he negotiated with Boston publisher James Munroe to edit a library series that would include a second edition of *Grandfather's Chair* (despite the first-edition copies that remained unsold), as well as a new volume of biographical sketches. Although he held out hope that the project might bring great profit, by 22 August 1841 Hawthorne was showing signs of strain from his inability to provide financial security for Sophia:

> Whatever may be thy husband's gifts, he has not hitherto shown a single one that may avail to gather gold. I confess that I have strong hopes of good from this arrangement with Munroe, but when I look at the scanty avails of my past literary efforts, I do not feel authorized to expect much from the future. Well; we shall see. Other persons have bought large estates and built splendid mansions with such little books as I mean to write. . . . Dearest, how much depends on those little books! (*CE*, 15:563)

Hawthorne's mention of "gold," resonating with the recent debates over the instability of paper currencies and the "hard" Democrats' belief in the intrinsic value of bullion, points to what he believed were his failures to produce with his pen something of real financial worth. Against this failed literary past, however, he sets the resplendent future he envisions for himself and Sophia. Like *Grandfather's Chair*'s rendition of young William Phips, who tells his wife "some time or other, he should be very rich, and would build a 'fair brick house' in the Green Lane of Boston" (*CE*, 6:58), Hawthorne confesses to Sophia that children's literature might be a means not only to the kind of financial success that would finally "authorize" his sense of worth as a writer, but also to the "large estates" and "splendid mansions" he imagines as representative of married life's domestic bliss.[44] Unfortunately, his worst fears would fulfill themselves: wary of cheating publishers, he consistently refused the terms offered him and eventually abandoned the plan.[45]

When, in the face of these financial failures, Elizabeth Peabody arranged for Tappan and Dennet to release the second edition in December 1841, with the new collection, *Biographical Stories for Children*, following in April 1842, Hawthorne found another opportunity to domesticate the world's Charleys. The plight of poor Edward Temple, an eight-year-old boy suddenly afflicted with a "disorder of the eyes" so severe that it renders him temporarily blind (*CE*, 6:215), makes up the "slender thread" of narrative weaving the new sketches together. Though the structure of the collection is similar to that of *Grandfather's Chair*, its bleak outlook stands in contrast to the homely comfort of Hawthorne's earlier volume.[46] Confined to a "darkened chamber, with a bandage over his eyes" (*CE*, 6:215), Edward passes the time by listening to his loving father's bedside stories, childhood biographies of famous figures ranging from Ben Franklin's account of stealing pier blocks to a Boswell anecdote of Samuel Johnson's youth. Once again, the purpose of the stories is didactic: Mr. Temple infuses his narratives with a heavy-handed morality intended to teach Edward such bourgeois values as love for family, deference to authority, respect for property, and proper roles for male and female.

Undoubtedly, *Biographical Stories* is another of Hawthorne's attempts to cultivate love in his readers as a means to literary success. In the preface, Hawthorne confesses that his hope for the efficacy of juvenile writing in regulating young literary tastes lies in the potential that the "sympathy of childish intimacies will attach itself to [the] famous names of history and literature," so that "when, hereafter, the reader shall learn the deeds of their manhood, it will be with a portion of interest which we feel in the lives of our early companions." Of course, lurking behind this assertion is a barely veiled desire to harness readers' affections, the "sympathy of childish intimacies," for his own gain—a hope that when his young readers do mature and hear of the deeds of *his* manhood, that is, the stories and books he has written and will write, they might feel enough stirring of interest about the life of their early literary companion to purchase and read his adult works. Not willing to conclude the preface without reiterating these hopes, he bluntly admits that, "in point of reputation to be aimed at, juvenile literature is as well worth cultivating as any other" because the writer, "if he succeed in pleasing his little readers, may hope to be remembered by them till their own old age—a far longer period of literary existence than is generally attained, by those who seek immortality from the judgments of full grown men" (*CE*, 6:213, 214).

Of all the stories in the volume, the sketch of young Samuel Johnson most clearly reflects Hawthorne's need to endear himself to a young audience. Mr. Temple begins the story as a parable to make peace when Edward, who is "inclined to be despotic" with his family's attentions, takes offense that older brother George does not spend every hour with him (*CE*, 6:239). Taking its inspiration from an anecdote in James Boswell's *Life of Johnson*, Hawthorne's sketch tells the story of "Sam," who, after having refused one day to help his sick father peddle books, returns to Uttoxeter as an adult, consumed by guilt and remorse. The original anecdote is extremely brief, but it powerfully affected Hawthorne's imagination.[47] His version is significant, not only because it serves as an example of bourgeois disciplinary intimacy at work in fiction (preaching love as a regulator for all human relationships, as it demonstrates the need for loving discipline in Sam's behavior toward his father and Edward's toward his brother), but also because it extrapolates this model to literary practice.

Hawthorne's authorial preoccupations make themselves clear as his lesson in filial obedience quickly turns into a troubled meditation on the state of the literary market. One day, Johnson's father, once a successful bookseller but now a sick, elderly man in "reduced circumstances," asks Sam to tend to his bookstall while he stays home to rest. Sam refuses, and his father, "too feeble, and too much out of spirits" to argue, leaves, but not before berating his son for allowing him to suffer the "noise and confusion of the market, when he ought to be in his bed." Sam's "heart" soon begins to "smite" him, the loving bond between son and parent causing him to think with guilt of his sick father standing among a "noisy crowd" (*CE*, 6:240, 241). Interestingly, as his remorseful imagination takes over and his sense of shame grows, Sam worries more about his father's book display than his ill-health:

> Sam seemed to behold him, arranging his literary merchandize [*sic*] upon the stall, in such a way as was best calculated to attract notice. Here was Addison's Spectator, a long row of little volumes; here was Pope's translation of the Iliad and Odyssey; here were Dryden's poems, or those of Prior. Here, likewise, were Gulliver's Travels, and a variety of little gilt-covered children's books, such as Tom Thumb, Jack the Giant-queller, Mother Goose's Melodies, and others which our great-grandparents used to read, in their childhood. (*CE*, 6:241–42)

While Sam first envisions a selection of canonical texts, both classical and contemporary, the next image, a variety of children's books, points to Hawthorne's own efforts to enter the juvenile market (this scene appears, after all, in the context of a collection in which he desperately attempts to sell his own stories to children). Furthermore, the "gilt" covering on these books evokes Hawthorne's search for a medium of intrinsic worth, marking children's literature as a kind of literary equivalent to the gold specie whose stability "hard" Democrats thought so crucial to the nation's financial well-being.

As he thinks over his father's stock, Sam manifests his ambivalence toward the literary market and frets over the discrepancy in caliber between the books and their intended purchasers, whom he imagines are "rude and ignorant country-people" incapable of understanding the texts' value. He envisions his father offering books, first to "the rude yeoman, who perhaps could not read a word," then to "the country squires, who cared for nothing but to hunt hares and foxes." The implausibility of these "yeomen" reading Addison, or these "squires" perusing Pope and Dryden, registers Hawthorne's personal sense of the reading public as a largely ignorant lot, grossly inadequate to the task of appreciating the literature available to them. Children do not escape his notice either: Sam envisions his father trying to interest "children, who chose to spend their coppers for sugar-plums or gingerbread, rather than for picture-books" (*CE*, 6:241–42). Hawthorne here conflates dismay at adults' purchasing habits with disappointment at unsuccessful attempts to capitalize on the sympathies of children—after all, few children could afford to buy books without their parents' money or approval.

Reflecting the frustrated author's obsession with the idea of these children growing up to be loyal customers, the second half of the story registers his concern for future prospects, as the narrative leaps forward in time. Fifty years later, the market remains as chaotic as ever, still "in very great confusion," with the "people of the village . . . trading, jesting, quarreling, and making just such a bustle as their fathers and grandfathers had made, half a century before" (*CE*, 6:247, 245). But invoking Dr. Johnson's return to the site of his father's bookstall, Hawthorne offers hope for the writer willing to brave the market's noise and confusion to earn a living. In a moment recalling the collection's preface—in which Hawthorne expresses his desire that young readers might remember him fondly in their old age—Mr. Temple reports: "On the very spot of ground, where [Johnson] now stood, some aged people remembered that old Michael Johnson had formerly kept his bookstall. The little children, who had once bought picture-books of him, were grandfathers now" (*CE*, 6:246).

Hawthorne likely saw in the anecdote of Johnson in the marketplace a ready-made lesson in authorship—perhaps recognizing, in Johnson's initial refusal to travel to Uttoxeter, his own ambivalence toward the literary market, and, in Sam's guilt, his shame at rejecting Munroe's terms at a time when impending marriage made him increasingly anxious for an adequate living. If he would not brave the market for one he loved, then what reason had he to enter it at all? In this sense, the sketch offered Hawthorne a chance for penance, an opportunity to exorcise his literary demons by providing him a way to confront his professional fears and to re-enter the market for Sophia. In early 1838, five years before *Biographical Stories,* he recorded in his American notebooks the desire to work up the Johnson anecdote into a story about facing past mistakes: "Dr. Johnson's penance in Uttoxeter Market. A man who does penance in what might appear to lookers-on the most glorious and triumphal circumstance of his life. Each circumstance of the career of an apparently successful man to be a penance and torture to him on account of some fundamental error in early life" (*CE,* 8:180). While Johnson's "fundamental error" is a breach of disciplinary intimacy, it is also a refusal to face the conditions of his father's profession—an irony given that Samuel Johnson would become one of England's most renowned writers. Yet Hawthorne's "Sam" does not at first recognize this truth because he thinks himself better than his father's customers. Conscious of "uncommon sense and ability, which, in his own opinion, entitled him to great respect from the world," young Sam paradoxically turns his back on the marketplace from which he will later wish to win literary respect (*CE,* 6:240). In Hawthorne's anecdote, then, each subsequent circumstance becomes an effort to atone for that initial slight; Sam ultimately returns to Uttoxeter, to the "noise and confusion" of the market, and, as a final act of penance, stands in the spot where his father's bookstall once stood. But if Sam's travails become a lesson to all would-be writers (including Hawthorne) in accepting the conditions of the marketplace in the name of those they love, the story also acts as an exhortation to Hawthorne's readers, entreating them for the love and acceptance he thinks crucial to the success of his career. Before ending his parable, in a moment where the story's moral and Hawthorne's literary anxieties merge, Mr. Temple implores his quarreling sons to heed Sam's lesson: "My dear children, if you have grieved—I will not say, your parents—but, if you have grieved the heart of any human being, who has a claim upon your love, then think of Samuel Johnson's penance" (*CE,* 6:248). Declining to confine the objects of affection to "parents" alone, Hawthorne widens the range of possibilities for disciplinary intimacy to include the relationship between author and reader. Given Mr. Temple's insistence that his children think upon "*any* human being who has a claim upon your love" (emphasis added), one might as well substitute "author" for "parent." For if a well-intentioned author, carefully crafting nurturing children's books that his audience might one day look back upon with nostalgia, does not deserve love and support, then who does?

Similarly, Hawthorne's complaints elsewhere in the narrative reflect his belief that, though his readers continually grieve his heart, he should have a claim on their love. In a self-conscious moment of moral rhapsodizing over "how dependent on one another God has ordained us to be[,] insomuch that all the necessities of mankind should incite them to mutual love," Hawthorne remarks that Edward, through his father's stories, learned to care for "his friends, and perhaps all the world, better than he ever did before." Hawthorne then adds, "[The son] felt grateful towards his father for spending the evenings in telling him stories—more grateful, probably, than any of my little readers will feel towards me, for so carefully writing those same stories down" (*CE*, 6:261–62). While Edward comes to understand how his father's stories strengthen the filial bond and increase his listeners' love for all those around them, Hawthorne protests that his own readers pay too little heed to him as an important storyteller in their lives.

Conclusion: "Very Capital Reading"

As such protestations suggest, it did not take Hawthorne long to realize that children's literature was not a panacea for his financial ills. In a 27 September 1843 letter to Samuel Coleman (editor of the *Boys' and Girls' Magazine*), he revealed his newfound misgivings about the genre:

> It would give me pleasure to comply with your request [to become a regular contributor for your magazine]; but it could not be done without interrupting other pursuits, and at a greater sacrifice than the real value of my articles. If I saw a probability of deriving a reasonable profit from juvenile literature, I would willingly devote myself to it for a time, as being both easier and more agreeable (by way of variety) than literature for grown people. But my experience hitherto has not made me very sanguine on this point. In fact, the business has long been overdone. (*CE*, 16:1)

While Hawthorne insinuates that a contribution would require more work on his part than the magazine would be willing to pay, he also wonders whether it would require more effort than warranted by the "real value" of any work he might produce. Recalling notions of intrinsic worth that led him to the children's genre in the first place, the self-deprecatory confession regarding the "real value of [his] articles" suggests a shift in attitude. Claiming that the market is "overdone," crowded with successful authors like Goodrich or "Mr. Abbot [sic]" (*CE*, 16:1), whose *Rollo* books of 1835 were a cultural force to contend with, Hawthorne admits that children's literature is a business like every other literary endeavor. In a sense, then, he appears to anticipate that accepting Coleman's offer would simply put him back where he began, in the position of a poorly paid magazine scribbler subject to all the abuses of the literary market, albeit this time at a children's magazine.

But even without immediate profit, Hawthorne's investment in children's literature continued. In 1850, he returned to the genre, beginning with the reissue of the *Grandfather's Chair* series and *Biographical Stories* as *True Stories from History and Biography*. Following the financial success of *The Scarlet Letter* (1850), Hawthorne saw a chance to revisit the juvenile market, essentially enacting in reverse his earlier literary plans—now using the success of his adult book as a way to insert himself into the children's market. He had been mulling this return for a while, writing to Mann (now his brother-in-law) as late as 8 August 1849, "I mean soon to comply with your kind invitation to come and see you . . . because I think of writing a school-book—or, at any rate, a book for the young—and should highly prize your advice as to what is wanted, and how it should be achieved" (*CE*, 16:293). More significantly, he may have come to realize that success in children's literature rested less in restricting readers' tastes to certain styles or subjects than in opening up spaces for new ones.[48] Revisiting the idea for the "Boys' Wonder-Horn" he had entertained since his earlier correspondence with Longfellow, the "book for the young" Hawthorne would next produce was not another set of the biographical and historical sketches but a collection of domesticated myths and fantasies for children, *A Wonder-Book for Girls and Boys*, and its sequel, *Tanglewood Tales* (1853). Thus, while earlier juvenile efforts had failed to "gather gold" (*CE*, 15:563), as investments in an accruing bank of ideas for the genre they were about to pay off. As he tellingly explains in *A Wonder-Book*'s preface: "The author has long been of opinion, that many of the classical myths were capable of being rendered into very *capital* reading for children" (*CE*, 7:3; emphasis added). At last, Hawthorne's long desire to build a link between "capital" (first-rate) literature and capital (monetary sales) could be realized.

An exchange at the end of *A Wonder-Book* confirms his sustained faith in the fame, financial success, and stability that children's literature might provide him. His stories at last concluded, intrepid mythologizer Eustace

Bright imagines himself riding the winged horse Pegasus across the Massachusetts countryside, visiting "brother authors" such as Longfellow, Melville, and Holmes, when Primrose waggishly intrudes upon his reverie, asking him whether they had not such an author already as their "next neighbor" (*CE*, 7: 169). Describing Hawthorne, that "silent man" whom "we sometimes meet, with two children at his side, in the woods or at the lake," she then observes, "I think I have heard of his writing a poem, or a romance, or an arithmetic, or a school-history, or some other kind of a book" (169). When Eustace then jokingly warns that, if "our babble were to reach his ears, and happen not to please him, he has but to fling a quire or two of paper into the stove" and their whole world "would turn to smoke, and go whisking up the funnel" (169–70), Hawthorne comes full-circle; a mature author enjoying literary fraternity and modest renown, he confronts his younger, more anxious self from "The Devil in Manuscript." But unlike Oberon's scornful dismissal of "school-books," Hawthorne's tongue-in-cheek depiction of himself as a "school-history" writer wielding "terrible power" (170) over Eustace and the children enacts the masculine and authorial self-assurance he had since found in juvenile fiction. When he crows to a friend in 1853, "I never did anything else so well as these old baby-stories" (*CE*, 16:649), his attitude is a far cry from earlier doubts about his writings' merit, and the feelings of "solitude" Oberon had voiced all those years before. Hawthorne would thus find his long-sought sense of belonging, not among men, but in the company of children.

The supreme irony, of course, is that men like Horace Mann, and the public institutions they helped to establish, continued to be instrumental in making these later successes possible. After Ohio, for instance, adopted the district model and passed a law providing tax funds for school libraries in 1853, Hawthorne's publishers, William Ticknor and James Fields, negotiated with the state's Commissioner of Common Schools for a wholesale order of approximately 8,500 books. In early 1856, they sent, along with a variety of children's fiction, poetry, and travel narratives, 1,400 copies of *True Stories from History and Biography*. It was the fourth largest lot in the order, and the second largest by an American author, ensuring that Ohio's schoolchildren would grow up with Hawthorne as a formative part of their adolescent education.[49] Such shipments not only remind us that publication venues were as crucial to Hawthorne's successes in the juvenile market as changing consumer tastes, but also provide an important addendum to accounts of his literary canonization via "interlocking system[s] of literary institutions that were themselves newly emerging" at the time.[50] Decades before

Houghton Mifflin's inexpensive *Riverside Literature Series,* which repackaged New England authors as texts for schools, solidified his "classic" status in American curriculum, antebellum district school libraries, along with the expansive markets for children's literature that they nurtured, enabled writers like Hawthorne to avoid Oberon's fate, and saved him from the ignominy of being "the obscurest man of letters in America."[51]

CHAPTER 3

"Contact with the World"

Elizabeth Palmer Peabody's West Street Bookshop

Henry David Thoreau voices a common refrain among critics of nineteenth-century print culture when he complains in his "Reading" chapter of *Walden* (1854) of "a work in several volumes in our Circulating Library entitled Little Reading" which the populace consumes with "saucer eyes, and erect and primitive curiosity, and with unwearied gizzard . . . just as some little four-year-old bencher his two-cent gilt-covered edition of Cinderella,—without any improvement, that I can see, in the pronunciation, or accent, or emphasis, or any more skill in extracting or inserting the moral."[1] Thoreau's lament over "Little Reading" registers long-standing assumptions not only about the poor character of popular literature and the questionable taste of those readers who peruse it, but also about the character of institutions that circulate such texts. He reiterates a complaint dating back to the beginnings of circulating libraries themselves in Boston, when they first began appearing during the second half of the eighteenth century. Far from inculcating edifying principles in readers, the creation, circulation, and consumption of light reading, Thoreau maintains, is a "sort of gingerbread," merely a sugary sweet that rots the mind instead of the teeth, resulting in a general "sloughing off of all the intellectual faculties" (105). Yet, with booksellers and distributors aiming only to make a profit, this bread is "baked daily . . . in almost every oven," and finds an eager audience more than willing to consume it (105).

But even as Thoreau complains about the processes of a print culture he sees as both corrupting and "provincial" (109)—one that refuses to grow up and embrace more than narrow interests—there had already been at least one well-known, local bookstore and library that rejected the "gingerbread" model of business, and without the reactionary insistence on a return to "classics" that Thoreau himself articulates when he composes his own reading list in *Walden*.[2] Founded in the summer of 1840 and remaining open until 1852, Elizabeth Palmer Peabody's West Street bookshop and foreign circulating library garnered seemingly universal praise from the residents of antebellum Boston who frequented it. The bookstore was "a part of the educational influences of the period," Thomas Wentworth Higginson, famous Boston resident and one-time frequent customer remembered fondly, a place where he himself had made "acquaintance" with various foreign books, both classical and contemporary, including the "relics of the French Eclecticism, then beginning to fade, but still taught in colleges" and "many of the German balladists who were beginning to enthrall [him]."[3]

Indeed, at the heart of Peabody's enterprise was the act of opening for customers an "acquaintance" with world literatures, exposing them to new ideas and literary experiences beyond those of New England. As Peabody would later describe it, "About 1840 I came to Boston and opened the business of importing foreign books . . . and then I came into contact with the world as never before."[4] This expansive, cosmopolitan notion of "contact with the world" was one of the driving impulses of her enterprise. By the time she established her bookstore, Peabody had come to view the idea of "contact" both as indispensable to fostering her customers' self-culture and as a corrective measure against the "spirit of coterie," the exclusive, self-interested circles that she saw pervading American life and letters. This chapter, therefore, investigates Elizabeth Peabody's career as a transcendentalist bookseller, lender, and publisher striving to forge a space within a male-dominated profession, and examines her efforts to "transcend" the coterie practices dominating business as usual in Boston. In the process, it argues that Peabody's search for "contact with the world" points to some of the larger concerns of transcendentalism with which she wrangled, encapsulating both her struggles as a woman trying to overcome obstacles to a career in literature and her interest in importing the foreign as a way to escape provincial American thinking.

My reading of Peabody is markedly different from earlier assessments of her career, which have tended to dismiss her as an eccentric and relatively minor figure in the antebellum scene. I join a recent body of criticism interested in Peabody as a source of insight into a wide range of important nineteenth-century issues, including, as Leslie Perrin Wilson points out, "Boston intellectual history, book trade history, library history, reform history, [and] women's history," not to mention transcendental attitudes toward antebellum print culture.[5] But while Wilson has examined the organization and daily operations of the bookshop, I am interested in reconstructing Peabody's initial vision of herself as its proprietor, and in how that vision deepens our own understanding of the relationship between gender, transcendentalism, and the literary marketplace.[6] Born out of her experiences as a woman intellectual within the patriarchal confines of nineteenth-century New England, and thus uniquely embodied in notions of contact and collaboration, Peabody's transcendentalism would find its apotheosis in her West Street bookshop and foreign circulating library. What is so interesting about Peabody is that although she would become the poster-child for charges of liberal New England intellectual fuzziness that critics of the movement heaped upon it, the bookstore reveals her as, in some respects, a much more sensible transcendentalist than many of her colleagues.[7] Ultimately, Peabody's enterprise offers us a more nuanced understanding of the varieties of American transcendentalism since, as it demonstrates, her brand of transcendentalism was practical and ethical, a kind of feminist cosmopolitanism that was as much a tool for coping with the gendered dimensions of the antebellum marketplace as it was a religious or philosophical orientation.[8]

At least part of Peabody's modern obscurity rests, as others have observed, on the fact that most of her efforts were in collaboration with, or on behalf of, other literary figures, thus tending to deflect attention away from herself and toward her contemporaries. Whether through her essays, translations, biographies, or bookstore, she continually sought to act as intermediary between some favorite associate, writer, or text, and the reading public she hoped would receive them.[9] When literary critics have mentioned Peabody, it has been in relation to people such as Nathaniel Hawthorne or Ralph Waldo Emerson—in other words, in connection with the great men, and sometimes women, in whose circles she moved. Not surprisingly, literary critics have tended to treat her bookstore as merely a stage where other, more significant players enacted their parts—the location, for instance, where Fuller held her famous conversation classes, or where George Ripley held the first discussions on what would be the Brook Farm experiment.

No doubt the critical neglect of Peabody has been perpetuated by the gendering of the literary canon itself, and by reliance on sources, such as Hawthorne, Emerson, and Henry James, each with extremely vexed relations to women and/in the marketplace, that enforce her secondary status. Emerson, for instance, described her as someone "who, by her constitutional hospitality to excellence, whether mental or moral, has made her modest abode for so many years the inevitable resort of studious feet, and a private theatre for the exposition of every question of letters, of philosophy, of ethics, and of art."[10] In positing her essential value as a "constitutional hospitality to excellence" and in dubbing her bookstore a "modest abode" and "private theatre," Emerson reinforces gendered notions of passivity, domesticity, and privacy that were, ironically, at odds with the expansive purpose of the enterprise; it was a business venture, a public endeavor designed both to make money and at the same time to actively foster a more open, and thus "transcendental," print culture. But, given such accounts, Peabody's fate as a footnote to American transcendentalism, it seems, was sealed.[11]

On the contrary, the bookstore and lending library obliged her to function as importer, bookseller, lender, publisher, educator, editor, and writer all at once, and in a way that made her a virtually omnipresent influence in the literary and intellectual circles of Unitarian Boston during the early 1840s. Although, in her search to disseminate a more moral literature than the character of the market had thus far allowed, she clearly sought to regulate certain types of popular, "trashy" texts her efforts did not necessarily translate into a vision of a world with fewer books in circulation. Unlike many of her male peers whose anxieties manifested themselves in desires to restrict the literary market, Peabody hoped to encourage a larger variety of texts than was currently available to the American reader, seeking a diverse and eclectic set of books, both domestic and foreign, to foster readers' self-development by promoting the exchange of ideas between the sexes and across cultural barriers. Profoundly affected by the gendered practices of both the literary market and the circles in which she moved, she harbored a transcendental vision of the book trade as inclusive and encompassing, rising above provincial ends and seeking increasing avenues to captivate the public interest and earn a profit without resorting to best-selling, but morally questionable texts. Envisioning her bookstore as an embodiment of her lessons in "contact," Peabody turned to bookselling, publishing, and importation as essential means to the dissemination of a new print culture, seeking success through an establishment that would rise above the spirits of coterie and exclusion she envisioned as threatening American cultural life.

Engendering Controversy

For Peabody, transcendentalism was inseparable from gendered dynamics of power precisely because even the most liberal-minded male intellectual was subject to restrictive, masculinist paradigms of thinking that could have potentially serious consequences for her efforts to collaborate with them. Indeed, the bookstore would be Peabody's own chance to restore "contact with the world" after what was the fantastic and catastrophic failure of the Temple School in Boston, a fraught collaboration with fellow (though, importantly, male) transcendentalist Bronson Alcott that essentially forced her into an almost unbearable, four-year social and intellectual exile in Salem. Her involvement with Alcott began in late 1834 with the opening of their school and ended in mid-1836 when she quit a few months before the publication of their *Conversations with Children on the Gospels* (1836), a transcript of weekly conversations Alcott held with their class, initially purporting to validate the truths of Christianity as uttered through the mouths of babes. Concluding with the abrupt dissolution of their partnership, her retreat to Salem for the sake of her reputation, a public outcry against the *Conversations,* the eventual collapse of the school, and the destruction of Alcott's teaching career, their collaboration reinforced the harsh realities of gender proprieties in antebellum New England and offered an important lesson on the viability of educational commodities in connection with them. Ultimately, however, it served to reinforce her commitment to contact, circulation, and exchange as absolutely essential to self-culture, helping to push her toward the foundational principles of her bookstore by hardening her resolve for "contact with the world," not merely for herself, but also for her customers.

Scholars have already outlined Peabody's life-long battles against what she saw as the problematic tendencies fostered by an otherwise timely and necessary self-culture movement: excessive individualism, or even downright egoism.[12] In her *Reminiscences* (1880), a lengthy biography of her former mentor, influential Unitarian minister William Ellery Channing, Peabody records detailed conversations with him on these misguided tendencies.[13] In one such conversation, Channing confesses his belief that the "danger that besets our Transcendentalists is that they sometimes mistake their individualities for the Transcendent" (Peabody, *Reminiscences,* 365). Although, on Peabody's prodding, he absolves Emerson of the tendency to confuse personal idiosyncrasy with universal human nature, Channing warns her that many of Emerson's "professed followers" had yet to recognize this problem (365). Assessing the direction of the transcendental movement, Peabody herself considers whether its introduction into Boston society might not have been better served by one of its "some what more conservative" members, wondering, for instance, if "perhaps Dr. [Frederick Henry] Hedge might have introduced Transcendentalism in such a way that it would not have become identified with the extreme Individualism which is now perhaps indelibly associated with it in America" (371).

While Peabody involved herself in every stage of the Temple School's development, functioning as its organizer, promoter, recorder, and, when worse came to worst, its fervent defender despite a serious falling out with Alcott, it is in the context of Alcott's growing egoism that we should understand her dissatisfaction with him during their Temple School years.[14] Most disconcerting to Peabody was the fact that, as a progressive endeavor built upon the principles of self-culture (seeking to remove all outside impediments to students' self-development and employing Socratic conversations to enable their voices), the school failed namely because of the masculine ego behind Alcott's supposedly transcendental practices. While it was ultimately Alcott's brazen intrusion, in a fit of suspicion that his assistant was turning against him, into her private correspondence that precipitated Peabody's final break from him, much of what soured her to their collaboration arose from his obvious failures to live up to the school's original aims.[15]

To better understand her mounting vexation with Alcott, one might look to the optimism expressed in the preface of the *Record of a School* (first edition, 1835), her original account of the school and its curriculum, composed from notes taken while observing its classes. By the time she published the book's second edition in 1836, Peabody would be on the defensive. She made several changes to the edition, and, after she had revised its preface, what was once a modest five-page introduction now ballooned to over 40 belabored pages of clarification on the school's principles and practices.[16] In the first edition, however, she lauds Alcott as a great "mediator" of the "influences of those great principles of spiritual self-culture," whose sole purpose is "removing inward and outward obstacles to their full and harmonious development" in his students. She also informs her readers proudly that while teaching as an employment "has been too often assumed . . . with avowedly mercenary ends, or at least for secondary purposes," Alcott's methods would remedy this problem because, in demanding "a better spirit, where it was wanting," they put children's educational and "spiritual" needs first.[17] All other things, she implies, would follow from this lofty "primary" premise of helping students cultivate their own minds, characters, and consciences.

By the end of the first year, she had begun to register serious disagreements with Alcott's classroom practices, even as some parents had grown uneasy about the school's curriculum, with its intense focus on mind, spirit, and soul almost to the exclusion of all other subjects.[18] For instance, Peabody tells Alcott in an 8 October 1835 letter that she "wanted to see if you did not change my opinions" about what she thought was becoming his deleterious obsession with introspection, "But a year's observation of your practice has not convinced me, and my own opinion and feeling have only grown more strong."[19] More troubling to both Elizabeth and her sister, Mary, was the fact that Alcott was growing downright manipulative with the children, orchestrating class discussions so that they would come to predetermined conclusions of his own choosing, rather than allowing the conversations to unfold on the students' terms, as both he and Peabody had intended. And this was only the tamest of the techniques he employed to coerce the students into agreement with his will. In some cases, he would goad the children into acts of disobedience in order to make individuals an example to the class, while, in others, he would indulge in corporal punishment, requiring that students beat *him* for their transgressions, which they then would have to do in front of the class, and often on the verge of tears.[20] Mary, for one, had watched these exploits with what she ironically termed "great interest," confessing to Elizabeth in mid-1836: "All you express of Mr. Alcott I respond to. . . . I have not by any means felt that he did not lead the minds of his scholars, though I know he does not intend to. I have heard them questioned out of their opinions more than once. I think these faults of Mr. A's have grown upon him very much and begun to appear very much in his whole manner."[21] Both women, therefore, feared that Alcott had become a subtle, yet substantial bully in the classroom, his disingenuous manipulations casting uncertainty not only on his abilities as the spiritual "mediator" that Peabody's *Record* preface had championed, but also on the school itself as a place dedicated to removing "inward and outward obstacles" to students' self-culture.

In mid-1836, Mary cautioned Elizabeth that the position was no longer worth the dangers it engendered. Alcott's domineering personality had spilled over to his professional relationship with Elizabeth, and he began to treat her more and more like his subordinate rather than as his collaborator. Although she continued to be crucial to the success and credibility of the school, it seems the fact that, under the terms of their initial arrangement, their relation "was not a partnership" was coming back to haunt her.[22] Mary was worried especially that Alcott—who was not about to change his ways—would damage the integrity of their next collaboration, *Conversations with*

Children, as a text dedicated to Christian self-culture, and with which her sister's professional and personal reputations were deeply intertwined: "You do not in your heart think he is quite honest always about his record and if I were in your place I should not be willing to have anything to do with it unless it can be a true record—You do not agree in all his measures, and [yet] you are obliged to sanction them tacitly or else explain the disagreement to people."[23] In another letter, Mary tells Elizabeth that she "would give the world if you were no longer in association with Mr. A" because "that book will not be honestly printed & if not you will suffer for it. It is your record. That is known—but if you gave it up to Mr. A to print you may be sure he will print it his own way." That he would alter the book to his liking given the chance was certain, not only given his dealings with the children and Peabody, but also as Mary recalls "being startled a year ago when you & Mr. A were discussing the record & disputing about a fact, by his saying he wished to have *the book a perfect one*—as if the truth might be sacrificed to that!" She therefore implores Elizabeth to be the one to guide the book to print, hoping "you are to do it all yourself & to correct the proofs."[24]

What ultimately doomed the school was, in fact, the publication of the first volume of *Conversations* in December 1836, after Elizabeth had left the school. While what had disturbed Peabody were his numerous violations of the principles of self-culture, she also correctly feared a reactionary fervor on the part of readers over the text's occasional indulgence in illicit subjects such as birth and circumcision. On 7 August 1836, after she had already gone, but before he had published the *Conversations,* she wrote him one final letter, noting the precariously gendered implications of their situation. She warns him that "many persons, liking the school in every other respect, think it is decisive against putting female children to it especially" (*Letters,* 180). Although she not did not agree with these sentiments and believed that girls as much as boys deserved the kind of education the school hoped to offer, Peabody tells Alcott that, still, "something of an impression was gratuitously taken up that I left the School" on account of its class discussions being inappropriate for mixed company, and, what was more, "it was thought I," as a woman, "ought to leave it" (180).

In the months leading up to Elizabeth's break with Alcott, even Mary had begun to think her sister's involvement improper, advising her that perhaps she "ought to be teaching *great girls.* That is your peculiar calling[,] your vocation." She implored her to leave Boston, to "go into the country," and to "take a class of country young ladies for almost no price." There she could "see the grass grow, and the brooks run & hear the wind in the trees," noting "there are enough interesting people in Concord & Margaret Fuller in Groton," although, from what we know of Fuller's country experiences, rural life was not exactly conducive to fostering the interests of intellectual women.[25] Of course, the last thing Elizabeth wanted to do after the vistas opened to her through contact with the likes of Channing and the rest of her Boston friends was retreat into rural Massachusetts, to some intellectual backwater in the countryside where she would find very little stimulation, only to be doubly confined by gender proprieties to a class of young girls. Reluctantly, however, Elizabeth capitulated to her sister's suggestion, taking over her girls' school in Salem when Mary herself returned to Boston in early 1839.[26]

Peabody did not think Alcott's discussions inherently "obscene," as one of the critics of *Conversations* would famously claim when it appeared in print, but she did find it ill advised that Alcott should *lead* his students into controversial topics, believing them forced upon the children by Alcott's misguided intentions rather than provoked by the spontaneous flow of their own conversation.[27] Addressing this issue of his repeated manipulations directly, then, she confesses in her 7 August 1836 letter that, although she thinks that "it is impossible to keep children ignorant and that it is better to lead their imaginations than to leave them to be directed by idle curiosity," she does *not* feel she "should ever have ventured so far myself," and she even calls a "great many" of his questions "quite superfluous" (*Letters*, 180). She left no doubt as to where the blame would lie for their impending disaster, should he insist on proceeding with his plans for publication. Having left the school, she tells him, "I am conscious of the effect of a few weeks' freedom from the excitement of being a part of the School, or taking down that exaggerated feeling which made every detail of it seem so very important to the great course of Spiritual Culture; and I never was under half the illusion in this respect that you were" (180–81).

In order to save her reputation as a lady, Peabody begged Alcott to omit all reference in the book to her involvement in his conversations. Calling forth traditional constructions of femininity, she tells him that she hoped that it "may be felt that I was entirely passive" in recording the transcripts. She also asks him to omit the questionable elements of the conversations (such as those on sex and birth), and to write his own preface to be placed before hers, further distancing her from the project by stating that "the Recorder did not entirely sympathize or agree" with him "in respect to the course taken," or something to that effect (181). She then concludes her letter with a remarkable commentary on the constraints placed upon women, telling Alcott that he "as a man can say anything; but I am a woman, and have feelings that I dare not distrust, however little I can *understand them* or give an account of them" (181; emphasis in original). Of course, Alcott largely ignored her warnings, rejecting them, it seems, as he might dismiss the impositions of a woman who did not know her proper place.[28]

When Alcott published the book over Peabody's objections, its fate, and that of the school, was sealed. Although he wrote his own introductory note and included Peabody's own preface distancing herself from the book, he still printed the text on his own terms, including all the questionable moments in an appendix at the end instead of removing them completely. Then, when he had made these changes, he sent review copies of the book to all the local newspapers. In a sense, Alcott neatly and noticeably packaged together and delivered all the materials that hostile reviewers would need to launch their savage attacks on him in the coming months. Apparently, there *were* some things that even a man could not say or write about. Though she had warned Alcott against publishing the manuscript in its current form, the book was, in Peabody's opinion, unfairly attacked as a moral abomination. One particularly galling assault called it a "more indecent and obscene book . . . than any other one we ever saw exposed for sale on a bookseller's counter."[29] Despite her reservations about Alcott's constant meddling, Peabody would hardly grant that the book was the worst *ever* in existence. It was, at least, a principled text, seeking to demonstrate the lofty educational ideal of allowing children to speak for themselves, however poorly Alcott put that ideal into execution.

Despite their numerous flaws, she believed there was unrecognized potential in Alcott's methods. In an 1837 letter to Horace Mann, in which she unflinchingly criticizes Alcott for the "great deal of nonsense about [him] all along," Peabody laments that his "disputed views" should overshadow the strength of his "general plans," which, even then, she still considered "wise." She believes that, despite his mistakes, "there is a current of the true method—an infusion of Truth—which I think neutralizes the error."[30] In one of her journal entries, she articulates the exact nature of this "Truth," offering a way to read the *Conversations* beyond merely as an account of Alcott's disingenuous manipulations:

> I thought Mr. Alcott's practical ability was much greater than he or any one else was inclined to give him credit for. That he could rouse the sense of justice and moral ideas practically in the minds of children to something like omnipotence, and this done the children's own wits would and did apply the principles to particular cases often in a superior manner to Mr. Alcott himself.

> My faith in his good influence was founded on the fact that he so truly roused their moral principles as to enable them to hold out and beat him in an argument upon special cases in which he concluded wrongly.[31]

Peabody marvels that Alcott, in love with his own voice and often arguing in the wrong, can still "truly rouse" the children's sense of "justice" and their "moral ideas" to something like "omnipotence," forcing that sense to assert itself and to triumph over his errors. The fact that this process takes place despite Alcott's misguidance—that the students themselves can "hold out and beat him in an argument . . . in which he concluded wrongly"—gives the episode an air of the transcendental. Even error, these conversations revealed, can function in the service of moral truth so long as it incites or inspires, offering the children something against which they might define themselves, some resistance against which they could instinctively respond and react. Her own collaboration with Alcott had, at least, taught her that much.

Ultimately, the debacle over the book forced Elizabeth to articulate to the world her own views on the school. In a short newspaper article, entitled "Mr. Alcott's Book and School," Peabody would lay out her case for the worth of Alcott's pedagogical practices, expressing in the process a transcendental manifesto on the circulation of ideas as essential to education. Articulating startlingly modern criticisms of the pedagogical status quo, she declares that "our actual Education, generally speaking," is "a violent imposition of the confessedly imperfect adult mind of the time upon the rising generation"—what a friend had described colorfully as the "steam-engine system" of educating children.[32] Adopting her own materialist analogy, she then informs the reader that, in a system merely presupposing a "dead capacity" in students "into which knowledge can be poured like material liquid," there is "no cultivation in the world—except by chance" (1). But Alcott's conversations with the children, and their victories over his wrong-headedness, suggest that they are not empty vessels into which elders can dispense their beliefs. In the process, his book proves conclusively that an alternative method of self-exploration "can be successfully pursued; that children can be interested in spiritual subjects, without doing violence to their natures; that it is easier to interest them . . . in such conversations, than to make them diligent in any other intellectual exercise" (1).

The worth of Mr. Alcott's book, therefore, lies in the "suggestive character" of its conversations, and the strength of Alcott as a teacher rests in the "cherishing influence" he exerts over the "spontaneous faculties of the mind" (1). It is this inspirational influence, she insists, that marks the "great value of the school" and constitutes the "very principle of education."³³ Ultimately, Peabody insists that while students may sometimes "go away from [Alcott's] school with a hundred fantastic notions," in the end it did them a great service because they left his classroom carrying "with them the first principles of the act of finding truth, by means of which all false notions are made temporary" (1). By attempting to foster their intellectual freedom, the school allowed students to explore in themselves "tendencies of mind to be encouraged or regulated," a process she believed was "the surest way to self-knowledge" (1). Even in his missteps, she contends, Alcott "allows the various associations [the children make] to act upon each other; knowing that the *universal* alone can survive a fair meeting. By observing one another the children learn what is invaluable—to see how the peculiarities of temper and disposition modify the understanding, and to discriminate the accidental from the absolute" (1; emphasis in original).

"No Worthless Books"

The problem, of course, was that it was not always a "fair meeting," and, in the face of masculine prerogative, for instance, the free exchange of ideas, the process of discriminating the "accidental" from the "absolute," might be stifled, as it was when Alcott bullied their students and warped the presentation of his and Peabody's pedagogical experiment; or as it was when male periodical editors denounced the *Conversations* out of hand as immoral without considering its high principles; or even as it was when Peabody was forced by notions of propriety to retreat to the backwaters of Salem. For generations of students, young and old, who had long been denied "contact" by the provinciality of their surroundings, then, the West Street bookstore would be a chance for intellectual cultivation without arbitrary imposition, a place where customers could leisurely browse, buy, and read books, or simply seize an opportunity to converse with the proprietor or any one of the personages that graced her premises. It also marked an opportunity for Peabody to combat the kind of provincial thinking that had relegated her to Salem in the first place, as she hoped to give voice to authors, texts, and perspectives overlooked or pushed out by the market's shortsighted practices. Her enterprise would resist, for example, what she saw as the literary industry's obsession with money at the expense of everything else, and its patriarchal structure, which thwarted not only women like her in their attempts to break into the publishing business, but also male writers like Hawthorne who struggled to find a place for themselves as authors in a role defined by male-female/publisher-writer power relations.[34]

Admittedly, Peabody's explicit motivations for opening a bookstore were, to quote one of her biographers, "something of a mystery."[35] But it would be just the thing she needed after Salem, where she could, essentially, "do nothing in the world by way of helping in the world." Confessing to Elizabeth Davis Bliss that Salem "seems another world than Boston" because its residents "care about nothing stirring—& read every species & form of transcendentalism as if it were Evil Lore," she jokes, "I like to hear from Boston folks—do they ever keep up foreign correspondences?" (*Letters*, 190). There is poignancy behind her humor; in poking fun at her isolation, the village's provinciality, and its residents' intellectual stagnation, she articulates a desperate yearning for the "world" beyond Salem's borders, as well as for "foreign correspondence" with it. Such cosmopolitan sentiments anticipate not only her foreign circulating library, but also the transcendental sensibilities informing the entire enterprise. In "foreign correspondence," or the search for continuities through comparative cultural study and the eclectic, unexpected connections it enables, Peabody sought the means toward the sounding of a more universal human culture, or as Bruce Ronda puts it, the sense of "belonging not simply to oneself or one's family but to the entire human race."[36] Committed to "stirring" correspondence even from the far recesses of Salem, she mentions at the end of this letter "negotiating with a publisher" to write a book containing "all my odd ends on education" (*Letters*, 190). This book did not materialize, but understandably so: why settle for a single book when nothing short of an entire bookstore might be enough to contain the "odd ends" that a competent teacher could provide, or a student might need?

While this book is not the same one that Peabody also intended to write for *The School Library*, still, her conversations with Mann, and intermediaries like him, on the subject of education could only have confirmed her decision to go into the "schoolbook" (in its broadest sense) business for herself.[37] In her 3 March 1838 letter to Mann, Peabody discusses his efforts to organize *The School Library*, while he was soliciting support for the state's common schools as Secretary of Education. She approved of his plan for the series, calling it "very interesting as well as wise," but she demurred at one particular aspect of it (*Letters*, 199). Mann intended that the Board itself choose the books for inclusion, but Peabody wondered whether the committee was really best qualified for the task. "[I]t seems to me that you think school committee men more important than *the teachers*," she tells him, "You will smile if I say you speak of teachers as if they were the schoolboys in comparison. You speak of the legislature & school committee men as choosing books. . . . Teachers are the best judge of books" (199; emphasis in original). Unfortunately, Mann's response was not very encouraging. He essentially dismissed her suggestion while complaining that there were currently no "suitable" books "fit to be recommended" for the series, even though in her letter Peabody had explicitly recommended Hawthorne as someone whose work more than qualified him to write for it (at least in her teacherly opinion).[38]

In a sense, then, Peabody's bookshop would be a chance to exercise her own judgment in the selection and recommendation of books. She would disseminate only "the most choice and valuable" texts "selected carefully by one who knows," as she would advertise them in one of the local papers—chosen by someone "who knows" presumably because she was first, foremost, and always a teacher.[39] In describing her bookstore to Samuel Gray Ward, Peabody echoes these sentiments, acknowledging that it was, in the words of one of her friends, "so desirable to have this foreign bookstore—where people could obtain information—& so desirable to have the matter so much in my own hands as for me to be able to have only that in my shop which *I chose*—& and could in a measure recommend."[40] Who better, after all, than a publisher, bookseller, *and* teacher to "render an inestimable service to the public," as the Board of Education had put it, "by the circulation of good books, at reasonable prices"? (*Second Annual Report*, 18). In her search for "good books," to take one example, one of her first acts as a publisher would be to ignore Mann's "school committee men" sensibilities and begin publishing Hawthorne's *Grandfather's Chair* series of children's books under her own imprint, although she happily stocked and advertised Mann's *School Library* as well.[41]

Choosing to begin her "first commercial enterprise" just as commerce itself "seemed about to be *reformed out*," that is, in the midst of vociferous debates over the perils of capitalism that marked the decades of 1830s and 1840s, Peabody embarked upon a literary establishment that she believed would contribute to the great works of moral, educational, and economic reform. In her 1841 letter to her friend, Samuel Gray Ward, Peabody offers a more detailed rationale for the enterprise. "This was the plan of my store," she writes, "that I should keep one in which were to be found no *worthless* books—shadows of shadows—& nothing of any kind of a secondary nature."[42] With these remarks on the moral and commercial value of her new enterprise, she articulates a desire to combat what she sees as a print culture promoting, to use her description of teaching in the preface to her *Record of a School*, "avowedly mercenary ends, or at least, secondary purposes," and thus indiscriminately circulating bad texts over good ones.[43] But if her notion of "no *worthless* books" in this letter to Ward is akin to Mann's plan for "good books" because they both seek to cultivate restraint in a print culture run amok, there are distinctions to be made between them nonetheless, as her differences with Mann on the selection of books also suggest.

With such considerations in mind—and after the debacle over the *Conversations*—Peabody was poised to tackle the state of antebellum print culture. By the time she decided upon the bookstore, she had already witnessed first-hand the kind of communal damage that the circulation of bad texts could cause. In early 1831, when she was teaching school in Boston with her sister, Mary, Elizabeth became aware of a scandal involving one of her "lovely and beloved" female pupils and a fast and loose set of young Boston men, whose antics Peabody claimed were inspired by the widely read English author Edward Bulwer-Lytton.[44] Perhaps now best known for the opening of his 1830 novel *Paul Clifford*, which begins "It was dark and stormy night," Bulwer-Lytton was then fashionable in Boston for his novel *Henry Pelham, or, The Adventures of a Gentleman* (1828), whose exposé of high-class life prompted interest in the hedonistic activities it decried.[45] The scandal was a formative experience; she returned to it nearly fifty years later, mentioning it not once, but twice in her *Reminiscences*. Declaring that news of scandal brought her into "intimate knowledge of the corruption of the imagination and life of some gifted young men of Boston," she confesses that it "was a frightful revelation to me to see crime committed . . . out of purely egotistical profligacy" (Peabody, *Reminiscences*, 320).

But those who distributed and promoted such books—editors, publishers, and booksellers—were generally thought to be culpable in the evils of the press and as bad in their tendencies as writers like Bulwer-Lytton. One periodical implored everyone involved in the production and distribution of books to consider the consequences of their actions, asking "those authors *who have consciences*, to weigh well what they write; with publishers, to consider beforehand what they publish; and with booksellers, to remember that readers, even female readers, have souls."[46] Some believed that industry practices made assembling an entire collection of good books impossible. Bronson Alcott himself had publicly attacked the character of most bookstores, declaring them "filled with their trash" and "a great field of temptation to children and youth":

> The child finds his way into one of them. Here is a pretty book—he wants this—the parent is unwilling to refuse him, and the book is bought; and what

is it? He would not be understood as saying that there were *no books* in our bookstores which were of the right character. Some, there indeed were, but they were few and far between. His own collection at his school room was small; and he did not believe it possible, he would again say, to find a large collection.[47]

While Peabody had learned not to trust his judgment—Alcott's low opinion of books led her to complain that he had no plan "to search the thought and views of other minds—in any faith that they will *help his own*. He only seems to look in books for what agrees with his own thoughts"—his were not isolated opinions.[48] At the very least, comments like these reveal the power that antebellum Americans attributed to the printed word, which, according to one editorialist, was "daily and hourly exerting its influences on the youthful mind of our country, whether perceived or unperceived."[49] By striking at character of print culture, therefore, reformers thought they were striking at the essence of the modern condition, and tackling the task of reform at one of its roots: the modern world *was* a reading world, after all.

Not surprisingly, new library ventures were exceedingly popular in the antebellum period, and several kinds of libraries existed simultaneously, with varying levels of access. First, there were traditional college libraries, which were not available to the general public. Then there were social libraries, private book collections acquired by groups of individuals joined together expressly for the purpose of forming their own library. The most prominent example of a social library was the Boston Athenaeum, founded in 1807, which quickly became one of the premier libraries in the country. It was very exclusive, to say the least.[50] There were also the circulating libraries, first established in Boston in 1765. These commercial enterprises, their proponents maintained, were democratic in principle, their goal being to "make available to persons of moderate means the sources of knowledge previously obtainable solely by the wealthy."[51] Since books at the turn of the nineteenth century were still relatively expensive to make and buy, these enterprises were very popular, distinguishing themselves not only by moderate subscription rates but also by their willingness to cater to women. Whereas an institution like the Boston Athenaeum restricted its membership to men (on one occasion, Peabody had to ask for special dispensation to conduct research there, seeking permission to borrow books on her own rather than through one of its male members), circulating libraries were willing to lend their articles to anyone who could meet their modest fees.[52] But if social libraries' membership costs and practices effectively restricted participation to the elite classes, circulating libraries' accessibility came at the cost of literary and cultural value. Aimed at making a profit, these libraries catered to what their critics claimed was the public's taste for pernicious forms of entertainment, namely novels and others fictions. Over time, they even trimmed their holdings, once dominated by newspapers, histories, and other nonfiction forms, until they carried fiction almost exclusively.[53] Not surprisingly, these libraries were stigmatized, especially when considered in connection with the "fairer sex." From the late eighteenth century onward, numerous texts condemned the image of the young woman who attempted to improve her mind through the stock of a circulating library.[54]

In fact, when Peabody informed her friends about her plans for such an enterprise, some hesitated to endorse it. Among those responses we have on record, Theodore Parker, for instance, admitted to Peabody that "the plan [for her bookshop] did not at first strike me so favorably as it did you."[55] William Ellery Channing was also cautious. Though he generally approved of her idea for a bookstore (apparently agreeing with her crusade for the necessary elevation of business, and telling her that such an endeavor might "partake of the dignity of literature"), he expressed reservations about her ideas for an accompanying circulating library. "The only objection I have to a circulating library," he tells her in a 22 June 1840 letter, "is the corrupt taste of readers, who often want books which one would not like to circulate" (quoted in Peabody, *Reminiscences*, 409). Channing, as Peabody remembered it, had on more than one occasion expressed his "fear that to lose oneself in imaginative sympathy with beautiful heroes and heroines, sympathizing as we always do with the noble, and gratified by the poetic justice which was dealt to all the characters, satisfied us with ourselves, though our own life was of a lower tone" (*Reminiscences*, 267). Essentially, Channing worried that the usual circulating library fare tended to foster complacence where there was a great need for continual self-improvement, the heart and soul of a Unitarian self-culture movement that saw the challenge of human life as a steady progression toward self-perfection. This was putting nineteenth-century fears of fiction in the best possible terms, since (as Thoreau's complaints at the start of this chapter also suggest) most objections centered on the moral degeneration and intellectual decay that novel-reading engendered in those who indulged it, especially women.

Peabody, however, took pains to reassure her friends that her plan was well within the bounds of propriety. For instance, she wrote to Channing: "On the first of August, I shall make my debut in the mercantile world, having made all my arrangements.... The plan is a very safe one. It will be hardly possible for any loss to accrue in any direction even if it does not succeed and there is every encouragement of success. Every body assures me they think it perfectly '*lady-like*.'"[56] Her emphasis on the "*lady-like*" dimensions of the endeavor, not to mention its "safety," indicates that she knew full well that others were worried a certain kind of trade might not only sully her image as a woman but also damage her social status, a distinction intimately connected with, and as equally rigid as, nineteenth-century constructions of gender. In claiming business for the realm of women, however, she posits it as a kind of a "debut" or coming of age for herself, comparing the opening of her store to the party at which a young woman is officially presented to society. Thus, business was not incompatible with proper gender roles, but merely a step in the full development of a woman.

The discussion of sex and business talent was in fact an ongoing issue between Peabody and Channing. In a 7 June 1840 letter, he offers his qualms about her entrance into the book trade, and, in a gendered moment of slippage between moral and commercial concerns, cautions her that in an "age of proprieties" difficulties may arise in her business efforts that she cannot anticipate (quoted in *Reminiscences*, 408). Despite being nonetheless "glad" to see what he calls an "experiment made by a woman equal to the task," perhaps she was not the woman he had in mind; he bluntly tells her that he "distrust[s]" her "business talent" (408). For her part, Peabody was quick to find evidence to the contrary, calling his attention to her early successes at the store. "I have now been a month in my new business and I think you will be interested to know how I get on," she writes him, "Well, I have sold a hundred dollars worth of books, the profit on which, together with your kind present, has covered all the expenses, and my getting under way." Then, responding directly to his doubts about her "talent" for business, she asks: "Now do you not think this proves quite a business talent? Nothing in a mercantile line could be as agreeable." Things were going so well, in fact, that she had big plans for the enterprise; she had "a great deal many orders on Europe" and had begun "to dream of the time when I shall go thither myself on direct transactions with the French and German bookstores."[57] Her bookshop, therefore, was a chance to silence her critics, to show them that not only did there exist large collections of good books in the world, as Alcott and others had denied there were, but also that she, a woman and teacher, would be the one to assemble and disseminate them.

While she was not the first woman to own and operate a circulating library in Boston, nor the only bookshop to sell foreign books, Peabody's enterprise would be an influential source for the dissemination of foreign literature in the city.[58] In an 1840 letter to Channing, Peabody explains one of the more tangible benefits of her establishment:

> I have ordered the two principal German periodicals, which having been retained a short while in the room to be examined by the subscribers, I shall allow to circulate with the other books. None of the Continental periodicals I have ordered are taken out [at] the University or Athenaeum, and this will be an attraction of the library. I shall have more than a hundred and fifty dollars worth of periodicals, which are to be circulated only among fifty subscribers. Therefore those who subscribe will have some real benefit.[59]

While one might bring books back from the continent (if one could afford to travel there) or subscribe to foreign periodicals oneself (again, if one could afford it), foreign texts were generally a scarce and expensive commodity in antebellum America. Indeed, mere months before Peabody opened her shop, Margaret Fuller lamented, in a 12 January 1840 letter to her friend Sarah Helen Whitman, the dearth of German literature available in the area: "There are few German books for sale in Boston, now Burdett has given up his shop. You will be more likely to find them at Behr's in New York. The vol of Tieck could not I presume, be bought, you might get it from the library of Harvard university, if you have a friend there" (*LMF*, 2:118).[60] Of course, the problem was whether one had a male connection at the university, since, like the Boston Athenaeum, the Harvard library was closed to the public at large and accessible only by men. Peabody's enterprise, therefore, would seek to counter such practices, making what were rare foreign commodities available to those interested in the materials regardless of their sex or affiliation, offering them literary "contact with the world" within a culture that largely excluded it.

Transcending West Street

Indeed, Peabody posits this notion of "contact" as a defining feature of transcendentalism itself. In an essay entitled "Plan of the West Roxbury Community" (1842), appearing in *The Dial* (1840–44), the transcendental periodical that was, for a time, published out of her own bookshop, she offers advice to Ripley and his Brook Farm associates as they embarked upon their utopian experiment (they had, after all, first discussed in her bookstore their plans for the commune). In the process, she warns against dangers inherent to the "spirit of coterie":

> Some may say, "already this taint has come upon them, for they are doubtless *transcendentalists*." But to mass a few protestants together and call them transcendentalists, is a popular cant. Transcendentalism belongs to no sect of religion, and no social party. It is the common ground to which all sects may rise, and be purified of their narrowness; for it consists in seeking the spiritual ground of all manifestations. . . . [I]t would be seen, if the word were understood, that transcendentalism, notwithstanding its name is taken in vain by many moonshiny youths and misses who assume it, would be the best of all guards against the spirit of coterie.[61]

Chafing at the term "transcendentalist" as a catch-all phrase for those seeking to counter troubling cultural tendencies, whether it be the growing materialism that worried the Brook Farmers or the cultural ignorance and provincialism that were her own concerns, Peabody asserts that the transcendentalist is not simply a nay-sayer. While those who gathered at Brook Farm were indeed all "protestants" because they dissented against the social and economic arrangements of their day, they were certainly *not* all "transcendentalists." To call them all by this name is to try to dismiss transcendentalism as nothing more than a coterie. Instead, the transcendentalist is one who embraces the vast potential of a human culture expanding above and beyond the bounds of self or nation. Aligning "coterie" with intellectual and spiritual "narrowness" that the transcendentalist flatly rejects, she asserts the necessity of expanding rather than contracting one's involvement in and knowledge of the world.

As a counter to the "spirit of coterie" threatening American life, and as a way to "transcend" the vices of its largely parochial print culture, Peabody's bookshop therefore sought to provide customers with an array of foreign materials and to allow their curiosity greater room for experimentation without resorting to the kinds of questionable texts already monopolizing circulation. In her *Dial* essay "A Glimpse of Christ's Idea of Society" (1841), the companion piece to her article on Brook Farm, Peabody makes a case for her transcendental model of education:

> Moral and Religious life should be the atmosphere in which the human being unfolds . . . . Thus only may he be permitted to freely act out what is within him; and have no temptations but necessary ones; and the intellectual apprehension follow rather than precede his virtue. This is not to take captive the will, but to educate it. If there were no wrong action in the world organized in institutions, children could be allowed a little more moral experimenting than is now convenient for others, or safe for themselves.[62]

In this context, one can argue that Peabody envisioned her bookshop as a kind of *right* "action in the world organized in [an] institution." If "education," in the grandest sense of the term, was a freeing of the will rather than the imposition of some set of ideas upon it (as the mishaps at the Temple School confirmed, and as she indicated in her published defense of Alcott), then the bookstore and foreign library would aim to achieve this lofty goal by offering nothing more than a place for "moral experimenting" using a method of both convenience *and* safety. It would offer convenience in the form of easy access to a variety of otherwise unattainable materials such as foreign-language texts, and its safety as an environment for experimentation came from the fact that Peabody only stocked books of which she herself approved, having considered them unquestionable in quality.

The bookstore offered customers several tiers of access to books, from the chance to purchase for themselves lavish editions of both classic and modern writers, foreign or domestic, to the opportunity to subscribe to her reading room for immediate access to new texts, to simply waiting to borrow, for a small fee, what books and periodicals she allowed to circulate.[63] Announcing a yearly subscription price of $5 or individual texts at 12 ½ to 25 cents a volume depending on their size, her foreign library's book catalogue for 1840, for instance, lists roughly 1,187 entries, initially consisting of 26 periodicals and collections of books arranged by language, most notably French, German, and English, but also Italian and Spanish. The library was, as the catalogue states, "on the increase," and would later grow to include texts in several other languages.[64] The list includes transcendental favorites such as Coleridge, Wordsworth, and Carlyle, prominent foreign periodicals in English, French, and German, as well as American journals such as *The Dial*, the *Christian Examiner*, the *Boston Quarterly*, and the *Western Messenger*, histories both ancient and modern, travel narratives, poetry, numerous English translations of foreign texts, including one of Peabody's own favorites, Herder's *Spirit of Hebrew Poetry*, and even novels in various languages.[65]

But Peabody did not merely sell books and distribute foreign texts; as one of the only female publishers in Boston, she also printed local talent.[66] In accordance with her pledge to circulate only books of the highest moral "worth," her first acquisition as a publisher was William Ellery Channing's *Emancipation* (1840). Channing gave her his manuscript, its copyright, and the rights to all possible profits resulting from its publication as a show of good faith in her enterprise, but the sales of the edition were not favorable. Although some would charge her with mismanaging the affair, according to

Peabody the problem was less a matter of business incompetence than of sexism and bookseller collusion:

> Very soon after this publication, Dr. Channing was written to by the Antislavery Societies of New York and Philadelphia for leave to print editions, each of twenty-thousand copies. He said it must not be done until my edition of a thousand copies had been sold. But I told him that I found booksellers would only take copies of me on sale to be accounted for in six months; for the publishers seemed to conspire to discourage a woman from attempts to publish; and I feared that if the popular tide was not taken at once, his dearest end—to serve the Antislavery cause—would be frustrated. I also said that if he did not, I should write to the Societies to go on with the cheap editions and risk the loss of mine. Mine, indeed, was never entirely sold. (*Reminiscences*, 412)

Suggesting that local booksellers "conspired" to discourage a woman from publishing by purchasing her goods only at discounted rates and even then postponing their payments, Peabody faced a choice between personal profit and much-needed exposure for Channing's greater cause (which 40,000 copies were sure to achieve, being an impressive number of volumes in circulation). While she kept to the principles of the bookstore, choosing to promote the "dearest end" of anti-slavery and, thus, the communal good over her own pecuniary interests, here, then, she came face to face with the specter of "coterie" in the shape of antebellum Boston's sexist publishing practices. She had to confront book publishers' masculine designs to keep a woman out of what they narrowly claimed as *their* business despite her best efforts to "transcend" them.[67] Certainly, it did not help that Channing, having visited Philadelphia, informed her, "My 'Emancipation' (which is yours in a sense) has been spread widely, and I believe done much good. It has been put into the hands of men of influence" (*Reminiscences*, 420–21). In attributing his book's success to "men of influence" (whether its male readers or the men who distributed it to them), he reproduces masculinist logic even as his parenthetical aside admits another possibility; the book *was* hers, not only in the sense that she held its copyright, but also in the signification that she, with "shrewd business sense," had accurately judged its popular demand where he had not, allowing it to find its way into the right men's hands in the first place.[68]

The opposition she faced from men within the industry is not surprising when one considers the rise of the "gentlemen publisher" in antebellum America. Even though the realities of business often clashed with such an ideal, this model, as Susan Coultrap-McQuin has noted, emphasized paternal, family-like relations with authors while espousing noncommercial aims, and envisioned the male publisher as society's moral steward.[69] The image solidified itself as chaos, competition, and profit in the industry increased, not to mention as the prevalence of professional women writers and their female readership became increasingly hard to ignore. Whether this formulation arose in response to the overwhelming female presence in the literary profession, or whether increasing female participation in the literary market resulted from the existence of a patriarchal structure with which many women were already comfortable, the power dynamic between "male" publisher and "female" author set the terms for much of women's and men's participation in the marketplace.[70] Perhaps, then, many of Peabody's male counterparts in Boston did not appreciate her efforts to upset the conventional order of literary business.[71]

Peabody continued to express her frustrations with an industry dominated by men whose practices were so much worse than she had anticipated. In a June 1841 letter to Channing, she details "disappointments in [her] undertaking" in both bookstore and library, writing, "I am disappointed because encouragements and expectations held out to me by those in the trade, with whom I conversed have not been acted up to." First, she was "curtailed of my plan of importing according to my own judgment by Wiley's refusing to give me more than ten days credit—too short a time to sell books, so I am obliged to limit myself to orders which makes my business smaller."[72] The Wiley referred to in the quotation is the New York publishing firm of Wiley and Putnam, where Peabody's cousin, George Palmer Putnam, and his partner, John Wiley, had agreed to act as agents in furnishing her with books.[73] The change in terms must have been galling for Peabody since the whole point of the enterprise was, as she indicates, to establish a bookshop guided by her "own judgment." Yet here was another man imposing himself upon her plans. Second, she was "disappointed" with respect to her circulating library because, here too, "Wiley has withdrawn his first agreement which was to let me have them on credit, to be paid only in January. So my library is at a stand still, and unless I can get a letter of credit on London, I shall have to sell it next winter."[74]

Similarly, she shared with Channing her dismay "in finding rules of the trade so bad morally, and the whole concern so rotten. I have obtained some insight into a deeply rooted evil in society that I would have appreciated no other way. But there is here and there a man who cares more for his conscience than for money. All such that I know are poor—small dealers."[75] Peabody's protests notwithstanding, most antebellum booksellers were, in fact, "small dealers." In 1850, there were only 1,720 booksellers in the nation, while the average lifespan for a bookstore was barely over one year.[76] At twelve years (1840–52), Peabody's was a long-lived enterprise, even as it would never rival the successes of bigger firms. But if her observations about "poor" book dealers simply reflect the material realties of the antebellum industry, in lamenting "rules of the trade" she found "so bad morally," and in identifying only "here and there a man" who fully understood such literary ventures as moral enterprises, Peabody expresses her frustration with *male* competitors who, more often than not, placed the "mercenary" or "secondary" aims of business before the "primary" one of self-culture. Ultimately, then, the "deeply rooted" industry "evil" of which she speaks is not the lack of capital or the economic instabilities that modern historians identify as endemic to the period, but rather what she came to understand as a spirit of masculine coterie. While some complained bitterly about what they saw as the literary market's increasingly feminized character, as Hawthorne did when he famously recoiled from its "mob of scribbling women" (*CE*, 17:304), Peabody saw it as a space of male prerogative (embodied in the male reviewers, editors, publishers, distributors, and booksellers with whom she had contact), which could be arbitrarily competitive, inhibitive, and restrictive.

Peabody's struggles with booksellers in Boston and Wiley and Putnam in New York are not the only problems worth noting. From January 1842 to July 1843, she published *The Dial*, having been suggested as successor by Margaret Fuller after the journal's financially troubled publisher, Weeks and Jordan, went bankrupt.[77] She inherited it in precarious financial condition; not only was Weeks, Jordan, & Co. "much in debt" financially to *The Dial*, but Fuller had also not been paid "a penny" in all her time as editor, overall journal subscriptions were down, and the journal was barely covering its publishing costs.[78] Peabody made several sensible suggestions as publisher. First, she issued a notice in the April 1842 issue in which she asked subscribers to help the journal by paying on time or in advance (a common refrain among periodicals with long lists of delinquent subscribers). Next, she asked them to send their money and names directly to her rather than the journal's agents in order to save on commission. Finally, hoping to rein in excessive publishing costs, she encouraged those who bought single issues to subscribe so that she could more accurately determine the number of copies to be printed.[79] Despite these management decisions, when Peabody failed to get the April 1843 issue to booksellers by the first of the month, Emerson changed publishers, hiring his own, James Munroe of Boston. Emerson seems to have blamed Peabody for the journal's continued woes, pointing to her April failure as evidence of what he believed were her generally "careless" policies with regards to *The Dial*'s distribution.[80] One cannot help but wonder, then, whether in his decision to replace the journal's female publisher with a male one, Emerson hoped that a more capable man might not improve the periodical's prospects—just as when Fuller resigned as editor and Emerson took over, Theodore Parker declared to him that *The Dial* could finally "grow up to vigorous manhood."[81]

Conclusion: "Transcendental Exchange"

When all was said and done, Peabody was not so easily deterred by such setbacks, or by narrow-minded opinions on the prospects of her business, and through her own persistence, as well as the help of various friends, what Channing had envisioned as merely a "resort for ladies" in fact became a bustling of intellectual exchange for those of both sexes. She was pleased to find "at the end of the first year that I had done *something*, notwithstanding the failure of my first plans" (Peabody, *Reminiscences*, 413; emphasis in original). One customer, Edward Everett Hale, called the store an "immense convenience" for "young Boston" in its determination to "keep more in the current of the flow of German and French life," and claimed that to "one who remembers how very 'English' the training of young Boston had been till now,—fed on Blackwood, Fraser, and the English quarterlies,—it will be seen that the opening of this modest reading-room for books printed in France and Germany, with a chance to meet those who read them most, was an enlargement of the means of education."[82] Another contemporary, George Bradford, called the bookstore "a sort of Transcendental Exchange" where people "young and old resorted . . . to talk with the learned and active-minded proprietor, to get the literary news of the day, the last word of philosophy, of religious literature and thought," as well as "questions then agitating the community."[83] Peabody's transcendental revolt against narrow-mindedness through the importation of foreign learning and the push for intellectual collaboration obviously had personal resonance in the sexism she faced, in so far as she understood it as symptomatic of a larger cultural parochialism, or "spirit of coterie," at work.

Peabody's example shows us that nineteenth-century American women could be positioned toward cosmopolitanism, attracted to the transcendental, by the necessities of their circumstances. In a culture largely refusing women any active participation in its intellectual life, it is not surprising that Peabody turned to importation as a means for intellectual fulfillment, filling in the process a market void that others in their short-sightedness had overlooked or denied. The bookshop became a place where Boston residents could go to satisfy their need for more than what the mainstream market had to offer, and where there were sure to be others who shared their interests. As Margaret Fuller reveals in a 7 November 1840 letter to Emerson, Peabody's business model actually worked: "Will you send to me at Miss Peabody's," she asks him, "the remaining volume's Pietro della Valle which she is to have in her Foreign Library, and foreign they will surely be.—The other day I was sitting there and two young ladies coming in asked first for Bettina and then for Les Sept Chordes &c—I suppose next time they will ask for Pietro and Munchausen" (*LMF*, 2:182). Fuller's wry comments about the popularity of Peabody's stock (the books were "foreign" indeed because she could never quite get her hands on the ones she wanted), and her minor competition with the other young ladies over their voracious desire for the same foreign literature, reveals that women devoured the cosmopolitan and the "transcendental" alternatives that Peabody provided them.

CHAPTER 4

"Conversation of a Better Order"
Margaret Fuller from the Classroom to *The Dial*

WRITING TO Elizabeth Peabody in 1836, and anxious for employment after her father's death, Margaret Fuller waxes prophetic about her literary ambitions:

> It is my earnest wish to interpret the German authors of whom I am most fond to such Americans as are ready to receive. Perhaps some might sneer at the notion of my becoming a teacher; but where I love so much, surely I might inspire others to love a little; and I think this kind of culture would be precisely the counterpoise required by the utilitarian tendencies of our day and place.... I hope a periodical may arise, by and by, which may think me worthy to furnish a series of articles on German literature, giving room enough and perfect freedom to say what I please.[1]

That periodical would be the transcendentalist magazine *The Dial* (1840–44), where Fuller would serve not only as a constant contributor, but also as editor, directing the journal through the first half of its existence. But if, in 1836, she imagined her future career as a union of writing and teaching, what did it mean for her to consider *The Dial* as such an enterprise? Exactly what roles would love, inspiration, "room enough," and "perfect freedom" of expression play in the intersections of periodical literature and education? How would the enterprises between her life at the time of this letter and the journal's inception—school-teaching in Providence and Conversations in Boston—culminate in a vision of periodical literature as a means of democratic education?

In their efforts to recover her work from canonical obscurity and champion her as the radical thinker she was, literary critics have focused on "multi-vocality" as the essence of Fuller's feminist agenda. A lengthy critical tradition, in fact, reads *Woman in the Nineteenth Century* (1845) as the culmination of her search for a voice that is, as one critic has called it, "subversive" and "polyphonic," resistant to masculine models of discourse monopolizing cultural conversation.[2] Numerous critics have elucidated Fuller's rhetorical style, tracing the influence on it of forms like conversation, and focusing on techniques such as dialogue, digression, mediation, and interruption, to name but a few.[3] But while scholars have found Fuller's conversational apotheosis in *Woman in the Nineteenth Century*, it is important to remember that Fuller was a periodical writer for the majority of her career; *Woman* itself began its life as the periodical essay "The Great Lawsuit" in 1843. Not only was the periodical, therefore, the form in which she worked until her untimely death in 1850, when employed as foreign correspondent for the *New York Tribune*, but it was also the means by which she began her career, editing *The Dial* from 1840 to 1842. In investigating the convergence of Fuller's multi-vocal style with the periodical genre, this chapter contends that her feminist pedagogy found its print analog in her role as editor.

In essence, it argues that Fuller's experiences as *The Dial*'s editor forced her, if not to rethink, then, at least, to recommit herself to some aspects of her conversational pedagogy over others, eventually shaping a new understanding of it that arose, in part, from her differences of opinion with Emerson regarding the magazine's direction. As their interactions attest, Fuller came to see her role as editor as less a "systematizing" influence (a phrase she often used to describe the productive conflict that was her conversational ideal) than as a safeguard for the free exchange of ideas (*LMF*, 1:87). Experiencing a shift in her understanding of what a "conversation of a better order," as she called it, might entail (*LMF*, 2:86), she concluded that, like the "plants of great vigor" and the "little, delicate flowers" she evokes in *Woman in the Nineteenth Century*, what participants needed from conversation was not intellectual rigor but rather "encouragement, and a free, genial atmosphere" suited to individual temperament (27). Whereas she initially sought to redirect discussion when it wandered away from her lofty aims, her exchanges with Emerson suggested to her how closely aligned such an attitude could be to a kind of masculine prerogative that suppressed opinions in accordance with its own sense of excellence, or "taste" as she termed it. Rather than seeking to restrict the magazine's submissions to only the best, Fuller hoped to allow for the greatest possible range of expression in its pages, and came to see the journal as a means to broaden the usual conversation, so to speak, however uneven these new contributions might be.

Ultimately, Fuller's shifting editorial priorities suggest yet another way in which she "reshapes and redefines the discursive field" of transcendentalism, aligned as it still is with Emerson.[4] Indeed, her role as editor is a crucial component of this redefinition, demonstrating, to use Steven Fink's terminology, the manner in which gender "limit[s]" and "reconfigure[s]" editorial authority when a woman sits in the "editor's chair" rather than a "solicitous, paternalistic literary gentleman." While the language of transcendentalism helped her "conduct business" as an editor—validating, for instance, her determination "not as a woman to act or rule, but as a nature to grow" (*Woman in the Nineteenth Century*, 20), and thus to defy the restrictions of a discourse Fink identifies as endemic to antebellum female editors—it also complicated these efforts.[5] Surely, she discovered this when Caroline Sturgis's father refused to allow his daughter to visit Fuller for fear of her transcendental reputation. Fuller responded with petulance to the "nonsense" about transcendentalism, asserting that an "active mind frequently busy with large topics" did not "interfere with domestic duties, cheerful courage and judgment in the practical affairs of life," and challenging "all in the little world which knows me to prove such deficiency from any acts of mine since I came to a woman's estate" (*LMF*, 1:314–15). But if these associations cut both ways, Fuller's editorship nonetheless reveals how educational imperative, radical feminism, and nascent free-market ideology all converge in transcendental literary enterprise. Unsurprisingly, then, Fuller's editorial style reproduces a "most distinctive development" of the antebellum market, enacting a literary and educational "marketplace of ideas" encouraged by a new-found faith in the din and clatter of free, democratic society.[6]

Conversations in Providence

Like others in an "age of conversation" seeking talk both as a fine art in its own right and as the basis of a literary style valorizing inspiration, spontaneity, and democratic availability as sources of power, Fuller easily found models among favorite foreign writers such as Goethe and Madame de Staël, as well as those closer to home, such as William Ellery Channing, Elizabeth Peabody, and Bronson Alcott, for whom she served as assistant in a four-month stint at the Temple School after Peabody's departure.[7] The chance to experiment extensively with her own conversational pedagogy, however, came when she accepted a position at the new Greene Street School in Providence, run by Alcott-enthusiast Hiram Fuller.[8] In the summer of 1837, she assented to the attractive proposal that she should teach "elder girls my favorite branches," including Latin, classical history, literature, rhetoric, and moral science, "for four hours a day,—choosing my own hours, and arranging the course,—for a thousand dollars a year" (*LMF*, 1:280). Such a flexible schedule and unrivaled salary could afford the "immediate independence" she longed for, despite any lingering preference for literary employment (280). While the reality of the position was more than she bargained for—she found herself attempting lessons to students of both sexes and of widely varying ages, from boys and girls of ten to full grown scholars of twenty years—Fuller found, as she tells a friend, "just what [she] wanted" when a group of "five or six maidens, from eighteen to twenty, intelligent and earnest," joined the school in search of "more advanced culture" (*LMF*, 1:322–23).[9]

These girls' journals record with keen insight their daily impressions of the school, its teachers, and its curriculum.[10] Remarking on the exercise of journal-keeping, Anna Gale, one of Fuller's "maidens," suggests the "Journals must be very nice keys by which, the teachers, can unlock the hearts, the characters, and as it were read the very thoughts of their scholars" (Kopacz, "School Journal," 100). Literary historians, however, value them not simply as "keys" to these young girls' interiority but also as records of Margaret Fuller's tenure at the school. Coming from young ladies "uncontaminated" by the "sense of threat" coloring male responses to Fuller, these journals are invaluable resources on her pedagogical method, revealing her to be a teacher commanding "great love and respect" as well as demonstrating a "deep understanding" of, and a regard for, the "intellectual and moral integrity of her students."[11] More importantly, they reveal Fuller's commitment to self-development, the "more advanced" moral and intellectual culture to which she hoped to introduce her students. While these journals demonstrate Fuller's vision of conversation as the "formation of a character," or "art in its highest sense," as Elizabeth Peabody described it, ultimately, the conversational exchanges they record are an important transitional phase in Fuller's rhetorical style, as she attempted to find the strategies best suited to female intellectual cultivation, not only to teach her young ladies to appreciate the life of the mind, but also to teach them to "systematize" it, that is, to change the way they think as the means to improving the condition of modern women.[12]

One of Fuller's "favorites branches," as it turned out, was female self-culture; she often offered lessons on subjects pertinent to women, such as history and literature, and on practical matters of importance to them such as the "rights of property" and "rent, insurance, wages, &c."[13] Fuller assured her students, for instance, that history "was a study peculiarly adapted to females. She said it was not to be expected that women would be good Astronomers or Geologists or Metaphysicians," given the social hurdles they faced in such fields, "but they could and are expected to be good historians" (Shuffelton, "Margaret Fuller," 42). "Let them be sea captains" this is not, but Fuller's expectation that her girls be "good historians" nonetheless widens the field of female possibility as she asks them to consider the lives of women such as Sappho, the poet, and Aphasia, wife of Pericles, rather than solely the exploits of classical antiquity's great men.[14] In this way, Mary Ware Allen informs us, history, "not very interesting in itself, was made so by Miss Fuller. She told us the names of some of the most distinguished women of Greece. There were but few, for the customs of the time did not permit them to mingle as much with society" (Allen, "School Journal," 2:18–19). Making it clear that the paucity of historical examples pointed not to an inherent lack of talent in the female sex but to cultural restrictions, the "customs of the time," Fuller encouraged her girls to find solace in past eruptions of women into public life despite concerted efforts to discourage them from it, much as she would advise readers in *Woman in the Nineteenth Century* that "the female Greek . . . is as much in the street as the male to cry, What news?" because they "are not so constituted that they can live without expansion. If they do not get it one way, they must another, or perish" (19).

Just as Fuller offered students unconventional lessons in female self-reliance, she spurned traditional methods of rote learning for a "chiefly conversational" mode that was "so different from every other" because, as Mary Ware Allen reports, it "required *thought* as well as *study*—and *conversation* as well as *recitation*."[15] As Allen relates it, Fuller "said it must not be our object to come and hear her talk. We might think it a delightful thing to her to talk to so many interesting auditors . . . but that was not the thing: she could not teach us so, *we* must talk and let her understand our minds" (Johnson, "Margaret Fuller," 135; emphasis in original). In her refusal to "teach us so," therefore, Fuller sought to remold the teacher/student relation from one in which the instructor simply imposed knowledge on students to a more reciprocal exchange in which students helped her, and themselves in turn, understand the processes and principles of their minds. In an explicit rejection of Locke's *tabula rasa*, Fuller argued that distinctions between students' intellectual capabilities rested upon the degree to which they cultivated their intrinsic potential: "One of the class asked Miss Fuller if she believed that the human mind was like a blank sheet of paper,—and she said, no, she despised the idea. She thought that everyone was capable of appreciating what is beautiful, in a degree, but some took more lofty views than others—and some cultivated their natural powers to a greater degree than others" (Allen, "School Journal," 1:16).

But such "lofty views" first required that Fuller encourage greater self-awareness among students and weaken socially conditioned impediments to the exercise of their native abilities. In her journal, Evelina Metcalf conveys Fuller's aim to "arouse our dormant faculties and break up the film over our mind. . . . She wished us to know what we could do and to collect our scattered senses" (Shealy, "Margaret Fuller," 51–52). And, on the first day of Fuller's rhetoric class, Mary Ware Allen recorded a question from a classmate, who asked if Fuller intended that they get their lessons "by *heart*" (Allen, "School Journal," 1:3; emphasis in original). Fuller responded in the negative. Memorizing lessons "by heart, as the expression is commonly understood," she explained, was "often only getting it by body" (3), a mere mechanical response that required little conscious mental engagement and with which the "heart had nothing to do" (4). Rather, she wanted them to get their lessons "by *mind*—to give [their] minds and souls to the work," and she told then that "[i]f there were any who thought they would not do this, who did not feel an interest in it, who did not feel willing to answer her questions, she wished them to leave the class—it would not displease her . . . even if there were only two left who really felt interested" (4; emphasis in original).

Beyond indicating dismay with a "banking" model of education antithetical to romantic sensibility, Fuller's discomfort with rote memorization, with "getting it by heart" (3), anticipates the resistance she would articulate with much greater force in *Woman in the Nineteenth Century*, where, in a testy exchange with the trader, she "doubts" the essentialist, sentimental ideology of women's true nature often espoused in opposition to women's rights:

"Am I not the head of my house?"
"You are not the head of your wife. God has given her a mind of her own."
"I am the head and she the heart."
"God grant you play true to one another then. I suppose I am to be grateful that you did not say she was only the hand. . . . But our doubt is whether the heart does consent with the head, or only obeys its decrees with a passiveness that precludes the exercise of its natural powers." (16)

Such arguments about the female "heart" reduced women to sensational bodies in need of masculine control. In the trader's formulation, the "head must rule over the heart; the two are not separate but equal powers."[16] Understanding this dynamic, Fuller challenges sentimental ideology's enervating influences by disassociating the image of the "heart" from the realm of female "natural power" and by suggesting that, far from enabling the "exercise" of intrinsic potential, such rhetoric fostered internalized "passiveness." In its most innocuous forms (such as in the commonplace, "getting it by heart"), then, sentimental rhetoric could encourage "scattered senses," as she tells her students in Providence, discouraging the mental faculties and producing a "film" over the mind (Shealy, "Margaret Fuller," 51). Even as nineteenth-century difference feminists attempted to use sentimental formulations as the basis for women's greater participation in public life, Fuller understood the ways in which sentimentality bolstered gendered "spheres" (to use the trader's own term) and encouraged male guardianship of women.

Because sentimentality was not the expression of female nature but rather a product of women's social conditioning, the real problem with it, as she told her students, was that it encouraged a "false modesty" (Allen, "School Journal," 1:2) that could retard self-development by inhibiting women from sharing and testing their ideas. Such delicate sensibilities were "false" in that Fuller believed them to be merely internalized social niceties, untrue to the natural self-confidence and the expansive self-potential that was the inheritance of every human soul. As Mary Ware Allen tells it, candid, unrestrained conversation was what Fuller wanted from her girls: "Miss Fuller said that a *great deal* would depend on the freedom with which we should express our thoughts. . . . She said a great difficulty, even with many fine minds, was a want of freedom to express their thoughts—that many minds were so profound, that it was hard to get at them—every thing seemed buried up" (2–3; emphasis in original). Self-culture, in this view, depended on an understanding that "true modesty consisted in not being ashamed that other people should know our ignorance, but in being ashamed of the ignorance itself" (2–3).

In an effort to "get at" the treasures "buried up" in her students' minds, Fuller employed her hallmark wit, the infamous sarcasm that her detractors interpreted, to use Emerson's words, as "sneering, scoffing, critical, [and] disdainful" (*Memoirs*, 1:203). Mary Ware Allen informs her family that Fuller "is very satirical, and I should think might be *very severe*," opining: "She is very critical and sometimes cuts us up into bits. When she cuts us all in a lump, it is quite pleasant, for she is quite witty; but woe to the one whom she cuts by herself" (Johnson, "Margaret Fuller," 135; emphasis in original). At times, Fuller sought to challenge her students and force them to think for themselves, even if this method might bruise egos and precipitate tears (which, on at least one occasion, it did).[17] Fuller's penchant for satire was not, as Emerson characterized it, the "play of superabundant animal spirits" in a woman otherwise known for her refined talents—a declaration reducing as effectively as any sentimental rhetoric could Fuller's intellectual capacities to bodily impulses in need of regulation (*Memoirs*, 1:203). But neither was it, as one modern critic has suggested, the indications of a novice teacher who "did not always have the discretion to keep her views to herself."[18] Rather, satire and sarcasm were what Bell Chevigny calls "deliberate creative act[s]" of "insistent agency" and "resistant female expression" in which Fuller gave new shape and meaning to her character through "defiant performances" of intellectual prowess.[19]

Ultimately, these verbal performances were intellectual strategies, self-conscious decisions to avoid the sentimentality she thought inimical to self-culture. While at the school, for instance, Fuller had praised Hiram Fuller as a man with the "ready sympathy" and the "pious, tender turn of thought" necessary to the "practical part" of schoolmaster, but she also worried that the "danger arising from that sort of education which [he] has unfolded" is that he "may not be sufficiently systematic and not observe due gradation and completeness in his plans" (*LMF*, 1:287). In other words, she was apprehensive that, while essential to students' practical well-being, too much sympathy might conflict with the severity of will necessary to cultivate all the departments of the intellect. Thus, in her farewell speech to the students on her last day at the school, Fuller explained the rationale for these uncompromising methods: if she "had sometimes been harsh, sometimes too ironical . . . the latter she had made use of, not to wound our feelings, but to awaken in us a sense of our deficiencies, to make us feel how little we knew, comparatively, and to stimulate us to exertion" (Johnson, "Margaret Fuller," 139).

In the end, Fuller's "Providence period" lasted only eighteen months. Many literary historians have concluded that Fuller disliked school-teaching and hated Providence—sentiments she seems to display in missives such as her 19 August 1838 letter to Lidian Emerson, in which she complains of "uncongenial pursuits and the oppressive intercourse with vulgar minds" (*LMF*, 1:341). But while Fuller expressed occasional chagrin with circumstances in Providence, to insist too forcefully upon such moments is to risk overshadowing the real satisfaction she took from her employment. Her letter to Lidian, for example, merely confesses a "wish" to "feel more joy at the prospect of escape" because she is not relieved to quit the school; as she says, "I cease from a noble effort to consult my own health and feelings" (*LMF*, 1:341), namely, a sense of exhaustion and a yearning to complete her long-delayed translation of Goethe. Similarly, in a letter written to William Henry Channing on the eve of her departure, Fuller reiterates her "dreams and hopes as to the education of women" despite the "unfeigned delight" she feels at leaving Providence (*LMF*, 1:354, 353). Read in this context, such letters leave little doubt that she saw Greene Street as a testing-ground for future educational efforts, rather than merely as a stop-gap until better opportunities came along. In leaving the school, in other words, Fuller was "not giving up on the idea of being an educator, but was leaving the classroom in Providence . . . to reach a wider audience."[20] Unsurprisingly, she would be teaching again within the year.

Boston and the "Animating Influences of Discord"

Holding up Fuller's conversations as a model for the "collaborative and noncoercive" discourse embraced by the "second wave of feminist theorists in the United States," Annette Kolodny has argued that, "as a *woman* speaking for women," Fuller sought to replace the "combativeness" of male rhetorical strategies in favor of a conversational ethic founded in conciliation, consensus, and mutual agreement.[21] But in suggesting that Fuller crafted a "discourse appropriate to feminism [that] rejected alike the authoritarianism of coercion and the manipulative strategies of the disempowered," such arguments tend to obscure the combative dimensions of her early conversational ideal, something more akin to what Elizabeth Hewitt calls "agonistic reciprocity" than the non-conflictual ethos championed by modern feminist critics.[22] Hewitt argues that, unlike Emerson, Fuller was "deeply cognizant of the necessary inequalities" informing friendship, viewing it as "essentially dissymmetrical" even as she "cannot eliminate a depiction of sociability that emphasizes friendship as reciprocity." In place of the perfect agreement sought by her transcendental companion, Fuller evinces nostalgia for the *polis*—"Oh, for my dear old Greeks, who talked everything—not to shine as in the Parisian saloons, but to learn, to teach, to vent the heart, to clear the mind!" (*Memoirs*, 1:107)—a democratic arena in which individuals could equally and directly vie for distinction, even as she recognizes the restrictions that, historically, had excluded women from participation in the public and intellectual realms.[23]

In this context, then, Fuller viewed true conversation as a series of mutually stimulating conflicts, a give-and-take process of self-development proceeding from what she would describe to Emerson in 1844 as the "animating influences of Discord" (*LMF,* 3:213).

This notion of "agonistic reciprocity" appears repeatedly in her friends' testimonies about the Boston Conversations. When he first heard of Fuller's plans, for example, Theodore Parker called them "excellent," anticipating they would supply a "defect" that overlooks "the art of conversation" in "the system of [female] education." In spurning the "dull" talk of Boston's best ladies, Parker suggests, Fuller will "do away" with their tendency to "'suckle fools and chronicle small beer,' or perhaps read a magazine or novel that will never excite a thought" because she "smites and kindles with all the force, irregularity, and matchless beauty of lightning."[24] Unlike the kind of banter that "suckles fools" as a mother nurses a child, Fuller's method is, for Parker, sublime rather than sentimental. Like "lightning," it both awes and terrifies, its power striking down useless prattle, much of what passes as decorous conversation in Boston, only to inspire new truth and meaning in the conflagration of the old. Parker's contention, finally, that only this kind of conversation can "*awaken* minds, to think, examine, doubt" (emphasis in original) harkens back to Fuller's own explanation to her students at the Greene Street school, her wish to "arouse [their] dormant faculties and break up the film over [their] mind," another aggressive metaphor that reveals Fuller's desire to jar her students out of complacency and to challenge their ideas (Shealy, "Margaret Fuller," 51).

Others follow this rhetoric with their own vivid descriptions of violent overtaking. While registering a similar "electric shock" in the face of Fuller's "unusual speaking power," Sarah Clarke, a regular participant in the Conversations, ultimately resorts to the language of combat to describe her method. For Clarke, Fuller's conversations are chivalrous warfare; she meets you "fairly" on the field and "breaks her lance upon your shield"; her eyes "pierced through your disguises"; her conversation is a siege in which one's "outworks" fall before her loquacious "assault," her words maneuvering like an army to penetrate one's "little shams and defenses." Recalling these conversations, Clarke reveals the "delight" she felt at such an "exhilarated" struggle, both "startling" in its tenacity and "rudely searching" in its aims, at least by the conventional standards of conversation that Fuller sought to overturn.[25] Like his sister, long-time friend James Freeman Clarke proclaims that Fuller was "fitted for the arena of conversation. Here she found none adequate for the equal encounter; when she laid her lance in rest, every champion must go down before it" (*Memoirs*, 1:105). For his part, Emerson describes her as a hunter. "Persons were her game," he tells us; they "fell" before her as mere "casualties" offering "no resistance," so easily had Fuller "disarmed" them with her talk (*Memoirs*, 1:213).

While one might claim that responses from the likes of Emerson and James Freeman Clarke register masculine discomfort with Fuller's power (Emerson even admits that "men thought she carried too many guns"), Fuller uses similar language to describe the Conversations (*Memoirs* 1:202). On one occasion, she states that her aim had always been to show students "where the magazines of knowledge lie, & leave the rest to themselves & the spirit who must teach and help them to self-impulse."[26] In another, even as she expresses delight at feeling herself "truly a teacher and guide" to her fellow conversationalists, she reveals dissatisfaction with her results. She is, she tells us, "never driven home for ammunition; never put to any expense; never truly called out. What I have is always enough; though I feel how superficially I am treating my subject" (*Memoirs*, 1:332). With this striking language, Fuller states her conversational ideal: she hopes for confrontation that might drive her to inner resources, to reliance on the innate powers that will allow her to return linguistic assault. In articulating the desire to be "called out," she deploys the terminology of dueling, presenting conversation as a chivalrous contest undertaken to vindicate character, a challenge that necessitates the outward manifestation of inner worth. But Fuller then confesses that these exchanges never put her to any "expense." Julie Ellison argues that, for romantics like Fuller, friendship is founded upon a "fantasy of compensatory self-indulgence," the belief in subjectivity "as a resource that, when expended, must be replenished or compensated," whether monetarily—such as in the form of the subscription fees charged for the Conversations—or emotionally—through extravagant displays of affection bestowed by its subscribers.[27] Her colleagues, however, do not live up to this exchange; they readily offer payment for that which costs Fuller nothing. In the process, they deprive her of the all-important opportunity to account for herself (to "call out," in this sense, is to speak, to engage in a self-conscious verbal performance that breathes life into individual character by giving form and meaning to previously inchoate impulses). What Fuller seeks in "animating . . . Discord" (*LMF*, 3:213), then, is life itself as the highest and greatest of arts.[28]

Anticipating these complaints about the Conversations, one of Fuller's grievances with teaching at the Greene Street School had been its lack of challenge. Her students' caliber was lower than she expected; in a word, she found them "miserably prepared," confessing: "I feel so perfectly equal to all

I do there, without any effort" (*LMF*, 1:292). That there seemed to be such a "vast gulf" between her and her pupils, a separation "wider than [she] could have conceived possible" (*Memoirs*, 1:177), was a fact that was not lost on the students themselves. Juliet Graves records in her journal: "She cannot exercise her brightest, highest powers, for they cannot be understood; and, when she is obliged to bury, as it were, that which is most congenial to her mind, and bring it to a level with the minds round her, it must be a most irksome task, so sadly cultivated as many of them are" (Johnson, "Margaret Fuller," 138). But if Fuller felt disappointment at her own "energies . . . much repressed" (*LMF*, 1:353–54) in the classroom, it was because she believed education to be a mutually stimulating experience, in which conversation worked to create, as she tells her girls, a kind of "pleasant" friction against which individuals might "exert" and, therefore, define themselves (Johnson, "Margaret Fuller," 135).[29]

But she was determined to get it right in Boston, where, as she had told Channing when she left Providence, "by the success I have already attained and by the confidence I now feel in my powers," she might enact her plans "to much greater pecuniary advantage and with much more extensive good results" (*LMF*, 1:354). In her notes on the Conversations' first meeting (held 6 November 1839), Elizabeth Peabody records that Fuller "merely meant to be the nucleus of conversation . . . & she proposed to be *one* to give her own best thoughts on any subject that was named, as a means of calling out the thoughts of others" ("Journal," 203; emphasis in original). As the "nucleus" of the group, offering her "best thoughts" to guide its conversation, she enacts what Julie Ellison calls the Romantic "interpreter" who performs "an allusive and mythologized autobiography . . . so that others may find their own 'law' through identifying with it."[30] Certainly, this accords with Emerson's sense of Fuller as "magnificent, prophetic, reading my life at her will," as an interpreter not only of European texts but also of the foreign realm of her friends' interior states (*Memoirs*, 1:215). Building on Ellison's claims, Sandra Gustafson argues that Fuller molds conversation into a "sentimental oral form" at once more authoritative and yet more democratic than any other available to her.[31] While I am hesitant to use the term "sentimental" to describe Fuller's conversational style given the scorn Fuller lavishes upon sentimentality in the Conversations—for instance, she "repelled the sentimentalism that took away woman's moral power of performing stern duty," as Peabody records of the first meeting ("Journal," 215)—I do find Gustafson's formulation of Fuller's anti-sentimental sentimentalism compelling as a way to understand the ethic of sincerity binding her Conversations.[32]

Believing that this ethic sometimes necessitated exertions of rhetorical dominance to achieve its aims, Fuller hoped to act as a kind of "conversational disciplinarian," stripping her students of the "verbal cosmetics" that acted as barriers to true self-expression, and compelling them to speak in what she believed was a "healthy, transparent" style.[33] As she explained to Sophia Ripley, her Conversations aimed to "systematize thought and give a precision in which our sex are so deficient, chiefly, I think because they have so few inducements to test and classify what they receive" (*LMF*, 2:87). Resolving to "lay aside the shelter of vague generalities, the cant of coterei [*sic*] criticism and the delicate disdains of *good society*" and to "turn back the current when digressing into personalities or commonplaces" so characteristic of the gossip or other forms of "low" talk paradoxically generated by "high" society, Fuller sought to regulate how these women talked as well as what they talked about (86–87; emphasis in original). In this way she hoped to produce what she called a "conversation of a better order" that compelled them to move beyond mere parroting of undigested opinion and toward rigorous examination and classification of ideas. Much like the "false modesty" she decried to her Providence students, for Fuller, the "cant of coterei criticism" that dominated polite circles was problematic because it represented the worst side of consensus; such narrow, self-interested jargon, masquerading as truth whilst disseminating amongst the upper ranks of society or trickling down through the lower, was not only inimical to individual thought but also harmful to women's interests, since the conventional wisdom of the day was, as Fuller says in *Woman in the Nineteenth Century*, "Girls can't do that; girls can't play ball" (24). The conflation of "cant" with "can't"—what Christina Zwarg describes as the fact that "women literally 'can't' realize the world envisioned by the high rhetoric of the culture" because that very culture, by necessity, must produce "cultural outcasts" against which to define itself, outcasts among whose ranks, Fuller reminds us, women traditionally were numbered—ensured that coterie criticism disempowered women even as they espoused it.[34]

Peabody's record of the meetings demonstrates Fuller's effort to disrupt coterie thinking, to undo both the "cant" and "can't" inhibiting women from self-construction. Fuller, she writes,

> thought it would be a good plan to take up subjects on which we knew words—& had impressions, & vague irregular notions, & compel ourselves to define those words, to turn these impressions into thoughts, & to systematize these thoughts—We should probably have to go through some mortifica-

tion in finding how much less we knew than we thought—& on the other hand we should probably find ourselves encouraged by seeing how much & how rapidly we should gain by making a simple & clear effort for expression. (Peabody, "Journal," 203)

In suggesting that the women "go through some mortification" in their conversations, Fuller does not simply mean that they must endure the embarrassment of having their ignorance revealed to all their fellow subscribers. Rather, she envisions the Conversations as a "system" of discipline, in which participants identify each other's weaknesses, the "impressions, & vague and irregular notions" they hold, while demanding they define, defend, or ultimately discard them as a means to linguistic self-empowerment. Probing subjects on which they had vague "impressions," sensations produced in them by the operation of some external influence upon the mind, Fuller sought to transform the women from passive subjects to agents by helping them to convert "these impressions into thoughts," and thus to bring the external into conformity with the powers of human consciousness. Fuller ultimately sees encouraging results in the "simple & clear effort[s] for expression" produced by these exchanges; in this way, she inducts the women not only into knowledge of "words" and their role in the linguistic creation of the self, but also into the kind of "effort," or disciplined struggle, necessary to utilize them.

Fuller, Emerson, and *The Dial*

When Fuller began her editorship of *The Dial* in the spring of 1840, she had just concluded her first series of Conversations, and, given its success, it seemed only natural that she would want to extend the model used there to it.[35] With *The Dial*, therefore, she also sought this "conversation of a better order" (*LMF*, 2:86), hoping to inspire readers to think "more deeply and more nobly" (*LMF* 2:126), and more systematically, than they had done before. In an 1840 letter, Fuller argues for the timeliness of such a periodical, especially given what she saw as the woeful state of American culture, whose influences created people she called "superficial, irreverent, and more anxious to get a living than to live mentally or morally," and whose propensities were in "no way balanced by the slight literary culture common here, which is mostly English, and consists in a careless reading of publications of the day, having the same utilitarian tendency with our own proceedings" (*Memoirs*, 2:26–27). In addressing what she saw as a widespread, yet "superficial diffusion of knowledge" (26), Fuller targets educational arrangements she sees as merely vocational, tailored to the demands of "getting a living." Recalling the language of her letter to Elizabeth Peabody, in which she imagines a new periodical that would act as "precisely the counterpoise required by the utilitarian tendencies of our day" (*Memoirs* 1:168), here Fuller envisions *The Dial* as one that could "call out" readers' "higher sentiments," help them to "live mentally and morally," and raise their thoughts above the banalities of everyday existence (*Memoirs*, 2:26–27).

But it is this vision of herself as a "conversational disciplinarian" that she would quickly temper when she edited *The Dial*. For instance, Fuller admits that she does not have terribly high hopes for what the publication might accomplish in this regard. Given the novelty of the experiment, she confesses in a 22 March 1840 letter to Channing, she is "not sanguine as to the amount of talent which will be brought to bear on this publication. . . . I am sure we cannot show high culture, and I doubt about vigorous thought" (*LMF*, 2:126). Instead of the "systematic" thought she typically sought as an end to her conversations, here, she declares, she would settle for "free action as far as it goes and a high aim," adding presciently, "It were much if a periodical could be kept open to accomplish no outward object, but merely to afford an avenue for what of free and calm thought might be originated among us by the wants of individual minds" (126). Her editorial disagreements with Emerson—which in a manner of speaking would outlast her own lifetime—aptly demonstrate how provocative the open-ended policy she would come to envision really was.

Fuller's posthumously published, two-volume *Memoirs* (1852) is a prime example of Emerson's editorial prerogative and is notorious for its efforts to sanitize Fuller's life, making it conform to nineteenth-century standards of female propriety.[36] In his "Conversations in Boston" chapter, Emerson insists upon the private character of Fuller's literary enterprises:

> In reporting the story of an affectionate and passionate woman, the voice lowers itself to a whisper, and becomes inaudible. A woman in our society finds her safety and happiness in exclusions and privacy. She congratulates herself when she is not called to the market, to the courts, to the polls, to the stage, or to the orchestra. Only the most extraordinary genius can make the career of an artist secure and agreeable to her. (*Memoirs*, 1:321–22)

In suggesting that Fuller "willingly . . . confined" herself to "the usual circles and methods of female talent" (322), Emerson casts her various market engagements as feminine, amateur endeavors not meant for widespread public consumption—even though both the Conversations and *The Dial* were sold by subscription. Her Conversations, according to one estimate, brought in nearly $500 a year from 1841 to 1844 (the 1841 mixed-company series alone brought in almost $600), and, while *The Dial* promised, though never paid, her $200 a year, her teaching at the Greene Street School in Providence had provided a yearly salary of $1000, a seemingly unprecedented sum for a female instructor.[37] Clearly, her activities were economic as well as intellectual enterprises. The problem, then, is that Emerson takes it upon himself to determine the ways in which a woman like Fuller should circulate in the antebellum marketplace, essentially crafting her into the kind of "literary domestic" her life refuted.[38]

Given his assertions about women finding "safety and happiness in exclusions and privacy," it not surprising, therefore, that, when Emerson turns to the subject of *The Dial*, he revises the journal's scope in accordance with conventional notions of womanhood inimical to Fuller's self-professed aims as its editor. Invoking what he deems the essentially domestic nature of womanhood, he reduces the journal to a "private and friendly service," one that, though "pretending" to broader spheres, was no less feminine (*Memoirs*, 1:322), and thus filled with much "juvenility, timidity, and conventional rubbish."[39] In his attempt to distance himself from a project with which he was deeply, though at times reluctantly, involved, Emerson points to the feminine character of Fuller's journal as an implicit justification for what he came to see as its failures, including its lack of a "large circulation" and what he considers its meager artistic quality (323). He contends that the journal, its pages filled by "scattered writers" who had "not digested their theories into distinct dogma, still less into a practical measure which the public could grasp," became so "eclectic and miscellaneous" that, in any one issue, an individual reader might find only a small fraction of its contents suited to his tastes and enjoyment (323). While Emerson thus laments *The Dial*'s miscellaneous character as the unintended consequences of poor planning and implies that he would have quickly focused its scattershot approach, Fuller, I argue, encouraged these elements as its guiding principle, growing more firmly committed to *The Dial* as a "free organ" (*LMF*, 2:126), in part because of editorial disagreements with Emerson.

Emerson's insinuations that the journal needed a "distinct dogma" through which to focus its contents is in direct contrast to the sense of freedom and impartiality that Fuller sought to cultivate as its editor. In her 22 March 1840 letter to Channing, she explains,

> A perfectly free organ is to be offered for the expression of individual thought and character. There are no party measures to be carried, no particular standard to be set up. A fair calm tone, a recognition of universal principles will, I hope pervade the essays in every form[.] I hope there will neither be a spirit of dogmatism nor of compromise. That this periodical will not aim at leading public opinion, but at stimulating each man to think for himself . . . (*LMF*, 2:126)

Fuller's renunciation of "dogmatism," "party measures," "particular standards," or any effort aimed at "leading public opinion" contrasts with Emerson's sentiments in a letter to her a few months later on 4 August 1840. "I begin to wish to see a different Dial from that which I first imagined," he writes, "I would not have it too purely literary. I wish we might make a Journal so broad & great in its survey that it should lead the opinion of this generation on every great interest" (*LRWE*, 2:322). To this end, Emerson wants to "court some of the good fanatics," as he calls the partisan and reform-minded, and "publish chapters on every head" (322). But rather than seeking the advocacy of "fanatics" on social, intellectual, and religious "interests," Fuller's journal, as she envisions it in her letter to Channing, would maintain a "fair, calm tone," allowing for an unbiased presentation of "individual thought" whose very articulation would demonstrate to readers what is possible through a "wise self-trust."[40]

What Emerson obscures in the *Memoir*'s account of *The Dial* is the fact that Fuller's involvement in the enterprise was, from the first, rooted in a gendered desire for free expression; it was very much an effort to find the means by which she might finally "say [her] say" (*LMF*, 3:58) within a marketplace whose practices restricted such exertions. This sense of constraint was, in fact, a problem that extended itself to the traditional, male-oriented literary forms available to her:

> For all the tides of life that flow within me, I am dumb and ineffectual, when it comes to casting my thought into a form. No old one suits me. If I could invent one, it seems to me the pleasure of creation would make it possible for me to write. . . . One should be either private or public. I love best to be a woman; but womanhood is at present to straightly-bound to give me scope. At hours, I live truly as a woman; at others, I should stifle; as, on the other hand, I should palsy, when I would play the artist. (*Memoirs*, 1:297)

Clearly, Fuller struggled with the "straightly-bound" binaries of public/private, masculine/feminine, and artist/amateur that Emerson so easily reinscribes in the *Memoirs*. In her 22 March 1840 letter, Fuller laments her own sense of what Channing had called "unemployed force," or, as she puts it, of "never, never in life" having "had the happy feeling of really doing any thing"—a feeling so intense that she "cannot think . . . that all men in all ages have suffered thus from an unattained Ideal" (*LMF*, 2:126). Thus, if hers was a problem of "calling" or vocation common to a generation collectively disenchanted with the failed promise of traditional professions, it was also a gendered one. As Emerson's account in the *Memoirs* attests, women of Fuller's class had few sanctioned vocations outside of the private, domestic roles of wife and mother.[41]

While Mark Vásquez identifies in Fuller's polyvocal style a kind of "novelistic" discourse blurring genres and cultural voices in a manner anticipating the heterogeneity of the American novel, I suggest that this category, "novel," obscures the periodical's significance as the form that best "suits" Fuller and to which she turns for "scope."[42] The medium's cultural significance cannot be understated; it was not only a "natural forum for the dissemination of general education," but also *the* "author-sustaining formation" on which American print culture rested, as well as one vital to women's public involvement in the social and intellectual discussions of their day.[43] The "open" form of the periodical, compared to the "closed" form of the book, could provide the means to encourage a kind of active and continuous conversation with readers, and contribute to a sense of the periodical as a "democratic and non-hierarchical" entity in which everyone could take part.[44] At the same time, Fuller sought in her own contributions to avoid what she disliked about the traditional essay form, recording in her *Dial* notebook that the "regular build of an Essay (maugre the unpretending name) is dangerous. . . . It tempts to round the piece into a whole by filling up the gaps between the thoughts with—words—words—words."[45] As a result, her essays experimented with fiction, fables, and literary dialogues, helping to develop a "considerably more versatile," hybrid essay format reflective of a give-and-take conversational style that sought to draw out opposing perspectives and that refused easy closure.[46]

In her role as editor, Fuller thus attempted to expand her conversational "scope," and this despite the irony that *The Dial*, as an organ of a transcendental movement, was (its name notwithstanding) doomed to be a coterie publication. Revising Joel Myerson's Emerson-centered history of *The Dial*, Larry Reynolds has argued that the journal should be understood not so much as the product of the minister-dominated Transcendental Club as an outgrowth of the "coterie publishing practices" of Fuller's own circle, since, for several years prior to the journal's appearance, she and her friends had been exchanging packets of letters, poems, journals, and essays that essentially "constituted the *Dial* in embryo form."[47] While such practices seem to suggest the substitution of one kind of coterie for another, the change was a widening of boundaries, moving from the interests of what was mainly a ministerial elite of college-educated men to the everyday hopes and dreams of men and women.[48] Capper suggests that Fuller made a bold choice in crafting *The Dial* out of what were essentially the private writings of mostly unknowns, using the low and obscure as the materials of American literature.[49] Elizabeth Peabody's delighted response to the first issue supports this decision. "It is domestic," she writes to Sophia Ripley, "giving the everyday state of feeling and thoughts of the writers."[50]

In its aims, then, Fuller's journal was expansive, aspiring to reach beyond local, coterie interests. In preparing *The Dial*'s inaugural issue, Fuller confesses to Channing on 19 April 1840:

> Things go on pretty well, but I dare say people will be disappointed, for they seem to be looking for the gospel of transcendentalism. . . . Mr Emerson knows best what he wants but he has already said it in various ways.—Yet I deem the experiment is well worth trying; hearts beat so high, they must be full of something, and here is a way to breathe it out quite freely.—It is for dear New England that I wanted this review; for myself, if I had wished to write a few pages now and then, I had ways and means of disposing them. (*LMF*, 2:131)

Though Fuller recognizes that Emerson's circle will be disappointed with the first issue (which, if we take Alcott's and Ripley's and Parker's initial responses, they were), she has a much broader audience in mind than the adherents of his particular dogma.[51] I use the term "dogma" to once again evoke Emerson's own use of it while discussing *The Dial* in his letters and the *Memoirs*. Fuller's own rejection of the "spirit of dogmatism" in her earlier letter to Channing, and her dismissal of a dogmatic "gospel of transcendentalism" in this one, suggest a more expansive understanding of the journal's potential, and of transcendentalism itself. That it was for "dear New England," a larger public than a small group of reform-minded Boston ministers, and that she was not afraid to buck expectations in this regard was further reinforced by the fact that she had told James Freeman Clarke in January that its cast would be "literary rather than Theological," as the minister club had initially envisioned it.[52] In this respect, she "transcended" even the aims of the transcendentalists themselves.

Joel Myerson has asserted that the journal was literary by default; in "rashly" taking "any promise of aid to be a firm commitment," Fuller had to rely on whatever available help she could find.[53] But Fuller's January missive to Clarke suggests otherwise, as does Emerson's 4 August 1840 to Fuller, in which he advises her not to make the journal "too purely literary" (*LRWE*, 2:322). Furthermore, Fuller's editor's note, "To Contributors," in *The Dial*'s July 1841 issue reveals that the journal would have by the end of its first year *too* many contributions from which Fuller might choose to fill its pages. Specifically, she apologizes for space limitations making it impossible for her to print all the submissions received: "We trust that our unknown friends are not greatly disappointed that so many of their requests are neglected, and their gifts apparently unheeded. Our space is limited, and much that is not without merit must lie unpublished." Still, she urges them "not to be deterred by omission of their articles," as it "was our hope that the perfect freedom guaranteed for the Dial would make it the means of developing young talent. We should like to hear from our friends again and again, and be the means of their serving an apprenticeship to the pen."[54] Thus, while Fuller had confided to Channing in March 1840 that she feared a lack of "room for choice" (*LMF*, 2:126) in the selection of contributions, she ultimately need not have worried. If anything, there would be too many options, rather than too few.

A similar, though unexpected, complication "crowded out" Emerson's "large" essay, "Thoughts on Modern Literature," from the allotted 136 pages of *The Dial*'s first issue, forcing it to wait until October when the second number appeared.[55] On 21 June 1840, Emerson wrote to Fuller, both to encourage her about *The Dial*'s prospects—she had expressed worry that the journal had as yet only 30 subscribers, and fretted about the first issue's quality—and, it seems, to chide her about the omission, which he saw as part of a larger editorial concern.[56] Demonstrating a kind of masculine, coterie attitude about which Fuller would grow increasingly sensitive, he writes:

> Can we not explode in this enterprize [*sic*] of ours all the established rules of Grub Street or Washington Street? leave out all the ballast or Balaam and omit to count pages? One hundred thirty six pages! Our readers, who, I take it, are the sincere & the sensible, will not ask, Are there 110 or 150 pages? but Is there one page? Every dull sentence vulgarizes the book and when we have inserted our gems from the papers of love & friendship we shall feel that we

have wronged our angels by thrusting them into unfit company. . . . Only with such friends as we have, and willing as three or four of us are to put the heart into what we write & sleep not, I think we ought not to be lax in our conditions of admittance for such a reason as to fill pages. (*LRWE*, 2:305–6)

While Emerson obviously meant to encourage Fuller in his characteristically hyperbolic style (for he did not seriously think the public would subscribe to a one-page journal), his sentiment suggests that, for him, the "conditions of admittance" into the journal were "gems" from "friends" sharing his own literary sensibilities. Implicitly, he thus chides Fuller for what he saw as her "lax" standards, her desire, as he judged it, to include the "dull" and "unfit," to simply "fill pages" for the sake of convention. What he wanted was a manly, independent journal that might out-compete its competition in refusing to play by conventional rules. It is, he imagines, an "enterprise" in both senses, an economic endeavor and bold undertaking that seeks to "explode" the hack rules of "Grub Street" or, closer to home, of "Washington Street"—Boston's publishers' row where *The Dial* was printed. In other words, it must reject the feminine timidity—a tendency he excoriates in "Self-Reliance"—which, he believes, characterizes Fuller's first issue. When, a month later, Emerson implores her, "I hope our Dial will get to be a little *bad*. This first number is not enough to scare the tenderest bantling of Conformity" (*LRWE*, 2:316; emphasis in original), he once again conflates conformity with feminine and childish dependence, a logic that Fuller would attack with vigor in *Woman*.[57]

Emerson demonstrates a similar masculine prerogative in another letter, written to Fuller on 30 March 1840 after Frederick Henry Hedge, one of the Transcendental Club's original members, who had helped envision *The Dial* several years earlier, declined to contribute to it.[58] Chagrined at Hedge's refusal to support *The Dial* for fear its transcendental associations might jeopardize his employment as minister, Emerson defends it and encourages Fuller's editorial efforts, confessing: "I would rather trust for its wit & its verses to eight or nine persons in whose affections I have a sure place, than to eighty or ninety celebrated contributors" (*LRWE*, 2:270). Certainly, the "eight or nine persons" he imagines in this letter is a larger circle than the "three or four of us" (*LRWE*, 2:306) he envisions elsewhere, but both are ultimately in line with an image of the journal as a "private and friendly service" (*Memoirs*, 1:322). Thus, although he excoriates Hedge for his conservatism and his timid retreat in the face of conventional pressures, Emerson nonetheless defends the magazine's worth primarily in terms of it as a reflection of friends "in whose affections I have a sure place," putting himself at the center of its interests. Writing to Hedge after assuming *The Dial*'s editorship, Emerson even confesses that he decided to take over the magazine because he valued it as an extension of his own tastes, as a "portfolio which preserves & conveys to distant persons precisely what I should borrow & transcribe to send them if I could" (*LRWE*, 3:37).

But as her subtle barb, "Mr Emerson knows best what he wants but he has already said it in various ways" (*LMF*, 2:131), in her letter to Channing suggests, Fuller had already begun to suspect that her willingness to commit to *The Dial* as an experiment in freedom of expression for its own sake, as a "way to breathe it out quite freely," whatever "it" might be, was increasingly at odds with Emerson's own designs for the magazine. Ironically, Emerson himself had begun to feel they had very different journals in mind. Even as he voices his wish that what he calls "our Dial" would be to be a "little *bad*," he forwards to her a piece by the "little heretic" Edward Palmer that he thought she should print, declaring: "It is good enough and yet I can easily guess that it is better for my Dial than for yours" (*LWRE*, 2:316). Fuller would articulate what she believed to be their exact difference when she resigned as editor, telling him in April 1842 that, under his guidance, the journal "cannot but change its character a good deal" since "you will sometimes reject pieces that I should not. For you have always had in view to make a good periodical and represent your own tastes, while I have had in view to let all kinds of people have freedom to say their say, for better, for worse" (*LMF*, 3:57–58).

Steven Fink argues that Fuller is not entirely accurate in characterizing herself here, since she was, in effect, an active and engaged editor, exercising considerable control over the journal's contents, with Thoreau's "The Service" being one of the more famous examples of her rejections.[59] In her letter to Thoreau, however, Fuller does not refuse to publish the essay so much as request that he "revise and resubmit" it, on the grounds that she might help him cultivate his own "voice." She tells him that while other pieces accepted were "more unassuming in their tone," and had an "air of quiet good breeding which induces us to permit their presence," his literary voice is "so rugged that it ought to be commanding" (*LMF*, 2:185). Thoreau chose not to resubmit the essay (nor did he attempt to publish it elsewhere); thus it is difficult to determine whether Fuller eventually would have published it. While she rejected Thoreau's submissions on other occasions, she had placed his poem "Sympathy" and his essay "Persius Flaccus" in *The Dial*'s first issue, and would print four additional poems in subsequent issues— and this despite the opinions of friends who were much less kind about his work. For example, in his journal, Emerson records Sam Ward's "objection" to Thoreau's verses, even though they "pleased" Emerson very much. James Freeman Clarke thought Thoreau's essay on "Flaccus" poorly written, while Theodore Parker was even more dismissive; he thought the essay "foolish" and derided Thoreau as merely imitating Emerson. One gets the impression that if Parker had had his say, *The Dial* would have printed nothing of Thoreau at all.[60] Still, as Fuller later explains to Emerson, although she did not publish all of Thoreau's submissions, or, at least, as many as Emerson would have liked her to publish, others' "disgust at Henry Thoreau's pieces" did not stop her from publishing some of them (*LMF*, 3:160).

If Fuller downplays her editorial prerogatives in her letter to Emerson, therefore, I suggest it comes from a growing sense that the general tendency and direction of the journal seemed more "narrow in its range" (*LMF*, 3:160) under his guidance than under her own. A December 1840 letter to Emerson provides further evidence of her desire to allow contributors "their say." In it, Fuller tells him that she has decided to print some of James Russell Lowell's sonnets, not because she liked them very much (indeed, she did not, claiming that his poems had the "fault of seeming imitated from Tennyson"), but because, "Though I have many short poems in my drawer I like better, yet I do not wish to discourage these volunteers who are so much wanted to vary the manoeuvres of the regular platoon" (*LMF*, 2:189). Accordingly, she demonstrates an important principle behind her decision to include his poems, as well as work from Thoreau, despite her feelings about their quality: a desire to "vary the manoeuvres" of the journal, that is, to allow more, and more diverse, voices into each number.

While Fuller's declaration about allowing "all kinds of people [to] have freedom to say their say" arguably carries an air of rhetorical posturing, I believe it holds a core of sincerity as well. This is not to deny that she did, in fact, make critical judgments as editor, to insist that her *Dial* was a sort of unmediated forum publishing all submissions, or even to claim that she was entirely consistent in her editorial principles. Rather, it is merely to suggest that she was becoming more sensitive to the need for a freer "organ" than was customary in the periodical literature of the day. In this sense, her letter to Emerson is a reconstruction of editorial aims as she had come to understand them by 1842. Did, for instance, the journal stand to challenge not only the conservative religious establishment, as the Transcendental Club originally envisioned it would, but also the patriarchal literary establishment, with its formulations of what was acceptable or appropriate to publish? Did it aim to destabilize or "transcend," as it were, the arbitrary and limiting notions of taste on which similar literary enterprises were often founded? Ultimately, the difference in their editorial styles was, as she would tell Emerson in another letter, a matter of degree; she wished her "tastes and sympathies still more expansive than they are, instead of more severe" (*LMF*, 3:161).

Narrow aims, she thought, were evident even in the journal's publication model. In her resignation letter to Emerson, Fuller addresses the recent appointment of Elizabeth Palmer Peabody as the journal's new publisher. Though Fuller finds her "more exact and judicious than I expected" in regard to the journal's financial management (*LMF*, 3:58), her appointment had its downside: "[A] connection with her offers no advantages for the spread of your work whatever it may be. But you have always thought the Dial required nothing of this kind" (*LMF*, 3:58). This was not an attack on Peabody so much as a simple statement of fact. As a small, local publisher she lacked either the capital or the distribution capabilities of a larger firm such as Carey in Philadelphia, and, indeed, Boston itself would not be a major publishing center until the 1850s.[61] In keeping with her conversational aims, Fuller wanted a journal with a wide circulation and as many readers and contributors as possible, while Emerson, whom she believed "always thought the Dial required nothing of this kind," seemed to imagine it merely as a vehicle for his friends' interests.[62]

From the journal's inception, Emerson had demonstrated in his recommendations what Fuller feared was a narrow sense of "taste," privileging certain contributions, such as those of his protégé, Thoreau, over others. He advised her, for instance, to print "very good" texts in type "a little large & glorious" in order to "betray some slight consciousness of what they carry" and to differentiate them from the "bad" (*LRWE*, 2:311) materials that might otherwise fill an issue.[63] Though he found the contents of the first issue generally "better" than he "feared" from Fuller's account of it, still, he thought the journal might be "greatly improved in its appearance & style" (311). Finding even its title page "very cautious now, pale face, lily liver," he suggests that she print it in "strong black letters that can be seen in the sunshine," adding, "If I were compositor, I think I should print it in larger" (311). Although Fuller responds that she would "defer entirely" to his "taste" in this regard (*LMF*, 2:146), she clearly does not concur with his opinion. She tells him that she, for her part, found the current type "neat and unpretending" and that she "did not know [he] attached great importance to externals in such matters, as [he did] so little in others" (146). In the end, she ignored these suggestions; after all, she, and not he, was the journal's "compositor."[64]

Emerson was left to implement these changes when he became editor himself. Originally, he had attempted to mollify Fuller's irritation at his criticisms: "I am sorry if I have pestered you with criticism on trifles.... It is not my wish to magnify print & paper beyond the sun & moon ... but Alcott & Thoreau talked it over here, & I judged the book from the ground that competition with other journals was attempted" (*LRWE,* 2:313). But, as editor, he eventually did set the magazine's title in very large "strong black letters that can be seen in the sunshine" (unlike Fuller's "neat and unpretending" title, which was made to share space with a subtitle enumerating the journal's miscellaneous character as a "Magazine for Literature, Philosophy, and Religion"). Emerson would also include his own name, "R. W. Emerson, editor," "magnified beyond sun and moon" in the journal's table of contents, whereas Fuller's name had been conspicuously absent from the issues she edited. Possibly, she chose anonymity to emphasize *The Dial* as a contributors' forum, rather than marking it as her own. Regardless, the choice reinforces the magazine's practice of printing its contributions anonymously, or simply with authors' initials, and also puts its focus squarely on ideas, rather than on the distraction of "personalities" that so often vexed Fuller in conversation (*LMF,* 2:87). Emerson, it seems, chose to leverage his growing literary reputation in an effort to boost the periodical's sales. In losing its "competition with other journals," the magazine's financial condition became more precarious.[65]

That the changes appear to be an attempt to put his stamp on the journal is bolstered by the fact that, in 1843, Emerson transferred publication duties to his own publisher, James Munroe, and removed Elizabeth Peabody, who had helped save the journal when its original publisher, Weeks, Jordan, and Co. went bankrupt in late 1841. One cannot help but wonder whether, in his decision to replace the journal's female publisher with a male one, Emerson hoped that a more capable *man* might not improve the periodical's prospects—just as when Fuller resigned as editor and Emerson took over, Theodore Parker declared to him that *The Dial* could finally "grow up to vigorous manhood."[66] Disappointed with its first issue, Parker lamented the fact that the magazine should have been given over to a "Miss Dial," when he wanted, in essence, a more "manly" periodical, what he called a "Dial with a beard."[67] He was not the only one to resort to these sorts of expressions to describe Fuller's *Dial.* Carlyle wrote to Emerson it was "all spirit-like, aeriform, aurora-borealis like," and wondered, "Will no *angel* body himself out of that; no stalwart Yankee *man,* with colour in the cheeks of him, and a coat on his back!"[68]

In cataloguing these disputes, I do not mean to oversimplify what was, in essence, a "complex, mutually empowering and interactive" friendship between Fuller and Emerson by reducing it to a good guy/bad guy dichotomy in their conversations on *The Dial*. Revising the scholarly understanding of this relationship, Christina Zwarg argues convincingly for the "feminist lessons" in reading, writing, talking, and translating that the two derived from their conversations together.[69] One of the direct results of their interactions was the "rudderless" moments of interpretive freedom characterizing Fuller's translations, a theory that provides a useful framework for understanding Fuller's editorship, more generally.[70] But while Zwarg emphasizes the "developing feminist trends" of Emerson's thought to recover a sense of "feminist agency" in his work, the lessons that Fuller learned through her conversations with him could be either positive or negative, as Zwarg demonstrates in describing Fuller's formulation of translation as distinct from Emerson's more traditional, masculine understanding of it as an exercise in linguistic mastery or control.[71] In this sense, if Fuller grew committed to *The Dial* as a kind of "rudderless" space of literary possibility, it was because Emerson, often encouraging and provocative, could at times also be autocratic in prerogative, seemingly blind to the gendered dynamics of his positions.

But if his early involvement with *The Dial* would be both a blessing and a curse for Fuller, his behavior in the mixed-company sessions of the Conversations could have only confirmed her beliefs in the importance of the journal as a "free organ" (*LMF*, 2:126). Given in the spring of 1841, these sessions were the first and only time Fuller allowed men to participate in her Conversations. Emerson remembers that Fuller "seemed encumbered, or interrupted, by the headiness or incapacity of the men . . . who fancied, no doubt, that, on such a question, they, too, must assert and dogmatize" (*Memoirs*, 1:347–48). As Tiffany Wayne observes, in his account of these sessions Emerson depicts Fuller as unflatteringly "dogmatic" even as he blames the men for hijacking the conversation; of course, as the sessions' other records testify, he seems to have been the chief dogmatizer in this regard.[72] In a 14 March 1841 letter to Fuller, Emerson jokes about his disruptive presence at a recent session, the younger participants afterwards asking what "possessed" him to "tease" her "with so much prose, & becloud the fine conversation? I could only answer that it was . . . chronic & constitutional with me, & I asked them in my turn when they had heard me talk anything else? So I silenced them" (*LRWE*, 2:384).

In monopolizing the conversation and good-naturedly "silencing" its other participants, Emerson evinces the kind of masculine rhetorical tendencies that Fuller had witnessed from her boys at the Greene Street School, although perhaps it took the mixed-company Conversations for her to realize how little might change from child to man. In her journal, Ann Brown recounts a Latin lesson in which "the boys were a *little* too rude. . . . One little boy, who always learns his lessons well, answers to[o] *many* questions and Miss Fuller is obliged to speak forcibly 'unto him.' I can well sympathize with him for when I know the answer to a question I can hardly wait for another to answer but I generally raise my hand" (Fergenson, "Margaret Fuller as a Teacher," 73; emphasis in original). While Emerson's ideal for the "healthy attitude of human nature," as he writes in "Self-Reliance," is the "nonchalance" of the "boy . . . in the parlour" who "cumbers himself never about consequences" (29), Fuller quickly learned that, in the context of female self-culture, such a model could be troubling indeed. Emerson's "rude" behavior, to use Brown's term, like the subtle but disruptive behavior of the one "little boy" who excluded his classmates from conversation by continually speaking over them, thus reinforced Fuller's belief in the need for "conversation of a better order" (*LMF*, 2:86) than the sort she was apt to find among even the most sympathetic of male friends.

The clearest articulation of Fuller's growing schism with Emerson over his "tastes" came in late 1843. After Emerson, now editor, rejected one of Fuller's translations, she writes to gently "scold" him:

> When I had care of the Dial, I put in what those connected with me liked, even when it did not well please myself, on this principle that I considered a magazine was meant to suit more than one class of minds. . . . I thought it less important that everything in it should be excellent, than it should represent with some fidelity the state of mind amongst us as the name of Dial said was its intent. . . . You go on a different principle; you would have everything in it good according to your taste, which is in my opinion, though admirable as far as it goes, far too narrow in its range. This is *your* principle; very well! (*LMF*, 3:160; emphasis in original)

Although Fuller no doubt published contributions she enjoyed, as any editor would, she asserts that this was in no way her essential "principle" of selection while editor of *The Dial*. Rather, she often "put in what those connected to [her] liked," even when the contributions did not "please" her. She solicited, as she informs Emerson, both writings from and those "recommended by" him, "Mr. Ripley, Mr. Parker, &c," and published much of it "without regard" for these men's "contempt" for or "disgust" at each other's literary tastes (*LMF*, 3:160). While Elizabeth Hewitt rightly suggests that this letter resists a distinctly Emersonian editorial policy claiming to "represent the excellence of individuals at the same time as it demands homogeneity in the name of a deeper identity that unites us all," it also demonstrates that conforming to some universalized standard of excellence was far less appealing to Fuller than representing "with some fidelity" what she saw as the varieties of transcendentalism around her.[73] Attempting to uphold a vision of a journal whose contributors, as George Ripley had articulated it in *The Dial*'s prospectus, "possess little in common but the love of intellectual freedom, and the hope of social progress," she determined that its contents should embrace a "wide and varied range of subjects."[74] Indeed, she even announces this eclecticism as the "principle" that had attracted her in the first place to the periodical, a genre which, as Fuller understood it, was heterogeneous by its very nature; she tells Emerson that a "magazine was *meant* to suit more than one class of minds" (emphasis added). As *The Dial*'s editor, therefore, Fuller aimed to capitalize upon the multi-vocal qualities inherent in the form as a miscellany whose contents are selected but not dictated by its editor.

Conclusion: "Old Gentlemanly Pace"

Several years earlier, Mary Ware Allen recorded in her Greene Street "School Journal" a "very pleasant conversation" in which "Miss Fuller" spoke "upon what woman *could* do" and prophesied the day when "the chief literature of this country, would be in the hands of women" (1:77–78; emphasis in original). In the entry, Allen expresses her doubts, not about female capabilities but rather about social expectations, suggesting that attitudes toward the fairer sex must undergo "great change" before such prophesies might come to pass, and similarly anticipating a corresponding transformation in the nation's literature necessary before its *belles lettres* might be properly considered products of women's "hands." But if Allen's skepticism registers her version of what Fuller had characterized as woman's peculiar problem of "casting [her] thought into a form" within a culture where "no old one suit[ed]" her (*Memoirs*, 1:297), Fuller herself would find the hope to escape patriarchal modes of thinking in the periodical genre, just as so many other female editors and contributors turned to it to fulfill their own personal, financial, cultural, and ideological goals.[75]

After all, by the antebellum period the periodical already was the nation's "chief literature," as well as one of the most "powerful means of educating— for good or for evil—the rising generation," as one editorialist put it, because their "indirect lessons" were so "much more effectual than the *schools* in forming the moral character of . . . children and students."[76] But some, like the aforementioned writer, also worried that the genre might work "for evil" as easily as "for good" precisely because its efficacy lay in its disavowing (even as it asserted) "much pretension to authority," thereby allowing periodicals to insinuate themselves "daily and hourly . . . whether perceived or unperceived" into households' most mundane reading habits.[77] Anxious about the way in which periodicals challenged conventional avenues of cultural authority and voiced a motley assortment of unsanctioned investments, this writer ultimately expresses his wish that "the press was as often controlled by wise and good men, as it is by witty and crafty politicians," a worry no doubt exacerbated by the exponential growth of periodicals in the early decades of the nineteenth century, as the genre grew in tandem with the rise and then entrenchment of political parties in the United States.[78]

This desire for stewardship of "wise and good men," or at least men who claimed to represent universal standards of wisdom and goodness, also suggests the difficulties Fuller confronted while editing *The Dial* with Emerson. Registering this struggle, Fuller's "A Short Essay on Critics" (1840) appears second in the journal's inaugural issue, after Emerson, dissatisfied with what Fuller had written, took it upon himself to write his own introduction. In retrospect, the essay, with its description of the "subjective class" and the effects such critics have on the state of periodical criticism, reads as an indictment of Emerson's editorial priorities, as much as a call for a "new critic-reader partnership."[79] Like the self-reliant child who "tries and sentences . . . in the swift, summary way of boys, as good, bad, interesting, silly, eloquent, troublesome," these subjective critics, Fuller tells us, "never dream of going out of themselves to seek the motive, to trace the law of another nature. They never dream that there are statues which cannot be measured by their point of view. They love, they like, or they hate . . . these statements they make with authority, as those who bear the evangel of pure taste."[80] Later in the essay, she recasts these arbiters of "pure taste" as that "coterie where some critic sits despotic, entrenched behind the infallible 'We'" ("Short Essay," 8), espousing their cant as if they spoke with universal intelligibility—an interesting characterization, surely, given that Emerson himself adopts the plural pronoun in his introduction, "The Editors to the Reader," immediately preceding Fuller's essay. Like many other female editors who eschewed using the royal "we" common among their male counterparts, Fuller thus seeks to avoid the authoritative paternalism marking traditional editor-reader relationships.[81] She does so not because she seeks sanction as a female editor in a culture demanding self-effacement from its literary ladies, but because such "despotic" proclamations, and the "coterie" assumptions informing them, undermined the idea of *The Dial* as an "organ" of "individual thought" (*LMF*, 2:126) and obscured the diversity of opinion among its editors, with Fuller, Emerson, and Ripley having in the end produced not one, but essentially three separate introductions to the issue.[82] Of course, hers was not yet the "sisterly editorial voice" attributed to many nineteenth-century female periodical editors; in her "Short Essay," Fuller's ideal standard of periodical criticism remains "manliness," such as when she envisions a true critic capable of speaking "man to man" on an equal level with his reader.[83]

But if, in her first issue as *The Dial*'s editor, Fuller unwittingly reproduces masculine language even as she assaults the literary status quo, her partnership with Emerson nonetheless pushed her toward a renewed sense of the virtues of an open, conversational style and the conviction that those virtues should translate to the periodical medium—so much so that, by the time she became literary editor for the *New York Tribune* in 1844, she declared: "Newspaper writing is next door to conversation, and should be conducted on the same principles" ("American Literature," 140).[84] Perhaps her new position at Greeley's popular periodical was not what some had envisioned for her, but while a few friends thought she "ought to produce something excellent," she is "satisfied," she tells us, "to aid in the great work of popular education" (*LMF*, 4:39). In her use of the term "excellent," Fuller is likely thinking of Emerson again, evoking the limiting sense of "taste" she believed characterized his aesthetic sensibility. If this move to the *Tribune* marked her arrival on the threshold of full literary professionalism, the transformation was one she understood not as the culmination of some elitist aesthetic commitment but one enabled by an expansive sense of the periodical genre's possibilities. Ultimately, she believed it could offer a form suited not only to her range of experiences as a woman, but also to what she calls in "American Literature" (1846) the "mixed race" of national life itself (123).

In this essay, Fuller articulates her unfolding sense of the periodical's potential, declaring that the "most important part of our literature . . . lies in the journals, which monthly, weekly, daily, send their messages to every corner of this great land, and form, at present, the only efficient instrument for the general education of the people" (137–38). While she describes the "Literary Review" as one of the forms most "creditable to a new country" (138), she finds none "which occupies a truly great and commanding position" because no periodical had yet fully embraced its democratic nature, allowing "free range in its columns, to all kinds of ability, and all ways of viewing subjects" (139). Many, like the genteel *North American Review*, "once the best" in her opinion, had already fallen into a kind of "old gentlemanly pace," ambling "along a beaten path that leads to no important goal" (139). Her evocation of a "truly great" journal, whose freedom of "range" encompasses what she calls "life, rich, bold, various" (139), harkens back to the editorial principles she articulated to Emerson, and yet her characterization of the *North American Review*'s old "gentlemanly pace" demonstrates how far she had come in identifying her problem as the same elitist, masculine prerogative against which she had been struggling all along.

In contrasting her editorial ideals with such narrow tastes, Fuller invokes Cornelius Mathews' "The Journalist" (1843), what she calls a "worthy account" in verse of her profession's "duties," declaring: "Editors, generally, could not do better . . . than to read and insert" its lines in their papers on a regular basis (140). In Fuller's reading, the poem is a panegyric to the periodical's "thousand broad sheets . . . / Filled with the people's breath of potency" (lines 3–4), glorifying the genre's ability to "fix upon the unnumbered gazers' view" (line 19), that is, the "people's" perspective (line 4), and "on the air its many-colored heart unfold" (line 24). Interpreting Mathews' poem for us, Fuller champions the "few editors of this country . . . who have been willing to have all sides fully heard" and to value the "sincere, characteristic and free" in whatever form it appeared (141–42). But the problem was that, in their current state of development, many "men do *not* look at both sides," as Fuller had warned in *Woman in the Nineteenth-Century* (72; emphasis in original). In an industry dominated by male editors and the gentlemanly publications they encouraged, the prospects for such transcendent principles were dim indeed.

Even so, she did not lose faith that literary enterprises like *The Dial* and the *Tribune* might serve as harbingers of a better day, marking the hours (hence, the title, *Dial*) until the "first faint streaks" of that new "dawn" ("American Literature," 124) when the periodical genre might achieve its full, democratic potential. As for herself, Fuller experiences bittersweet satisfaction at the prospect that, although those who "foresee" this future should not live to share in its "glories," their "every act and word, uttered in the light of that foresight, may tend to hasten or ennoble its fulfillment" (124). In language evoking both the "free, genial atmosphere" (*Woman in the Nineteenth Century*, 27) she prescribes for women, and the hopes, articulated to Peabody all those years earlier, for a periodical with "room enough" and "perfect freedom" to write what she pleased (*Memoirs*, 1:168), Fuller offers this compensation for teacher, author, and editor: "Whether we introduce some noble model from another time and clime, to encourage aspiration in our own, or cheer into blossom the simplest wood-flower that ever rose from the earth, moved by the genuine impulse to grow, independent of money or celebrity . . . the spirit of truth, purely worshipped, shall turn our acts and forbearances alike to profit" ("American Literature," 125).

Finally, while Fuller trades certain kinds of capital (financial and cultural, "money" and "celebrity," respectively) for others (the spiritual, or "truth, purely worshipped"), her desire for "profit" nonetheless reveals how closely aligned her transcendental feminism is with the impulse for market reform. Even as she announces "no man of genius writes for money" (126), she admits that it is "essential to the free use of his powers"—in fact, she had once told Peabody that she was "perfectly willing" to write "to pay the seamstress" or to "get command of time" (*Memoirs,* 1:168). In calling for a "genuine impulse to grow" ("American Literature," 125), therefore, she hopes to cultivate not only men and women who might learn to "look at both sides," but also a literary industry not determined by the narrow interests of publishers who, regarding literary production as a mere "matter of business," ask authors "only to give [them] what will find an immediate market" (126). In Fuller's estimation, this pursuit of the "immediate," or the ready-made, is also the pursuit of the short-sighted; in doing so, publishers lose the chance to invest in new voices, and the potential markets they represented. But if literary enterprises like *The Dial* or the *Tribune,* as she envisioned them, sought to alter current industry practices, they simultaneously aimed to teach the industry's consumers "how to cherish the nobler and rarer plants, and to plant the aloe, able to wait a hundred years for its bloom, or its garden will contain, presently, nothing but potatoes and pot-herb" (126). With these sentiments, Fuller comes full circle, encouraging publisher and public alike to find value beyond the utilitarian impulses of their day.

CODA

"The Sun is but a Morning Star"

MANY OF THE thorny issues we identify as unique to our own pedagogical moment, such as standardized textbooks, the rise of new media in the classroom, or even "No Child Left Behind," have analogs in the experiences of the nineteenth-century American transcendentalist circle. Figures such as Horace Mann, Nathaniel Hawthorne, Elizabeth Peabody, and Margaret Fuller were deeply interested in the principles, practices, and problems of democratic education, aspiring to cultivate a literature leaving no child—or adult, for that matter—behind. While modern schools in the United States must be staffed by systematically trained and institutionally sanctioned teachers, in the unregulated, decentralized world of antebellum America, schools were not infrequently filled with aspiring authors, literary men and women who sought the financial stability of teaching while simultaneously claiming it as moral grounds for the pursuit of greater literary fame. In their wish to combine communal good with individual benefit, these transcendentalists are manifestations of the impulse uniting the antebellum author to its modern educator counterpart: the fervent desire to make a living by making a difference.

In the absence of codified pathways to publication or institutional means of support (such as university presses, or state-sanctioned textbook publishers, to name but two), however, antebellum educator-authors relied by necessity upon coterie practices to achieve their literary ambitions. Once again,

I use "coterie" with caution, since the transcendentalists themselves often excoriated the term; I invoke it not to summon the stigma of "self-serving insularity" they rejected, but rather to delineate writers whose associations acted as *de facto* "protective or defensive measures" against alienating economic circumstances.[1] In this book, therefore, I have positioned Peabody's circle and its investments (both cultural and financial) in education as an ethical alternative to literary business-as-usual, even as coterie practices constituted the substance of an antebellum print culture that emphasized heartfelt social obligations as a means to earn a living in a free, and increasingly impersonal, market.

When, in the midst of *Biographical Stories,* for instance, Hawthorne mentions a "new book, called THE FLOWER PEOPLE, in which the snowdrops, the violets, the columbines, the roses, and all that lovely tribe, are represented as telling their secrets to a little girl" (*CE*, 6:250–51), he engages in a kind of loving tribalism, to use his own metaphor. Hawthorne intends both to self-promote (by capitalizing on Mary Peabody Mann's reputation in local circles) and to teach nature's secrets (or, at least, bourgeois morality in the garb of nature) to a blooming generation of readers. Puffing Mann's popular children's book *The Flower People* (1842), he declares its power to stimulate children's imaginations, to open their minds' eyes as it were, despite all impediments, such as his protagonist Edward's debilitating blindness: "The flowers talked sweetly, as flowers should; and Edward almost fancied that he could behold their bloom, and smell their fragrant breath" (251). Recreating for Edward the experience of family reading—his father recounts the collection's titular biographies, while his adopted sister Emily repeats the stories she had read in Mann's book—the scene embraces bourgeois educational practices understood as exceeding, though never quite effacing, the insular concerns of class, party, or region. In other words, just as Mary Peabody Mann uses the imagined space of the domestic garden to introduce little girls to a cosmopolitan world, so too does Hawthorne use the home as the starting point for equally fanciful flights.[2] Yet, even as Peabody's circle understood such ideological formations as a transcendental value system rising above class investments, their literary-pedagogical enterprises were nonetheless ineluctably linked to the development of bourgeois identity.[3]

Obviously, not all educational practices are equal, and one might easily excoriate the transcendentalists' unknowing complicity in consolidating bourgeois consciousness, or, to take another instance, reject someone like Bronson Alcott's preference for corporal punishment, with his insistence on having his students whip *him* to teach them sympathy and discipline (did it really hurt them more than it hurt him?). But while granting the historical specificity of transcendentalist education, one might just as easily recognize the way its proponents used education to expand the market for literature, or recuperate some useful lessons from these enterprises, such as the importance of ethical character in liberal society, the value of pluralism, and the necessity of distrusting social, political, or religious dogma. Additionally, one might embrace the transcendentalists' belief that all education must become self-learning to have any lasting effect, or their faith in what Robert Milder calls "revolution-by-consciousness," the idea that changing the world first begins by changing minds.[4]

While others may have argued more passionately for the value of transcendental pedagogy in today's classrooms, I am content to contribute an anecdote to the cause of revisiting the transcendentalists' investments.[5] Take New York state's recent standardized test controversy, in which a passage administered as part of the state's eighth-grade reading comprehension exam left some students scratching their heads, test skeptics crying foul, the state's education department recanting (announcing it would strike the section from students' scores), and the excerpt's original author both denouncing the educational publishing industry and yet defending the sale of his work to them. Adapted quite loosely from one of Daniel Pinkwater's children's novels by Pearson PLC, the world's largest educational publisher, "The Hare and the Pineapple" concerns a race between these titular characters, with various forest animals weighing in on the pineapple's prospects, convinced, as a moose says, that he must have a "trick up his sleeve" to win. He doesn't. Although all the animals cheer him on, the pineapple never moves from the starting line and the hare wins the race easily. The animals then eat the pineapple, and the moral of the story, as stated by an owl, is: "Pineapples don't have sleeves." Following this story, the exam asks students several multiple-choice questions, including why the animals ate the pineapple and which animal in the story is the "wisest." Children, parents, and even teachers were confused.[6]

Amidst outcry against the exam, there is, at least, this silver lining: students' responses to the test might be taken to validate the pedagogical investments of the transcendentalists more than 170 years later. Some students thought that the animals could have eaten the pineapple because they were hungry. Although, according to the exam, this answer is incorrect, the story never says they weren't, and pineapples, after all, *are* tasty. Others wondered whether the "wisest" question was a trick, perhaps intuiting that while the owl is, conventionally, the "wisest" of animals, the story subverts this possibility.[7] After all, declaring "Pineapples don't have sleeves" hardly constitutes wisdom, especially when the owl mistakenly cheers for the pineapple along with the other animals. Maria Tatar compares the students' reaction to "The Emperor's New Clothes," claiming, "It's a wonderful case, with all these children pointing at the emperor. . . . That no adults seem to have noticed this is really interesting."[8] To this analysis, I would add another analogy: Alcott's *Conversations with Children*. Like Peabody's defense of the Temple School amidst its headmaster's foibles, we too might find encouragement in the way in which the children's responses bolster the truth of transcendental pedagogy, or to use Peabody's own language, in the way in which the test "so truly roused their moral principles as to enable them to hold out and beat [Pearson] in an argument upon special cases in which [it] concluded wrongly."[9] What the controversy exposes, then, is that children are not clean slates onto which individuals or institutions can transfer their characters, but rather that they bring their own insights and investments to the conversation. In this age of teaching-to-the-test, not unlike the nineteenth century's world of rote memorization, it should remind us, as Fuller told her students in Providence, to "despise" the idea of the mind as a "blank sheet of paper" (Allen, "School Journal," 1:16).

Pedagogical implications aside, what interests me most about the controversy is how the specter of the "sell out" emerging from it reproduces an enduring obsession of the romantic literary-educator. In his published response to the debacle, Pinkwater cites this email from an eighth-grader: "Listen, I love your work, but seriously? Selling out to the state test?"[10] On the one hand, Hawthorne himself—who described his own fanciful children's fiction as the "Child's Budget of Miscellaneous Nonsense," just as Pinkwater declares himself an "advocate of nonsense,"—could not have wished for a more ideal child-reader.[11] This reader's sentimental investment in the literary text demands that the author take "seriously" his own humorous writing, and obscures while simultaneously enabling that writing's commodity status, since someone had to invest in the book by purchasing it before the child could learn to love it. On the other hand, the child articulates so damning a criticism that Pinkwater feels the need to defend himself, claiming to have told him or her: "You bet I sold out. . . . You'd do the same thing if you were a writer, and didn't know where your next pineapple was coming from." In their exchange, both reader and author position "selling out" as an unabashed cash-in, prompted by economic necessity and, in a sense, beneath the dignity of "serious" literature. The exchange also presents us with additional complexities since, in both the student's and the author's formations, education becomes a form of "selling out"—the child blames the "state test," while

Pinkwater faults educational publishing companies like Pearson for editing "all the pleasure" out of texts (presumably, under the guise of better educating children).[12]

What so distresses authors like Pinkwater in the twenty-first century, no less than romantics like Margaret Fuller in the nineteenth, is the reality that "selling out" might precipitate, as Fuller calls it, "mutilation" by editors or publishers entitled to do what they want with their newly acquired texts. "I would gladly sell some part of my mind for lucre," Fuller informs Peabody in a letter on her prospects for teaching and writing, "but I will not sell my soul . . . I am *not* willing to have what I write mutilated" (*Memoirs*, 1:168). If such denunciations about pressure to "sell her soul" seem a tad melodramatic by modern standards, Fuller's fears of "mutilation," at least, were well-founded. Practices of censorship were rampant in the antebellum literary industry; editors felt no compunction in altering authors' texts without their consent—as James Russell Lowell did when he famously removed the last sentence from an installment of Thoreau's *Maine Woods* that he found too pantheistic. (Thoreau was so furious that he withdrew the rest of the text from Lowell's *Atlantic Monthly*).[13] These concerns are more relevant than ever, if "The Hare and the Pineapple" is any indication of modern educational publishing practices. Pinkwater describes his excerpt as "edited out of any resemblance to what I wrote . . . edited to where not a single word of it was mine, just the name [on the story]."[14] Among the changes made by Pearson was their decision to substitute for Pinkwater's original eggplant a pineapple, altering in the process the story's moral: "Don't bet on an eggplant." One wonders what educational purpose such a change serves. Are eggplants (like tomatoes, to quote a line from the movie *Elf* [2003]) just "too vulnerable" for children?

In responding to the controversy, Pinkwater paints a grim picture of modern educational publishing. He calls companies like Pearson "money grubbing," claiming that they "overcharge for this stuff and sell it over and over again and underpay the poor authors they buy it off of," adding, "Publishing in general is not a moral industry, and specialized publishing like this where they have a captive audience, and God knows what kind of longstanding relationships, might be less moral yet."[15] Having purchased the rights to the story over a decade ago for a small sum, Pearson has reused the passage in other states' tests since 2007, and its contract with New York state alone will earn it $32 million over five years. Pinkwater's preoccupation with the morality of publishing and his complaint about "captive audience[s]"—referring as much to authors at the whim of the few companies controlling the nation's educational markets as to the schools and children they target—recall antebellum reformers' own laments (like Mann's assault on the self-interested motives of educational publishers), although it is important to note that their cries were directed at the laissez-faire practices of a private industry seemingly loosened from traditional institutions and social bonds. Thus, while Pinkwater depicts Pearson as embodying an industry in moral decline, whose "dirty money" only gets "dirtier" as government control tightens and standardized tests' stakes increase, the experiences of Mann, Hawthorne, Peabody, and Fuller should dispel for us this myth of decline; the publishing industry, educational or otherwise, is no "dirtier" than it ever was.[16]

Antebellum literary reformers answered these vexing problems by becoming market intermediaries themselves—some, like Fuller, as editors; others, like Peabody, as booksellers; and still others, like Mann, as superintendents and advisory board members—in the hopes that individual character might reshape the practices of market culture, transforming it from within. But if, given the institutionalization of professional authorship, the consolidation of publishing houses, and the "reprivatization" of social authorship practices, today's industry makes such avenues seem less feasible, these reformers encourage us to dream of alternative arrangements, to harness new media, as they once did, and, at the very least, to determine for ourselves when vision might trump revenue, as Richard Henry Dana Jr. did when *The School Library*'s "school-master gone crazy" approached him about adapting *Two Years Before the Mast*.[17] Additionally, they raise compelling questions about earning one's living in an industry that, to this day, uneasily balances both pedagogical and economic incentives. How might one respond to publishers who use "making a difference" as a way to reduce author costs, as Mann did when he confessed to Dana that his compensation would be "small," or as modern companies do when they tell writers, "A lot of authors are contributing these things [for free] because it's for the betterment of our children"?[18] Conversely, does payment justify editorial doctoring in the name of didactic ends, as Mann intended for Dana Jr.'s text, and as Pearson did with Pinkwater's story? Is it, in fact, "mutilation" for editors and publishers to wantonly adapt literary texts to accommodate perceived audiences, or is it merely the failure of their changes to reach that supposed audience effectively that is the problem? And who should get to make these freighted decisions? There are, of course, no easy answers, as both Fuller's authorial comments on "mutilation," and Peabody's disagreement with Mann over the role of "*the teachers*" and "school committee men" in selecting books for *The School Library*, suggest (*Letters*, 199).

I conclude this book with these anecdotes not only because they dramatize issues persisting in our own day, but also because the lens of education provides a useful means for re-imagining the transcendentalist movement itself. Indeed, its various educational enterprises invite further study, offering new contexts for transcendentalism and literary genre; children's literature, for example, represents a frontier beyond the nonfiction forms usually associated with the circle. To view their careers in this way thus overturns longstanding assumptions about transcendentalists' aversion to writing fiction, helping to render visible once again the children's literature that is, along with its concern for childhood sensibility, one of transcendentalism's legacies.[19] Beyond this, these considerations suggest a different canon than the Emerson-Fuller-Thoreau one that now predominates. While the Hawthorne and Mary Peabody Mann pairing I discuss earlier accords with the constellation this book outlines, another formulation might place Hawthorne's more fanciful works, *A Wonder-Book* (1852) and *Tanglewood Tales* (1853), in conversation with other transcendental children's authors. What might one glean in reading him against Caroline Sturgis Tappan, whose whimsical *Rainbows for Children* (1848) was, along with *A Wonder-Book*, a great favorite of William James, and whose *Magician's Show Box* (1856) was issued by Hawthorne's same publisher, Ticknor and Fields?[20] Similarly, what might we gain in juxtaposing him against Christopher Pearse Cranch (arguably the nation's first children's novelist), whose *Last of the Huggermuggers* (1856), about a boy's adventures as a cast-away among giants, and its sequel, *Kobboltozo* (1857), were composed in the same fashion as Hawthorne's juvenile texts, with the father testing his stories upon his children as he wrote them?[21] At the very least, such couplings enrich our understanding of American juvenile literature's shift from the moralistic to the fantastic by positioning Hawthorne within a network of transcendentalists equally engaged in metamorphosing the genre.

So deeply rooted in the transcendental circle was this fascination with children's literature that even intellectuals such as Margaret Fuller listed it among their authorial ambitions. She once informed Elizabeth Peabody of a hope to translate Tieck's "Little Red Riding Hood for children," adding, "If it could be adorned with illustrations, like those in [Carové's] the 'Story without an End,' it would make a beautiful little book. . . . There is much meaning that children could not take in; but, as they would never discover this till able to receive the whole, the book corresponds exactly with my notions of what a child's book should be" (*Memoirs*, 1:169). Fuller's theory of what a "child's book should be" is obviously fertile ground, as is her interest in

Austin's translation (London, 1833) of Friedrich Wilhelm Carové's "Kinderleben oder das Mährchen ohne Ende" [The Story without an End] (1830). She doubted whether the book "could be done in Boston" (*Memoirs*, 1:169), but, given the popularity of German literature among its liberal circles, the city was perhaps one of the few markets in which such an edition would be sure to find an audience.[22] And, although she never produced this translation, Fuller maintained her investment in children's literature, reviewing juvenile books (including Hawthorne's works and at least one translation of German stories for children) in both *The Dial* and the *New York Tribune*.[23]

Furthermore, Fuller's desire for a "beautiful little book" encourages us to reconsider transcendental attitudes toward the material experience of reading. Of course, illustrations were, from the beginning, a market necessity in the book industry as a whole, and not merely in children's books. Hawthorne, for one, attributed disappointing sales of the first edition of *Grandfather's Chair* in part to a failure to procure his desired illustrations, while Cranch described his own "bantling" edition, for which he drew the sketches, as the sort of "typographic dandyism and display" that "infantine America loves." But the belief that "infantine America" required the visual as a precondition for intellectual engagement had also been part and parcel of Anglo-American early educational pedagogies since at least Locke in the late seventeenth century, and certainly of the Romantic and Pestalozzian theories of childhood development invigorating antebellum America. Speaking against contemporary juvenile literature's heavy-handed didacticism, Fuller observed that Americans had become "so fond of instruction, that we forget development," that is, so preoccupied with forcing moral lessons into the experience of childhood reading that we often neglect that the child must be allowed to "stretch its limbs" on its own terms, in accordance with the "nature in which it must find its root." Similarly, "beautiful" editions might help "infantine America" in yet another way, allowing its imagined national community to grow, to stretch its "infantine" limbs, as it were, both by providing new reading materials from cultures other than its British antecedents and also by enabling the shared material and aesthetic pleasures of reading itself.[24]

Finally, such enterprises offer new prospects for studying the educational imperatives influencing the antebellum literary market beyond the transcendental circle. Because those who wrote, published, or disseminated literature for money did so "without entirely abandoning the wellspring of social inspiration," pedagogical enterprises such as the ones described in this book continued to dominate the market well into the last decades of the nineteenth century. Education suffused market exchanges, for instance allowing the industry to promote itself in terms of sociability—such as when publishers pitched their commodities to "friends of education." By mid-century, schoolbooks comprised 30 to 40 percent of all books published in the nation. In the decades beyond, education remained a perennial theme of publishers' series; these series not only rose in number, but also constituted a greater percentage of all series published. Even those firms whose successes we associate with *belles lettres,* understood as cultivating an "autonomous world of art and pleasure" divorced from cultural or political action, earned a substantial portion of their business from educational texts. Therefore, this book positions Peabody's circle as vanguards and representatives of wider industry trends so that, in successive studies, we might investigate how pedagogy invigorated other writers and literary circles, as well as other genres, in antebellum America. After all, this "sun is but a morning star."[25]

NOTES

Introduction

1. "Notices and Intelligence: The School Library," *Christian Examiner* 27.1 (September 1839): 133; emphasis in original.

2. Ibid., 134; emphasis in original.

3. Elizabeth Peabody to Horace Mann, 3 March 1838, in *The Letters of Elizabeth Palmer Peabody*, ed. Bruce Ronda (Middletown, CT: Wesleyan University Press, 1984), 200. Subsequent references to this edition, hereafter cited as *Letters*, will appear in parentheses.

4. Lesley Ginsberg, "Hawthorne, Grace Greenwood, and the Culture of Pedagogy," *Nathaniel Hawthorne Review* 36.1 (Spring 2010): 47.

5. David Paul Nord, *Faith in Reading* (New York: Oxford University Press, 2004); Thomas Augst, *The Clerk's Tale* (Chicago: University of Chicago Press, 2003), 35, 32; Mark G. Vásquez, *Authority and Reform: Religious and Educational Discourses in Nineteenth-Century New England Literature* (Knoxville: University of Tennessee Press, 2003), 66–67.

6. See Leon Jackson, *The Business of Letters: Authorial Economies in Antebellum America* (Stanford, CA: Stanford University Press, 2008), 43. For another discussion of the antebellum literary industry's ethical dimensions, see Michael Everton, *The Grand Chorus of Complaint: Authors and the Business Ethics of American Publishing* (New York: Oxford University Press, 2011).

7. Ronald Zboray and Mary Saracino Zboray, *Literary Dollars and Social Sense* (New York: Routledge, 2005), xix–xx.

8. Nathaniel Hawthorne, "The Old Manse," in Vol. 10 of *The Centenary Edition of The Works of Nathaniel Hawthorne*, eds. William Charvat, Roy Harvey Pearce, and Claude Simpson, et al. (Columbus: The Ohio State University Press, 1974), 31. All subsequent references to Hawthorne's writings are to this edition, hereafter cited as *CE*, with volume and page number.

9. A pioneer in the discipline of history of the book, William Charvat took for granted the antagonism between literary artist and market. See "Literary Economics and Literary History," rpt. in *The Profession of Authorship in America, 1800–1870*, ed. Matthew Bruccoli (New York: Columbia University Press, 1992), 292. In the 1980s, Michael Gilmore refined this formulation, arguing that American romantics such as Melville, Hawthorne, and Emerson were deeply ambivalent about the marketplace, harshly critical of the new economic order, and yet still drawn

to it. See Gilmore, *American Romanticism and the Marketplace* (Chicago: University of Chicago Press, 1985), 8. Similarly, William Rowland Jr. has argued that it was these writers' sense of alienation from the market that, ironically, gave their literature its appeal with the nineteenth-century reading public. See William Rowland, Jr., *Literature and the Marketplace: Romantic Writers and their Audiences in Great Britain and the United States* (Lincoln: University of Nebraska Press, 1996), 5.

10. Perry Miller, *The Transcendentalists: An Anthology* (Cambridge, MA: Harvard University Press, 1950), 106. For an overview of this *"annus mirabilus,"* see Barbara Packer, "The Transcendentalists," in *The Cambridge History of American Literature, Volume Two: Prose Writing, 1820–1860*, ed. Sacvan Bercovitch (New York: Cambridge University Press, 1994), 376–91.

11. Theodore Parker described Peabody as "a Boswell" whose "office" was to "inquire and answer, 'What did they say?'" as she moved among the age's literary greats. Quoted in Bruce Ronda, *Elizabeth Palmer Peabody: A Reformer on Her Own Terms* (Cambridge, MA: Harvard University Press, 1999), 1; for further discussion of Peabody's role as intermediary, see also Mark Vásquez, "Declaration and Deference: Elizabeth Palmer Peabody, Mary Peabody Mann, and the Complex Rhetoric of Mediation," in *Reinventing the Peabody Sisters*, eds. Monika Elbert, Julie Hall, and Katharine Rodier (Iowa City: University of Iowa Press, 2006), 45–60, and John Idol, Jr., "Elizabeth Palmer Peabody: A Tireless Hawthorne Booster," in *Hawthorne and Women: Engendering and Expanding the Hawthorne Tradition,* eds. John Idol, Jr. and Melinda Ponder (Amherst: University of Massachusetts Press, 1999), 36–44; for Mann and education, see Megan Marshall, *The Peabody Sisters: Three Women Who Ignited American Romanticism* (Boston: Houghton Mifflin, 2005), 4; for "High Priest," see Mary Tyler Peabody to Horace Mann, 26 August 1837, *Horace Mann Collection*, microfilm edition, 40 reels (Boston: Massachusetts Historical Society, 1989), reel 4; "no right to be idle" is cited in James R. Mellow, *Hawthorne in His Times* (Baltimore: Johns Hopkins University Press, 1998), 4–5; for "justice to your character" see Margaret Fuller to Elizabeth Peabody, 26 December 1844, in Vol. 3 of *The Letters of Margaret Fuller,* ed. Robert Hudspeth (Ithaca, NY: Cornell University Press, 1984), 254 (subsequent references to this edition, hereafter cited as *LMF* with volume and page number, will appear in parentheses); for "faithful booster" see Charles Capper, *Margaret Fuller: An American Romantic Life, Vol. 1* (New York: Oxford University Press, 1992), 189; for more on the Peabody–Fuller relationship, see Capper, *Margaret Fuller*, 1: 317–18, and Ronda, *Elizabeth Palmer Peabody*, 156–58.

12. Charles Capper, "'A Little Beyond': Transcendentalism in American History," in *Transient and Permanent,* ed. Charles Capper and Conrad Wright (Boston: Massachusetts Historical Society, 2000), 28.

13. In examining this irony, I take my lead from Ronald and Mary Saracino Zboray, who remind us that most antebellum authors wrote "to fulfill social responsibilities to their specific surrounding coterie" of colleagues, family, and friends, while the market played a "mere supporting role" in their efforts. For this reason, the "role of coteries" must be "kept front and center" in any study of antebellum authorship, should one wish to "deal adequately" with the realities of literary production or dissemination, even for those writers who aspired to or attained much wider ends. See *Literary Dollars,* 204.

14. David Dowling, *The Business of Literary Circles in Nineteenth-Century America* (New York: Palgrave Macmillan, 2011), 20. See also his discussion of the transcendentalists on 91–144.

15. For enrollment and literacy rates, see Gerald Moran and Maris Vinovskis, "Schools," in *A History of the Book in America, Volume 2: 1790–1840,* eds. Robert Gross and Mary Kelley

(Chapel Hill: University of North Carolina Press, 2010), 290, and Mary Kelley, "Introduction" to "Section III. Educating the Citizenry," in *A History of the Book in America, Volume 2,* 269. Common-school reform in New England, for instance, tended to emphasize such things as modernized schoolhouses, Pestalozzi-influenced curriculum, adequate teacher training, standardized texts, and even a distinctive national literature appropriate to children.

16. Wesley T. Mott, "Education," in *The Oxford Handbook of Transcendentalism,* ed. Joel Myerson, et al. (New York: Oxford University Press, 2010), 153.

17. Jonathan Messerli, *Horace Mann: A Biography* (New York: Knopf, 1972), 306–7; Joseph Kett, *The Pursuit of Knowledge Under Difficulties* (Stanford, CA: Stanford University Press, 1994), 80, 86–87.

18. For reform as progressive or conservative, see C. S. Griffin, *Ferment of Reform, 1830–1860* (New York: Crowell, 1967), Ronald G. Walters, *American Reformers, 1815–1860* (New York: Hill and Wang, 1997), and María Carla Sánchez, *Reforming the World: Social Activism and the Problem of Fiction in Nineteenth-Century America* (Iowa City: University of Iowa Press, 2008), 10.

19. Vásquez, *Authority and Reform,* xvi.

20. Sánchez, *Reforming the World,* 4–5.

21. Horace Mann to Elizabeth Palmer Peabody, 10 March 1838, *Horace Mann Collection,* microfilm edition, 40 reels (Boston: Massachusetts Historical Society, 1989), reel 5.

22. Kenneth Price and Susan Belasco Smith, "Introduction: Periodical Literature in Social and Historical Context," in *Periodical Literature in Nineteenth-Century America,* ed. Kenneth W. Price and Susan Belasco Smith (Charlottesville: University of Virginia Press, 1995), 3. Also see John Tebbel, *A History of Book Publishing in the United States: Volume 1* (New York: R. R. Bowker, 1972); and William Charvat, *Literary Publishing in America, 1790–1850* (Amherst: University of Massachusetts Press, 1993).

23. For "liminal," see Isabelle Lehuu, *Carnival of the Page: Popular Print Media in Antebellum America* (Chapel Hill: University of North Carolina Press, 2000), 3–13. For "little publics" (and discussion of antebellum publishers' market segmentation strategies), see Sarah Wadsworth, *In the Company of Books: Literature and Its 'Classes' in Nineteenth-Century America* (Amherst: University of Massachusetts Press, 2006), 1. For "cottage industry," see Tebbel, *History of Book Publishing,* 75. For more on nationalizing print culture and its pitfalls, see Ronald Zboray, *A Fictive People: Antebellum Economic Development and the American Reading Public* (New York: Oxford University Press, 1993).

24. Ralph Waldo Emerson, "Fugitive Slave Law Address," cited in Price and Belasco Smith, "Introduction," 3.

25. Washington Irving, *The Sketch-Book of Geoffrey Crayon,* ed. Haskell Springer (Boston: Twayne Publishers, 1978), 105.

26. Samuel Goodrich, *Recollections of a Lifetime* (New York: Miller, Orton, and Mulligan, 1856), 2:387–88; 1:86.

27. For "hobby" and "one or two classes," see "Discussion on School Libraries," *American Annals of Education* 6.12 (December 1836): 553; for "multiplicity of school books," see "Schools in Massachusetts," *American Annals of Education* 7.3 (March 1837): 101; for "feature of the era," see Goodrich, *Recollections,* 2:382–83; for the United States' outstripping Europe in school books, see Tebbel, *History of Book Publishing,* 222. For example, Murray's *English Reader* (1799) was the most-bought book in the English-speaking world (selling an estimated 20 million copies by mid-century), rivaled only by the likes of McGuffey, whose *Eclectic Readers* series had

sold 7 million copies from its publication in 1836. See Charles Monaghan and E. Jennifer Monaghan, "Schoolbooks," in *A History of the Book in America, Volume 2: 1790–1840*, eds. Robert Gross and Mary Kelley (Chapel Hill: University of North Carolina Press, 2010), 309, 314–15.

28. As Charles and E. Jennifer Monaghan point out, "textbooks" in a modern sense would not come into use until the twentieth century. See "Schoolbooks," 305. For more varieties of schoolbooks, see Moran and Vivoskis, "Schools," 298–301, and Monaghan and Monaghan, "Schoolbooks," 305–7.

29. "The Periodical Press, Generally," *American Annals of Education* 8.6 (June 1838): 286.

30. Horace Mann, "On District School Libraries," in *Lectures on Education*, rpt. in *American Education: Its Men, Ideas, and Institutions*, ed. Lawrence Cremin (New York: Arno Press, 1969), 301. Subsequent references to this text will appear in parentheses.

31. See Lawrence Buell, "American Civil War Poetry and the Meaning of Literary Commodification," in *Reciprocal Influences: Literary Production, Distribution, and Consumption in America*, ed. Steven Fink and Susan S. Williams (Columbus: The Ohio State University Press, 1999), 123–38; Sheila Post-Lauria, "Magazine Practices and Melville's Israel Potter," in *Periodical Literature in Nineteenth-Century America*, ed. Kenneth W. Price and Susan Belasco Smith (Charlottesville: University of Virginia Press, 1995), 115–32, and *Correspondent Colorings: Melville in the Marketplace* (Amherst: University of Massachusetts Press, 1996); Wadsworth, *In the Company of Books*, 11.

32. "Instruction and Education in Families: Influence of Sisters," *American Annals of Education* 8.10 (October 1838): 447.

33. Elizabeth Palmer Peabody, *Reminiscences of Rev. Wm. Ellery Channing, D. D.* (Boston: Roberts Brothers, 1880), 412. Subsequent references to this edition will appear in parentheses.

34. See Michael Winship, "The Transatlantic Book Trade," in *Reciprocal Influences: Literary Production, Distribution, and Consumption in America*, ed. Steven Fink and Susan S. Williams (Columbus: The Ohio State University Press, 1999), 98–122; Meredith McGill, *American Literature and the Culture of Reprinting* (Philadelphia: University of Pennsylvania Press, 2003).

35. Margaret Fuller, "American Literature," in *Papers on Literature and Art* (New York: Wiley and Putnam, 1846), 2: vii. Subsequent references to this edition will appear in parentheses.

36. Charles Capper, *Margaret Fuller: An American Romantic Life, Vol. 2* (New York: Oxford University Press, 2007), xv.

37. Wadsworth, *In the Company of Books*, 13.

38. Horace Mann, "Necessity of Education in a Republican Government," in *Lectures on Education*, rpt. *American Education: Its Men, Ideas, and Institutions Series*, ed. Lawrence Cremin (New York: Arno Press, 1969), 161.

39. Margaret Fuller, *Woman in the Nineteenth Century*, Norton Critical Editions, ed. Larry Reynolds (New York: W. W. Norton & Co, 1998), 93. Subsequent references to this edition will appear in parentheses.

40. Peabody cited in George Cooke, *An Historical and Biographical Introduction to Accompany The Dial* (Cleveland: Rowfant Club, 1902), 1:148; for "citizen of the world," see *LMF*, 1:295; For "intensive" and "extensive," see David Hall, "Uses of Literacy in New England, 1600–1850," in *Cultures of Print: Essay in the History of the Book* (Amherst: University of Massachusetts Press, 1996), 87–88, and Lehuu, *Carnival on the Page*, 18–19, 132–33.

41. Mary Kelley, *Public Woman, Private Stage: Literary Domesticity in Nineteenth-century America* (New York: Oxford University Press, 1984). More recently, Kelley has complicated this public/private formulation by arguing that late-eighteenth- and early-nineteenth-century

American women found in education the "key both to [their] entering civil society and to the influence they exercised as makers of public opinion," even as they continued to be excluded from participation in the political realm of the state. See *Learning to Stand and Speak: Women, Education, and Public Life in America's Republic* (Chapel Hill: University of North Carolina Press, 2006), 15.

42. Messerli, *Horace Mann*, 336.

43. Anne Rose, *Transcendentalism as a Social Movement, 1830–1850* (New Haven, CT: Yale University Press, 1981), 207–8.

44. Robert Milder, "The Radical Emerson?" in *The Cambridge Companion to Ralph Waldo Emerson*, ed. Joel Porte and Saundra Morris (New York: Cambridge University Press, 1999), 55.

45. Lawrence Buell, "Transcendentalist Literary Legacies," in *Transient and Permanent: The Transcendentalist Movement and its Contexts*, ed. Charles Capper and Conrad Wright (Boston: Massachusetts Historical Society, 1999), 605–6.

46. Ronald J. Zboray and Mary Saracino Zboray, "Transcendentalism in Print: Production, Dissemination, and Common Reception," in *Transient and Permanent: The Transcendentalist Movement and its Contexts*, ed. Charles Capper and Conrad Wright (Boston: Massachusetts Historical Society, 1999), 320, 354.

47. Ralph Waldo Emerson, "Self-Reliance,' in Vol. 2 of *The Collected Works of Ralph Waldo Emerson*, ed. Joseph Slater, et al. (Cambridge: Belknap Press of Harvard University Press, 1979), 29; for "small dealers," see Elizabeth Palmer Peabody to William Ellery Channing, June 1841, in "Biography of Elizabeth Palmer Peabody" [manuscript draft] by Mary Van Wyck Church, pages 410–11, Massachusetts Historical Society.

Chapter 1

1. Sarah J. Hale, *The Juvenile Budget Opened; being Selections from the Writings of Dr. John Aikin* (Boston: Marsh, Capen, Lyon, and Webb, 1840), 7. Subsequent references to this edition will appear in parentheses.

2. "The School Library. Introductory Essay, Prefatory of the Plan," in *Life and Voyages of Christopher Columbus* (Boston: Marsh, Capen, Lyon, and Webb, 1839), xlvi–xlvii, ix. Subsequent references to this text will appear in parentheses.

3. Sarah Robbins, *Managing Literacy, Mothering America: Women's Narratives on Reading and Writing in the Nineteenth Century* (Pittsburgh: University of Pittsburgh Press, 2004), 40, and "Remaking Barbauld's Primers: A Case Study in the Americanization of British Literary Pedagogy," *Children's Literature Association Quarterly* 21.4 (Winter 1996): 158.

4. To Richard Henry Dana Jr., Mann described the contents of *The School Library*'s adult series as works of a "more standard character." See Charles Adams, *Richard Henry Dana: A Biography* (Boston: Houghton Mifflin, 1890), 2:120. Leslie Howsam defines "standard" works as popular texts that "publishers and booksellers identified as likely to remain in print for some years and to command a steady readership." See Howsam, "Sustained Literary Ventures: The Series in Victorian Book Publishing," *Publishing History* 31 (1992): 10.

5. Margaret Ezell, *Social Authorship and the Advent of Print* (Baltimore: Johns Hopkins University Press, 1999), 125–26, 138.

6. For "sacred adherence," see *Second Annual Report of the Board of Education, together with the Second Annual Report of the Secretary of the Board* (Boston: Dutton and Wentworth, 1839), 20.

For "neat," see *First Annual Report of the Board of Education, together with the First Annual Report of the Secretary of the Board* (Boston: Dutton and Wentworth, 1838), 13. For "broad wastes," see *Third Annual Report of the Board of Education, together with the Third Annual Report of the Secretary of the Board* (Boston: Dutton and Wentworth, 1840), 57. Subsequent references to all three editions will appear in parentheses.

7. McGill, *American Literature and the Culture of Reprinting*, 7.

8. For *The School Library*'s origins, see Raymond B. Culver, *Horace Mann and Religion in the Massachusetts Public Schools* (New York: Arno Press, 1969), 41–54.

9. Mann, "On District School Libraries," 270, 271–72; also see *Third Annual Report*, 51.

10. For "neat," see *First Annual Report*, 13; for 15 to 20 percent, see Horace Mann, "District School Libraries," *Common School Journal* 2.5 (2 March 1840): 71. Subsequent references to this text will appear in parentheses. For $57.50, see Mann [1840], Draft of a letter explaining the activities of the Board of Education since its formation, *Horace Mann Collection*, microfilm edition, 40 reels (Boston: Massachusetts Historical Society, 1989), reel 5. Louise Hall Tharp claims that this estimate is for only 50 titles, but, at 40 and 75 cents per volume, 100 volumes would cost $57.50. See Tharp, *Until Victory: Horace Mann and Mary Peabody* (Boston: Little, Brown, and Company, 1953), 146.

11. Orestes Brownson, "The School Library," *Boston Quarterly Review* 3.2 (April 1840): 228–29.

12. Horace Mann to George Bancroft, 11 July 1839, George Bancroft Papers, Massachusetts Historical Society. Mann refers here to both the large number of completed manuscripts ("in esse" means "in actuality") and proposals ("in posse" means "in potentiality") received.

13. Marsh, Capen, Lyon, and Webb to Horace Mann, 27 and 28 December 1838, *Horace Mann Collection*, microfilm edition, 40 reels (Boston: Massachusetts Historical Society, 1989), reel 5.

14. "The School Library," in *Third Annual Report*, 27.

15. For Hawthorne's text, see "The School Library," in *Third Annual Report*, 31. For Mann's response to Hawthorne's fiction, see Horace Mann to Elizabeth Palmer Peabody, 10 March 1838, *Horace Mann Collection*, microfilm edition, 40 reels (Boston: Massachusetts Historical Society, 1989), reel 5. For plans to publish "History of the Pilgrims, by a Lady," see Marsh to Mann, 13 March 1839, *Horace Mann Collection*, microfilm edition, 40 reels (Boston: Massachusetts Historical Society, 1989), reel 5. For Mary Peabody submitting the book for Mann's consideration and his response, see Mary Tyler Peabody to Horace Mann, 20 May 1838, and Mann to Peabody, 4 June 1838, *Horace Mann Collection*, microfilm edition, 40 reels (Boston: Massachusetts Historical Society, 1989), reel 5. Neither volume was published.

16. Ultimately, its publishers issued, or at least proposed to issue, contributions from the Board's own members as well as its family and friends. For instance, they advertised contributions by Board members Jared Sparks, Edward Everett, and Robert Rantoul Jr., as well as their associates, Everett's brother, Alexander Everett, his sister, Sarah P. E. Hale, and Mann's confidante, Elizabeth Peabody.

17. Horace Mann to Samuel Gridley Howe, 21 July 1839, *Horace Mann Collection*, microfilm edition, 40 reels (Boston: Massachusetts Historical Society, 1989), reel 5.

18. Mann, [1840] Draft of a letter explaining the activities of the Board of Education since its formation, *Horace Mann Collection*, microfilm edition, 40 reels (Boston: Massachusetts Historical Society, 1989), reel 5. By 1840, when Mann offers this comparison, the first two series, or 95 volumes, of Harper's *School District Library* could be bought for $38. By 1846, Harper's *School*

District Library contained six series and 212 titles, for over 295 volumes in total. See Eugene Exman, *The Brothers Harper* (New York: Harper & Row, 1965), 109. For *School District Library* catalogues, including pricing, see 383–87.

19. Quoted in Exman, *Brothers Harper*, 130. Octodecimo (18mo) and duodecimo (12mo) refer to book page sizes, produced by folding printed sheets into 18 or 12 leaves (36 or 24 pages), respectively. *The School Library*'s publishers issued volumes of its *Juvenile series* in the cheaper 18mo format, while those in the adult series appeared in the more expensive 12mo format. Publishers often used what they could acquire most cheaply as contents for their series formats (Ezell, *Social Authorship*, 135), and Harper & Brothers was no exception, placing their own authors in the *School District Library*, as well as duplicating titles between their various library series. Robert Freeman observes that over fifty percent of the titles in the *School District Library* were duplicated from Harper's earlier *Family Library*, and that over eighty percent of their library titles, in general, were reprints of popular British works (a common practice in the absence of international copyright). See Freeman, "Harper & Brothers' Family and School District Libraries, 1830–1846," in *Libraries to the People*, ed. Robert Freeman and Robert Hovde (Jefferson, NC: McFarland & Co., 2003), 27.

20. "The School Library," in *Third Annual Report*, 31–32.

21. Zboray, *A Fictive People*, 11. John Tebbel observes that for the $1 cost of a single book, a buyer might purchase "five loaves of bread, twelve pounds of beef, or a third of a gallon of brandy. Even one of the cheapest books, at eighteen and one third cents, was equivalent to two-dozen eggs or twenty quarts of milk" (*History of Book Publishing*, 217).

22. Zboray, *A Fictive People*, 4. In its *Second Annual Report*, the Board remarked that the costs of obtaining books from urban centers such as Boston could be prohibitively expensive (19), and Mann recorded in his *Third Annual Report* that many residents were often forced to rely on the unreliable stock of itinerant salesmen, much of which was remainders, books "no longer salable at the bookstore nor inquired for at the circulating library" (73). For further confirmation of his views, see Zboray and Zboray, *Literary Dollars*, xxii–xxiii.

23. *Third Annual Report*, 57. In the category of "public" libraries, Mann included university, mechanical and scientific institute, town, and social libraries; he omitted from his estimates circulating and Sabbath school libraries, since most of their books, he contended, were "confessedly ill-adapted" for general use (82). Sabbath libraries, he believed, tended to be too denominational in nature, while circulating libraries were known to contain large stocks of "pernicious" fictions, romances, and novels (82, 72).

24. Rev. Gorham D. Abbott to Rev. Sylvester Holmes, 24 May 1838, *Horace Mann Collection*, microfilm edition, 40 reels (Boston: Massachusetts Historical Society, 1989), reel 5.

25. In 1838, Mann got into a heated public debate with Frederick Packard, Secretary of the American Sunday-School Union, when he rejected John Abbot's *Child at Home* (1834), which Packard had offered as part of a library sold by the ASSU to common schools. Animosities flared when Mann "hastily" dismissed the text, asserting it would "not be tolerated in this State, as a District School Library book" because its orthodox religious lessons would be "in the highest degree offensive" to the state's more liberal denominations, such as Unitarianism. See Horace Mann to Frederick Packard, 18 March 1838, *Horace Mann Collection*, microfilm edition, 40 reels (Boston: Massachusetts Historical Society, 1989), reel 5. State law prohibited public schools from using books "calculated to favor the tenets of any particular sect of Christians" (*Second Annual Report*, 20). In the controversy that followed, Packard repeatedly and publicly accused Mann of attempting to secularize the schools' curriculum, while Mann's supporters countered

that such accusations were simply a case of sour grapes on the part of a publisher denied the chance to peddle its denominationally divisive books to the state's schoolchildren. For more on this controversy, see Culver, *Horace Mann and Religion*, 55–110; Tharp, *Until Victory*, 147–49; Messerli, *Horace Mann*, 309–15; and Anne Boylan, *Sunday-School: Formation of an American Institution, 1790–1880* (New Haven, CT: Yale University Press, 1988), 52–59.

26. For "book-makers & sellers," see Horace Mann to C. E. Stowe, 15 March 1842, *Horace Mann Collection*, microfilm edition, 40 reels (Boston: Massachusetts Historical Society, 1989), reel 6. For "seek anxiously," see Horace Mann, "An Historical View of Education," in *Lectures on Education*, rpt. in American *Education: Its Men, Ideas, and Institutions*, ed. Lawrence Cremin (New York: Arno Press, 1969), 260–61. In his opinion, these "short-sighted, selfish" men, "manufacturer[s], author[s], compiler[s], copyright owner[s], vender[s], peddler[s], or puffer[s]," of any of the hundreds of school-books," cared only for the "success of [their own] reading book or primer" (261–62).

27. John D. Pierce to Horace Mann, 30 September 1839, *Horace Mann Collection*, microfilm edition, 40 reels (Boston: Massachusetts Historical Society, 1989), reel 5. Mann had reviewed the same book, *Town's Spelling Book*, unfavorably in the *Common School Journal*.

28. For "small," see Adams, *Richard Henry Dana*, 1: 119; for pay relative to labor, see Zboray and Zboray, *Literary Dollars*, 38; for "fair chance of profit," see Nathaniel Hawthorne to Henry Wadsworth Longfellow, 12 January 1839, in *CE* 15: 288; for "quite repaid," see Sarah P. E. Hale to Edward Everett, 23 January 1841, Hale Family Papers, Sophia Smith Collection, Smith College, North Hampton, Mass.; for payment of $142.50, see Thomas H. Webb to Sarah P. E. Hale, 27 May 1841; for "better than . . . expected," see Sarah P. E. Hale to Alexander Everett, 10 June 1841, Hale Family Papers, Sophia Smith Collection, Smith College, North Hampton, Mass. No doubt, she was pleased that the published had managed to pay her at all. For "common laborer's wages," see Theodore H. Palmer to Horace Mann, 23 December 1839, *Horace Mann Collection*, microfilm edition, 40 reels (Boston: Massachusetts Historical Society, 1989), reel 5. While Palmer's *Teacher's Manual* was not a contribution to *The School Library* per se, it was published by Marsh under Mann's instructions. Palmer's response to the terms of publication are an enlightening example of the way in which the reality of such arrangements could conflict with the value an author assigned his or her own work, even when popular education was ostensibly its aim.

29. Mann once described her as a "noble woman" of "Humanity . . . benevolence, conscientiousness, & reverence." See Horace Mann to George Combe, 13 October 1841, *Horace Mann Collection*, microfilm edition, 40 reels (Boston: Massachusetts Historical Society, 1989), reel 26.

30. Charles and Catharine Sedgwick to Horace Mann, 2 November 1838, *Horace Mann Collection*, microfilm edition, 40 reels (Boston: Massachusetts Historical Society, 1989), reel 5.

31. For "1500 copies" and "no risk" see Henry Wadsworth Longfellow to George Washington Greene, 4 September 1840, in Vol. 2 of *The Letters of Henry Wadsworth Longfellow*, ed. Andrew Hilen (Cambridge, MA: Belknap Press of Harvard University Press, 1966), 245–46. For 10 percent, see Zboray and Zboray, *Literary Dollars*, xxi. While a lucky author might get 15 percent or more, many authors were far worse off than 10 percent. Indeed, it was not uncommon for authors to assume the burden and risk of financing their books' publication. For more, see Charvat, *Literary Publishing in America*, 41–44, and Tebbel, *History of Book Publishing*, 210. As a stipulation of their agreement with the Board, however, Marsh, Capen, Lyon, and Webb agreed that "the enterprise should be undertaken wholly at the publishers' risk, neither the

Board nor the State having any pecuniary interest in it" (Mann, "District School Libraries," 70).

32. Longfellow owned his own plates, leasing them to publishers while dictating the terms of his royalties. See William Charvat, "Longfellow's Income from his Writings, 1842–1852," rpt. in *The Profession of Authorship in America, 1800–1870*, ed. Matthew Bruccoli (New York: Columbia University Press, 1992), 155–67, and Tebbel, *History of Book Publishing*, 211–12.

33. *Letters of Henry Wadsworth Longfellow*, 2:246.

34. Washington Irving to Marsh, Capen, Lyon, and Webb, 15 April 1839, in Vol. 25 of *The Complete Works of Washington Irving*, ed. Ralph Alderman, Herbert Kleinfield, and Jennifer Banks (Boston: Twayne Publishers, 1982), 14. Governor Everett had suggested a "general history of the discovery & colonization of the continent of America, condensed in one volume." See Edward Everett to Washington Irving, 7 Nov 1839, *Edward Everett Papers*, microfilm edition, 54 reels (Boston: Massachusetts Historical Society, 1972), reel 26. This letter appears to be misdated in Everett's letterbook; given the date of Irving's own response, the letter was most likely written in November 1838.

35. George Bancroft to Horace Mann, 9 June 1839, *Horace Mann Collection*, microfilm edition, 40 reels (Boston: Massachusetts Historical Society, 1989), reel 5. Mann encouraged Bancroft to submit his book to the Board's review, telling him: "I doubt not, it would be highly agreeable to them to examine your works. . . . My impression is, that it would have no competitor, tho—of this I am not quite sure." See Horace Mann to George Bancroft, 11 July 1839, George Bancroft Papers, Massachusetts Historical Society. Governor Everett, on the other hand, was not so sanguine. Having received the first two volumes from Bancroft, and a query from his publisher, James Brown, he declined to endorse the history for *The School Library*. Although "emphatically & warmly" in favor of Bancroft's work, he claims that it "contains some speculations on important points in which I do not concur" and that, as it was not written "expressly for a Common School Library," it had assumed "a somewhat different form" than their library series required. If corrected and "compendiously printed," however, he should "cheerfully consent" to its inclusion in the series. See Everett to James Brown, 4 June 1839, *Edward Everett Papers*, microfilm edition, 54 reels (Boston: Massachusetts Historical Society, 1972), reel 26. The history did not appear in the library. As Bancroft's letter to Mann indicates, he had hoped to place it "in the form I have given it," thus aligning him with at least one other author, Henry Dana Jr., who declined to efface his work in exchange for the Board's sanction. Dana took offense at Mann's recommendations for emending his book, *Two Years Before the Mast* (1840). He thought Mann a "school-master gone crazy," recording in his journal that he had never seen "such an exhibition of gaucheness and want of tact in [his] life" (Adams, *Richard Henry Dana*, 1:119). For more on Dana and Mann, see Messerli, *Horace Mann*, 345–46. For Dana's journal entry, see Adams, *Richard Henry Dana*, 1:117–20.

36. David Kaser, *A Book For A Sixpence: The Circulating Library in America* (Pittsburgh: Beta Phi Mu Chapbooks, 1980), 87; Freeman, "Harper & Brothers' Family," 38.

37. "Notices and Intelligence: The School Library," *Christian Examiner* 27.1 (September 1839): 134.

38. For the "carnivalesque" dimensions of antebellum print culture, see Lehuu, *Carnival on the Page*.

39. Patricia Crain, *The Story of A: The Alphabetization of America from* the New England Primer *to* The Scarlet Letter (Stanford, CA: Stanford University Press, 2000), 44–45; 74–75; 101.

40. Ibid., 75.

41. In so characterizing the method of *The School Library*, I borrow phrasing from Richard Brodhead, who describes what he terms "disciplinary intimacy," or discipline through love, as a bourgeois "strategy . . . for a superior introjection of authority." See Brodhead, *Cultures of Letters: Scenes of Reading and Writing in Nineteenth-Century America* (Chicago: University of Chicago Press, 1993), 21. For the way in which educational books, like alphabet primers, encouraged internalization of bourgeois values, see Crain, *Story of A,* 9–10, 85–91, 103–40. For the growing importance of play to antebellum understandings of childhood development, see Karen Sánchez-Eppler, *Dependent States: The Child's Part in Nineteenth-Century American Culture* (Chicago: University of Chicago Press, 2005), 3–18.

42. McGill, *American Literature and the Culture of Reprinting,* 29. For "text-image festival," see Crain, *Story of A,* 83.

43. For "tasteful," see "Art. IX. The School Library," *North American Review* 50.107 (April 1840): 512; for "superior," see "The School Library," *Common School Journal* 2.7 (1 April 1840): 107; for "numerous," see "The School Library," *Common School Journal* 4.7 (1 April 1842): 106; for "treat," see E. B. H., "Art VI. The School Library," *Christian Examiner* 27.3 (January 1840): 387. This abundance is not limited to illustrations. For instance, an advertisement promotes the "copious Index of twenty-two pages" included in its edition of Paley, while the "Specimen Pages" appended to another advertisement provide examples of the series' "copious" entries for readers to admire. See "The School Library," *Common School Journal* 2.7 (1 April 1840): 107, and *The School Advertiser No. II,* "The School Library," in Horace Mann, *Lectures on Education* (Boston: Marsh, Capen, Lyon, and Webb, 1840).

44. "The School Library," *Connecticut Common School Journal* 3.10 (15 March 1841): 1. Similarly, another advertisement trumpets the library's "numerous Cuts and Engravings" while assuring us that these illustrations will appear only "in such of the volumes as the subjects may require." Cited in "Common School Library," *Common School Journal* 1.2 (15 January 1839): 30.

45. For "autographs," see "The School Library," in *Third Annual Report,* 26. For use of autographs to "authorize" editions and combat reprinting, see McGill, *Culture of Reprinting,* 17. For handwriting (in the form of diary keeping) and character formation, see Augst, *The Clerk's Tale,* 19–61. For the pseudoscience of graphology and the marketing of autographs, see Samantha Matthews, "Gems, Texts, and Confessions: Writing Readers in Late-Victorian Autographic Gift-Books," *Publishing History* 62 (2007): 55–56, 59–60.

46. Quoted in "Common School Library," *Common School Journal* 1.2 (15 January 1839): 30.

47. For "exceedingly moderate," see E. B. H., "Art. VI. The School Library," 395. For "cheaper," see "The School Library," in *Third Annual Report,* 32.

48. "Art. IX. The School Library," *North American Review* 50.107 (April 1840): 512. For more on books and conspicuous consumption, see Zboray, *A Fictive People,* 11; Jeffrey D. Groves, "Judging Books by their Covers," in *Reading Books: Essays on the Material Text and Literature in America,* ed. Michele Moylan and Lane Stiles (Amherst: University of Massachusetts Press, 1996), 93; Lehuu, *Carnival on the Page,* 84–85; and Wadsworth, *In the Company of Books,* 124–25.

49. For more on Ticknor and Fields' "house styles" as marketing practice, see Groves, "Judging Books by their Covers," 75–100, and Wadsworth, *In the Company of Books,* 161–91.

50. For "newly arranged" and "modifications," see "The School Library," in *Third Annual Report,* 26, 27. For "mere republication" see E. B. H., "Art. VI. The School Library," 389. The reviewer also compliments the "American Editor" of Duncan's *Sacred Philosophy of the Seasons* for "important alterations" such as the "occasional insertion of fine passages from some of our own

writers, and the substitution of a few unexceptionable religious papers, in place of those that might offend some particular faith or feeling" (394).

51. McGill, *Culture of Reprinting*, 93, 14, 3, 23.

52. See Robbins, "Re-Making Barbauld's Primers," 161. For more on American editions of Barbauld's *Lessons with Children,* see Robbins, *Managing Literacy,* 40–49.

53. Sarah J. Hale, *Things by Their Right Names* (Boston: Marsh, Capen, Lyon, and Webb, 1840), 3. Subsequent references to this edition will appear in parentheses.

54. Michael Winship, "Manufacturing and Book Production," in *A History of the Book in America, Volume 3: The Industrial Book, 1840–1880,* ed. Scott Casper et al. (Chapel Hill: University of North Carolina Press, 2007), 50.

55. Elisa Tamarkin, *Anglophilia: Deference, Devotion, and Antebellum America* (Chicago: University of Chicago Press, 2007), xxvi–xvii.

56. Ibid., xxvii, xxiv.

57. For "spirit of party," see Horace Mann, "Conclusion of Introduction," *Common School Journal* 3.1 (1 January 1841): 15; for cultural uniformity and the common-school movement, see Carl Kaestle, *Pillars of the Republic: Common Schools and American Society, 1780–1860* (New York: Hill and Wang, 1983), 70–72, 134–35.

58. For the "public reach of home-based teaching" that was the aim of "domestic literacy narratives," see Robbins, *Managing Literacy,* 67, 69.

59. Messerli, *Horace Mann,* 445–47.

60. For "learning to be white" in Whittier's *Snow-Bound,* see Angela Sorby, *Schoolroom Poets: Childhood, Performance, and The Place of American Poetry, 1865–1917* (Durham: University of New Hampshire Press, 2005), 35–67; for whiteness and democracy, see *Schoolroom Poets,* 42, and Valerie Babb, *Whiteness Visible: The Meaning of Whiteness in American Literature and Culture* (New York: New York University Press, 1998), 125.

61. Wadsworth, *In the Company of Books,* 187.

62. Nahum Capen, *Memorial of Nahum Capen, of Boston, Massachusetts, on the subject of international copyright,* 28th cong., 1st sess., 15 Jan 1844, H. Doc. 61, p. 9.

63. Lehuu, *Carnival on the Page,* 101. For sentimental economy of exchange, see Lehuu, 78, 98.

64. Robbins, *Managing Literacy,* 2, 16.

65. Emma Embury, *Pictures of Early Life* (Boston: Marsh, Capen, Lyon, and Webb, 1839), 35. Subsequent references to this edition will appear in parentheses.

66. Mary Peabody Mann, *Life of Horace Mann* (Boston: Lee and Shepard, 1904), 151–52.

67. "The School Library," *Common School Journal* 1.12 (15 June 1839): 181; emphasis in original.

68. For "interruption," see Marsh et al., to Sarah P. E. Hale, 11 March 1841; for "vigor," see Thomas H. Webb to Sarah P. E. Hale, 27 May 1841; for "sanguine," see Sarah P. E. Hale to Alexander Everett, 10 June 1841, all from Hale Family Papers, Sophia Smith Collection, Smith College, North Hampton, Mass. For attempts to abolish the Board, see Culver, *Horace Mann and Religion,* 127–62, and Messerli, *Horace Mann,* 326–34; for sanction, see Mary Mann, *Life of Mann,* 132–33, and Tharp, *Until Victory,* 164; for "hot water," see Sarah P. E. Hale to Edward Everett, 23 January 1841, Hale Family Papers, Sophia Smith Collection, Smith College, North Hampton, Mass. In announcing the cessation of the *Common School Journal* in 1852, William B. Fowle suggests that the firm of Marsh, Capen, Lyon, and Webb had been "ruined in consequence of undertaking the preparation" of *The School Library.* See Fowle, "The Last Number,"

Common School Journal 14.25 (15 December 1852): 369. For "sympathy," see Horace Mann to George Combe, 28 February 1842, *Horace Mann Collection*, microfilm edition, 40 reels (Boston: Massachusetts Historical Society, 1989), reel 26.

69. In 1844, for instance, *The School Library* was implicated in the "Common School Controversy," a public feud begun between Mann and conservative opponent Edward Newton, a former member of the Board of Education who had resigned in protest over the library during the Packard controversy. For more, see Culver, *Horace Mann and Religion*, 181–88, and Messerli, *Horace Mann*, 409–21.

70. J. Pickering to Horace Mann, 7 February 1843, *Horace Mann Collection*, microfilm edition, 40 reels (Boston: Massachusetts Historical Society, 1989), reel 38. The confusion, it seems, was not confined to Capen's new libraries. In early 1843, the state legislature mistakenly reported that the Board had approved 250 books by various firms for use in school libraries. One of the books, *Elegant Extracts*, had been attacked in the local papers for its inappropriate content. See Thomas H. Webb to Horace Mann, 8 February 1843, *Horace Mann Collection*, microfilm edition, 40 reels (Boston: Massachusetts Historical Society, 1989), reel 7, and Culver, *Horace Mann and Religion*, 174–77.

71. William Fowle and Nahum Capen to Horace Mann, 21 October 1842, *Horace Mann Collection*, microfilm edition, 40 reels (Boston: Massachusetts Historical Society, 1989), reel 6.

72. *Sixth Annual Report of the Board of Education, together with the Sixth Annual Report of the Secretary of the Board* (Boston: Dutton and Wentworth, 1843), 11.

73. For the purchase of *The School Library* by Harper & Brothers, see Exman, *The Brothers Harper*, 252, and Freeman, "Harper & Brothers' Family," 38–39; for commission by Secretary of State to provide libraries for New York school districts, see Exman, *The Brothers Harper*, 106–10, Freeman, "Harper & Brothers' Family," 38; for "whiggism," see Orestes Brownson, "The School Library," *Boston Quarterly Review* 3.2 (April 1840): 226; for Mann's strong public and cross-denominational support, see Messerli, *Horace Mann*, 315, 326, and 332–35.

74. Thomas H. Webb to Sarah P. E. Hale, 19 October 1846, Hale Family Papers, Sophia Smith Collection, Smith College, North Hampton, Mass.

75. "Editor's Table," *Godey's Lady's Book* 21.10 (October 1840): 190–91.

76. Sarah P. E. Hale's royalty statements for 1883–98 (Hale Papers, Sophia Smith Collection, Smith College, North Hampton, Mass.) indicate that her estate continued to benefit from her two editions in *The Massachusetts School Library* well beyond the volumes' original publication date. Indeed, they kept selling until at least the end of the century; from January 1874 through January 1883, the volumes earned $882 in royalties. While Harper & Brothers stopped reprinting the edition of Columbus thereafter, the Balboa volume still brought in $109 in the next eight years (from 5 January 1883 to 5 June 1891), another $64 from 19 January 1892 to 5 July 1893, $79 from 5 July 1893 to 31 December 1896, and $26 in 1898.

77. For literacy training, fiction, and legitimization of antebellum women writers, see Crain, *The Story of A*; Robbins, *Managing Literacy*; and Sánchez-Eppler, *Dependent States*.

78. E. B. H., "Art. VI. The School Library," 387.

Chapter 2

1. Irving, *Sketch-Book*, 105.

2. I borrow the term "bibliomania" from Ronald Story, "Class and Culture in Boston: The Athenaeum, 1807–1860," *American Quarterly* 27.2 (1975): 188.

3. In a letter to his friend George Hillard, Hawthorne describes the "concocting of schoolbooks" and other genres as "what is called drudgery" (*CE*, 16:23). Lesley Ginsberg observes that he often described his adult fiction in "hardly more elevated" a fashion. See Ginsberg, "Hawthorne," 50. In his letter to Hillard, Hawthorne also mitigates the severity of this description by phrasing it "*what is called* drudgery" (emphasis added), although he does not specify who calls it this; for this reason, I am inclined to read this claim as another one of his characteristically self-effacing comments about his writing, rather than as an indication of any particular animus toward children literature as a genre.

4. Roy Harvey Pearce, "Historical Introduction," in *True Stories from History and Biography*, vol. 6 of *The Centenary Edition of the Works of Nathaniel Hawthorne*, ed. William Charvat et al. (Columbus: The Ohio State University Press, 1972), 288.

5. See, for instance, Nina Baym, *The Shape of Hawthorne's Career* (Ithaca, NY: Cornell University Press, 1976), 86–88; Elizabeth Goodenough, "*Grandfather's Chair:* Hawthorne's 'Deeper History' of New England," *The Lion and the Unicorn: A Critical Journal of Children's Literature* 15 (1991): 27–42; Gillian Brown, "Hawthorne's American History," in *The Cambridge Companion to Nathaniel Hawthorne*, ed. Richard H. Millington (New York: Cambridge University Press, 2004), 121–42; and Ginsberg, "Hawthorne," 47–71. In a 21 March 1838 letter to Longfellow, with whom he hoped to write a children's book, Hawthorne speculates on the importance of their collaboration: "Possibly we may make a great hit, and entirely revolutionize the whole system of juvenile literature" (*CE*, 15:266).

6. Laura Laffrado, *Hawthorne's Literature for Children* (Athens: University of Georgia Press, 1992), 7–8.

7. In her study of nineteenth-century responses to fiction, Nina Baym argues against the "essential premise on which our history of the American novel is based, that the nation was hostile to fiction," claiming that the U.S. was, in fact, a "nation of novel readers." See *Novels, Readers, and Reviewers: Responses to Fiction in Antebellum America* (Ithaca, NY: Cornell University Press, 1984), 14.

8. Magazine editors such as Goodrich paid Hawthorne about $1 per page—when they paid him at all. For the 27 pieces used in Goodrich's *Token*, Hawthorne received a total of $380. For Hawthorne's *Token* earnings, see J. Donald Crowley, "Historical Commentary," in *CE*, 9:497; for more on Hawthorne and his editors, see Lillian B. Gilkes, "Hawthorne, Park Benjamin, and S. G. Goodrich: Three-Cornered Imbroglio," *Nathaniel Hawthorne Journal 1971* (Middleton, CT: Microcard Edition Books, 1971), 83–112.

9. Hawthorne quit the magazine mere months after accepting his position, citing Goodrich's parsimony; see *CE*, 15:236.

10. The full title is *Peter Parley's Universal History on the Basis of Geography, for the Use of Families* (Boston: American Stationer's Company, 1837). Unsurprisingly, Hawthorne declined a second project from Goodrich when he was offered only $300 to write a lengthy volume "on the manners, customs, and civilities of all countries." See Samuel Goodrich to Nathaniel Hawthorne, 13 December 1836, as quoted in Julian Hawthorne, *Nathaniel Hawthorne and His Wife* (Boston: Houghton Mifflin Company, 1884), 1:138. Sarah Wadsworth suggests that the subsequent success of *Universal History*, which went through numerous editions and reportedly sold over one million copies, and of the *Peter Parley* series more generally, "must have been galling [to Hawthorne], considering they appeared at a time when he, having been paid so little for writing them, was diligently but unsuccessfully attempting to earn a living by his pen." See *In the Company of Books*, 29.

11. McGill, *Culture of Reprinting*, 223.

12. For detailed discussions of antebellum American publishing practices, see Frank Luther Mott, *A History of American Magazines, vol. 1* (New York: Appleton, 1930); William Charvat, *Literary Publishing in America;* and Tebbel, *History of Book Publishing, volume 1.*

13. McGill, *Culture of Reprinting,* 222.

14. Mann, "On District School Libraries," 295, 275 (the latter quoted from Mann's *Third Annual Report*).

15. Horace Mann to Elizabeth Palmer Peabody, 10 March 1838. The letter's full text appears in Wayne Allen Jones, "Sometimes Things Just Don't Work Out: Hawthorne's Income from *Twice-Told Tales* (1837), and Another 'Good Thing' for Hawthorne," *Nathaniel Hawthorne Journal 1975* (Englewood, CO: Microcard Edition Books, 1975), 21–23.

16. Horace Mann to Elizabeth Palmer Peabody, 10 March 1838, cited in Jones, "Sometimes Things," 21–23. Still, Peabody convinced Mann to refer Hawthorne to his publisher, Nahum Capen. In late March 1838, Hawthorne informed Longfellow that he had "overtures from two different quarters, to perpetuate children's histories and other such iniquities"—presumably referring to Mann and Capen, or perhaps Peabody and Mann (*CE*, 15:266). Capen placed advertisements in the local papers in September and December of 1839, announcing the upcoming publication of "*New-England Historical Sketches,* by N. Hawthorne. Author of 'Twice-Told Tales,' &c," as part of *The School Library* series (quoted in Pearce, "Historical Introduction," in *CE*, 6:291). Unfortunately, nothing further would come of it. In an 18 December 1839 letter to Sophia, Hawthorne complained that Capen "torments me every now-and-then about a book which he wants me to manufacture"—a sentiment no doubt exacerbated by the drudgery of Hawthorne's customhouse work, which virtually precluded him from writing (*CE*, 15:388).

17. The *Grandfather's Chair* series comprised three separate volumes published between December 1840 and March 1841. The titles and publication dates for the first editions are *Grandfather's Chair* (December 1840, but dated 1841), *Famous Old People* (January 1841), and *Liberty Tree* (March 1841).

18. It seemed to Hawthorne that the collaboration on "The Boys' Wonder-Horn" would be "far more credible" than any of his other literary plans, "and perhaps quite as profitable" (*CE*, 15:266).

19. See, for instance, Hawthorne's 16 May 1839 letter to Longfellow, or his 20 April 1840 letter to John O'Sullivan, in *CE*, 15:310–11, 447–48. Hawthorne's tenure at the customhouse taught him that the cost of making a good living was an almost complete inability to write; indeed, the manuscript for *Grandfather's Chair* was one of the few things he had been able to produce during the period. Ironically, Hawthorne had thought the appointment would provide the perfect opportunity and material for writing. For more, see Hawthorne's 11 January 1839 letter to George P. Morris, written shortly after accepting the job, in *CE*, 15:285.

20. Mellow, *Hawthorne in His Times,* 122.

21. Andrew Preston Peabody, "Twice-Told Tales," *Christian Examiner and General Review* 24 (November 1838): 182–90; rpt. in *Nathaniel Hawthorne: The Contemporary Reviews,* ed. John Idol Jr. and Buford Jones (Cambridge: Cambridge University Press, 1994), 35.

22. See David Levin, *History as Romantic Art: Bancroft, Prescott, Motley, and Parkman* (Stanford, CA: Stanford University Press, 1959).

23. Mann, *Third Annual Report,* quoted in "On District School Libraries," 273, 273–74.

24. Wadsworth compares Hawthorne's "relatively prosaic Parley-like historical sketches" unfavorably to his more "innovative" myths to a trace a "radical concurrent transformation of the juvenile literature market." See *In the Company of Books,* 26. Patricia Valenti similarly sug-

gests that, as his career progressed, Hawthorne would learn to abandon the "established boundaries" and "generic conventions" that had "constrained juvenile literature and his possibilities for success in that arena." See "'None But Imaginative Authority': Nathaniel Hawthorne and the Progress of Nineteenth-Century (Juvenile) Literature in America," *Nathaniel Hawthorne Review* 36.1 (Spring 2010): 12.

25. Richard Brodhead argues that school reformers such as Mann sought to revolutionize the education system by molding the common school into a kind of "second home." See *Cultures of Letters*, 24.

26. Brown, "Hawthorne's American History," 122; Laffrado, *Hawthorne's Literature for Children*, 5.

27. See Elizabeth Palmer Peabody's 3 March 1838 letter to Horace Mann (*Letters*, 199–200); and Hawthorne's 4 June 1837 letter to Longfellow (*CE*, 15:253).

28. On 5 April 1842, Peabody advertised "remnants of *Famous Old People* and *Liberty Tree*, first editions at ½ price," in the *Boston Daily Advertiser;* see *CE*, 6:295 fn. 19.

29. Hawthorne would repeat this sentiment in his 25 March 1843 letter to Horatio Bridge; see *CE*, 15:681–82.

30. For examples of this logic, one might look to the ample supply of editorials in the *United States Magazine and Democratic Review*, a political journal and literary magazine founded in October 1837 by Hawthorne's friend John O'Sullivan. One editorial locates the "moral" of the Panic in the national "sin" of the credit system and its paper monies, which it likens to the immorality and excess of gambling; see "The Moral of the Crisis," *United States Democratic Review* 1.1 (October 1837): 108, 110. Essentially, this editorial argues that the so-called "elasticity" championed by proponents of paper money actually makes such currency prone to fluctuations of the most violent and disastrous excess; in the writer's view, what the currency, and by extension the nation, needs is not elasticity but the stability found in a currency of "intrinsic value" (here, specie), whose value exists beyond manipulation and above external turmoil (114). For further discussion of "hard" Democrats and their hostility toward the banking system, see Naomi Lamoreaux, *Insider Lending: Banks, Personal Connections, and Economic Development in Industrial New England* (New York: Cambridge University Press, 1994).

31. Laffrado, *Hawthorne's Literature for Children*, 20.

32. According to Brodhead, the antebellum fascination with sensationalized scenes of beatings, floggings, and whippings was vital to a large-scale, bourgeois consolidation of cultural power through which corporal punishment became a "sign of [the] insufficiency" and "inferiority" of "rival [cultural] formation[s]," "first of the older patriarchal New England culture," and then of the "Irish immigrant" and "Southern planter class" cultures. See *Cultures of Letters*, 26.

33. Baym, *Shape of Hawthorne's Career*, 91.

34. Whereas I argue that Hawthorne harnesses the home-centered pedagogies dominating educational reform, Goodenough claims he complicates the progressive notions of childhood on which such efforts were premised—placing him outside the middle-class cultural agenda that Brodhead describes. Grandfather's approbation of Cheever's methods, in her view, represents Hawthorne's own "ambivalent view of the child," as well as his belief in "opposing pedagogical approaches for different species of children" ("Hawthorne's 'Deeper History,'" 37, 32). But this assertion is hard to reconcile with Grandfather's description of the corporal punishment, the children's reactions to it, or his own teaching methods. Goodenough herself concedes that the description lies in "direct contrast to the instructional space created by the outer 'modern' frame" of the book (37).

35. *CE*, 6:84. For a discussion of Hawthorne's willingness to manipulate the emotions of female readers as an assertion of authorial power, see Leland Person, "Hawthorne's Early Tales: Male Authorship, Domestic Violence, and Female Readers," in *Hawthorne and the Real: Bicentennial Essays*, ed. Millicent Bell (Columbus: The Ohio State University Press, 2005), 125–43.

36. Brodhead, *Cultures of Letters*, 40.

37. Grandfather refers to William B. O. Peabody's *Life of Cotton Mather*, vol. 6 of *The Library of American Biography*, ed. Jared Sparks (Boston: Hilliard, Gray, and Co., 1836).

38. For another treatment of Hawthorne's interest in Mather, see Christopher Felker, *Reinventing Cotton Mather in the American Renaissance: "Magnalia Christi Americana" in Hawthorne, Stowe, and Stoddard* (Boston: Northeastern University Press, 1993).

39. Quoted in Mellow, *Hawthorne in His Times*, 142.

40. For a discussion of Charley, and Hawthorne's anxieties about the unfeeling nature of boys, see Ken Parille, "Allegories of Childhood Gender: Hawthorne and the Material Boy," *Nathaniel Hawthorne Review* 36.1 (Spring 2010): 112–37, and especially 113–18. For "boyhood" itself as a problem in nineteenth-century America, see his *Boys at Home: Discipline, Masculinity, and the "Boy Problem" in Nineteenth Century American Literature* (Knoxville: University of Tennessee Press, 2009).

41. Hawthorne's feelings about "the mob" are well documented. For example, see Michael Colacurcio, *The Province of Piety: Moral History in Hawthorne's Early Tales* (Durham, NC: Duke University Press, 1995), 130–53, 406–23, esp. 415, and 634 fn. 14; Larry J. Reynolds, "'Strangely Ajar with the Human Race': Hawthorne, Slavery, and the Question of Moral Responsibility," in *Hawthorne and the Real: Bicentennial Essays*, ed. Millicent Bell (Columbus: The Ohio State University Press, 2005), 40–69, and esp. 48–49; not to mention the countless discussions of what Hawthorne termed the "d—d mob of scribbling women" (*CE*, 17:304) by critics such as Nina Baym, Michael Newberry, and others.

42. "Preparatory Study of History," *American Annals of Education* 8.3 (March 1838): 104, 106.

43. For a discussion of Hawthorne's investment in such standards of bourgeois domesticity, see T. Walter Herbert, *Dearest Beloved: The Hawthornes and the Making of the Middle-Class Family* (Berkeley: University of California Press, 1993). Herbert suggests that, while the "Hawthornes' stubborn commitment to home schooling formed a sharp contrast . . . to Horace Mann's leadership in the creation of public schools," they "shared with [him] a belief in disciplining children through nurturing love rather than applications of the rod" (xix). If Mann was intent upon molding public schools into a second home, as Brodhead argues, then Hawthorne was equally invested in turning the home into a kind of loving school. For more on loving "domestication" as the province of children's literature, see Karen Sánchez-Eppler, "Hawthorne and the Writing of Childhood," in *The Cambridge Companion to Nathaniel Hawthorne*, ed. Richard H. Millington (New York: Cambridge University Press, 2004), 143–59; for love and nationalism, see Gillian Brown, "Hawthorne's American History," 121–42.

44. The phrase "fair brick house" is from Cotton Mather's *Magnalia*, a source with which Hawthorne was intimately familiar. See *Magnalia Christi Americana, Books I & II*, ed. Kenneth Murdock (Cambridge, MA: Belknap Press of Harvard University Press, 1977), 280. As Hawthorne's letter suggests, his investment in children's literature, along with the riches he conjures out of it for Sophia, might be understood as yet another compensatory fantasy of treasure marking him as a "paper money man" of the sort David Anthony has identified, albeit in a manner varying from the "tabloid" manhood at work in *The Blithedale Romance* or the attempt to put

"race into service as a means of negotiating fiscal insecurity and masculine dispossession" distinguishing *The House of Seven Gables*. See *Paper Money Men: Commerce, Manhood, and the Sensational Public Sphere in Antebellum America* (Columbus: The Ohio State University Press, 2009), 148, 157. In other words, even as Hawthorne continually excoriates the modern, paper and credit economy, seeking in children's fiction a kind of literary analog to political hard metalism that might secure him much-deserved wealth, his early children's writings nonetheless are, to use Anthony's language, a "speculative project" undertaken to relieve himself of "debtor embarrassment" (Anthony, 60).

45. See Crowley, "Historical Commentary," in *CE*, 9:523. On 16 September 1841, Hawthorne joked to Sophia, "if [Munroe] cheats me once, I will have nothing more to do with him, but will straightway be cheated by some other publisher—that being, of course, the only alternative" (*CE*, 15:573). For more on Hawthorne's feelings about Munroe, see his 27 September 1841 letter in *CE*, 15:580–81.

46. Noting this contrast, Laffrado argues that *Biographical Stories* is Hawthorne's effort to "write his enclosed condition, write his attempt at living his resignation" in the face of constricting personal circumstances and repeated career failures (*Hawthorne's Literature for Children*, 63).

47. James Boswell recounts the incident thus, in Samuel Johnson's own words: "I refused to attend my father to Uttoxeter-market. Pride was the source of that refusal, and the remembrance of it was painful. A few years ago, I desired to atone for this fault; I went to Uttoxeter in very bad weather, and stood for a considerable time bareheaded in the rain, on the spot where my father's stall used to stand. In contrition I stood, and I hope the penance was expiatory." See *Life of Johnson* (Oxford: Oxford University Press, 1980), 1357. For Hawthorne's career-long interest in this scene from Johnson's life, see Gloria Erlich, *Family Themes and Hawthorne's Fiction* (New Brunswick, NJ: Rutgers University Press, 1984), 127, and Helen Deutsch, *Loving Dr. Johnson* (Chicago: University of Chicago Press, 2005), 197–207.

48. Wadsworth argues that over-saturation of the market with Peter Parley–like children's texts would lead Hawthorne to "new modes of juvenile writing," as in *A Wonder-Book*. See *In the Company of Books*, 32.

49. Michael Winship, *Ticknor and Fields: the Business of Literary Publishing in the United States of the Nineteenth Century* (Chapel Hill: Hanes Foundation, Rare Book Collection/University Library, University of North Carolina at Chapel Hill, 1992), 11–12.

50. Richard Brodhead, *The School Of Hawthorne* (New York: Oxford University Press, 1986), 53.

51. *School of Hawthorne*, 58–59; *CE*, 9:3.126–27.

Chapter 3

1. Henry D. Thoreau, *Walden*, ed. J. Lyndon Shanley (Princeton, NJ: Princeton University Press, 2004), 104–5. Subsequent references to this edition will appear in parentheses.

2. Quite literally, Thoreau's remedy for the state of modern publishing consists in a return to the "classics" of literature; he defends the ancient literature of Greece and Rome, read "in the original," as the "noblest recorded thoughts of man" (*Walden*, 106, 100).

3. Thomas Wentworth Higginson, *Cheerful Yesterdays* (Boston: Houghton Mifflin, 1898), 86.

4. Quoted in George Cooke, *Historical and Biographical Introduction*, 1: 148.

5. Leslie Perrin Wilson, "'No Worthless Books:' Elizabeth Peabody's Foreign Library, 1840–1852," *Papers of the Bibliographical Society of America* 99.1 (March 2005): 118.

6. A version of this argument appears in Derek Pacheco, "'One Great Moral Enterprise': Literature, Education, and the New England Marketplace, 1830–1845" (Ph.D. Dissertation, UCLA, 2006). For a related reading of Peabody's bookstore, see also Dowling, *Business of Literary Circles*, 117–44.

7. In his biography of her life, Bruce Ronda argues that Peabody is a "practical intellectual," going so far as to declare her one of the few "practitioners of praxis" in her circle. See *Elizabeth Palmer Peabody*, 4–5. Nina Baym has argued that Peabody was not a transcendentalist per se but rather a feminist "millennial thinker." See "The Ann Sisters: Elizabeth Peabody's Millennial Historicism," *American Literary History* 3.1 (Spring 1991): 28. While the significance of the feminism inherent in Peabody's Christian vision should not be understated, it is unnecessary, I think, to distinguish between the terms "Christian" and "transcendentalist" with regard to her, particularly as transcendentalism itself was not monolithic but rather eclectic and heterogeneous. In a sense, Peabody represents one point in a range of Christian-centered transcendentalisms including the likes of William Ellery Channing (who was older and whose transcendentalism was more moderate in several respects than Peabody's) or Theodore Parker (who was younger and more socially and intellectually extreme in many of his attitudes), both of whom were her close friends and confidants. Ultimately, Peabody's life disrupts, as Ronda suggests, a scholarly affinity for clearly defined literary categories, a propensity to organize "literary and cultural history through divisions and discontinuities rather than . . . continuities and connections." See Ronda, "Elizabeth Peabody and the Fate of Transcendentalism," in *Reinventing the Peabody Sisters*, ed. Monika Elbert, Julie E. Hall, and Katharine Rodier (Iowa City: University of Iowa Press, 2006), 232.

8. For a discussion of what Monika Elbert calls the "impassioned (feminine) voice" of Peabody's transcendentalism (206), see "Elizabeth Peabody's Problematic Feminism and the Feminization of Transcendentalism," in *Reinventing the Peabody Sisters*, ed. Monika Elbert, Julie E. Hall, and Katharine Rodier (Iowa City: University of Iowa Press, 2006), 199–215. I prefer the term "feminist" to "feminine" or "feminized" when discussing Peabody's transcendentalism because, while it was impossible for Peabody to completely escape certain conventional, bourgeois notions of women's "place," still, her understanding of transcendentalism was wrapped up in the promise of female intellectual equality that would "transcend" arbitrary constructions of gender. I also prefer the term "feminist" because I want to avoid any associations with the term "feminization" as either a kind of dilution of more rigorous styles of cultural thought, or as an essentialist logic that posits inherently masculine and feminine concerns or modes of expression. For a seminal discussion of the term "feminization," see Ann Douglas's *The Feminization of American Culture* (New York: Alfred Knopf, 1977). Finally, I use the term "cosmopolitanism" for a specific reason as well. Peabody's bookstore and foreign circulating library appear remarkably similar in principle to historian David Hollinger's definition of the term as:

> the desire to transcend limitations of any and all particularisms in order to achieve a more complete human experience and a more complete understanding of that experience. The ideal is exactly counter to the eradication of cultural differences, but counter also to their preservation in parochial form. Rather, particular cultures and subcultures are viewed as repositories for insights and experiences that can be drawn upon in the interests of a more comprehensive outlook on the world. In so far as a particular ethnic heritage or philosophical

tradition is an inhibition to experience, it is to be disarmed; in so far as that heritage or tradition is an avenue toward the expansion of experience and understanding, access to it is to be preserved.

See Hollinger, "Ethnic Diversity, Cosmopolitanism, and the Emergence of the American Liberal Intelligentsia," *American Quarterly* 27.2 (May 1975): 135.

9. See Diane Brown Jones, "Elizabeth Palmer Peabody's Transcendental Manifesto," *Studies in the American Renaissance* (1992): 195, and Ronda, "Print and Pedagogy: The Career of Elizabeth Peabody," in *A Living of Words: American Women in Print Culture*, ed. Susan Albertine (Knoxville: University of Tennessee Press, 1995), 35; for the gendered necessity of mediation, see Vásquez, "Declaration and Deference," 45–65, and *Authority and Reform*, 87–112.

10. Margaret Fuller, *Memoirs of Margaret Fuller Ossoli*, eds. Ralph Waldo Emerson et al. (Boston: Phillips, Sampson and Company, 1852), 1:321. Subsequent references to this edition, hereafter cited as *Memoirs* with volume and page number, will appear in parentheses.

11. One late-nineteenth-century historian of Boston literally does this, relegating Peabody to a footnote at the end of a chapter on transcendentalism. See George Bradford, "Philosophic Thought in Boston," in *The Memorial History of Boston: Including Suffolk County, Massachusetts, 1630–1880*, ed. Justin Winsor (Boston: J. R. Osgood and Co., 1880), 2:329.

12. For instance, see Susan H. Irons, "Channing's Influence on Peabody: Self-Culture and the Danger of Egotism," *Studies in the American Renaissance* (1992): 121–35, and John B. Wilson, "A Transcendentalist Minority Report," *New England Quarterly* 29.2 (June 1956): 141–58.

13. His thoughts on the subject carried special weight with Peabody because she saw him as one of the fathers of American transcendentalism. Asserting that, in the movement's history, she knew "of no name older," Peabody concludes that, when Emerson and Carlyle began to "quicken our Boston thinking" in the early 1830s, "at last Dr. Channing's spiritual philosophy had begun to pervade society." See *Reminiscences*, 364.

14. For a discussion of Peabody's initial enthusiasm for the school, see Josephine Roberts, "Elizabeth Peabody and the Temple School," *New England Quarterly* 15.3 (September 1942): 497–508. Even years after their collaboration's dissolution, Peabody could not help but feel exasperated with Alcott's egoism. In August 1840, one month into her new bookselling business and four years after she had left the Temple School, she notes rather smugly that others in town still discussed "Mr. Alcott & his wild sayings." Worrying about the potential pitfalls of the transcendental mindset, she fears Alcott is "ruined by 'self-esteem' as the phrenologists say. Some one has said he was a spiritual dandy. He does not know the line between universal mind and Alcolism and calls a good deal of the latter by the name of the former." See Elizabeth Peabody to William Ellery Channing, August 1840, in "Biography of Elizabeth Palmer Peabody" [manuscript draft] by Mary Van Wyck Church, page 405 (5), Massachusetts Historical Society.

15. Peabody lived with Alcott and his family while she worked at the Temple School because he could afford to pay her so little. The arrangement, however, came to an abrupt close when he and his wife pried into Peabody's personal correspondence, looking for evidence that Peabody was turning against Alcott amidst their intensifying professional disputes. When Alcott confronted her with the letters, Peabody determined that his unprecedented violation of her privacy required her to withdraw from his household. For more, see Marshall, *The Peabody Sisters*, 324–25.

16. For further discussion of Peabody's 1836 preface and her defense against charges of egoism at the school, see Irons, "Channing's Influence on Peabody."

17. Elizabeth Peabody, *Record of a School* (Boston: James Munroe, 1835), iv–v.

18. Peabody quickly recognized this rumbling of discontent among parents whose children, she tells Alcott, were "being talked about by the whole city," and she warned him that such gossip could have no positive outcome. See Elizabeth Peabody to Bronson Alcott, 8 October 1835, in *Letters*, 152. But even Channing began to have doubts over the details of the school's management, particularly regarding "the degree to which the mind of the child should be turned inward." He warned Peabody that the "soul is somewhat jealous of being watched, and it is no small part of wisdom to know when to leave it to its impulses, and when to restrain it." See William Ellery Channing to Elizabeth Peabody, 24 August 1835, quoted in Peabody, *Reminiscences*, 356–57.

19. *Letters*, 152. Like Channing, Peabody felt that Alcott's emphasis on introspection, combined with his questionable habit of having his students read their private journals aloud, gave students a forced self-consciousness (the overwrought tendency toward self-analysis) unbefitting the needs of their development, and fostered an undesirable "moral competitiveness" among them: "I think you are liable to injure the modesty and unconsciousness of good children, by making them reflect too much upon their actual superiority to others" (152). "Moral competitiveness" is Ronda's term; see *Elizabeth Palmer Peabody*, 125. For more on Peabody's growing disagreements with Alcott, see Marshall, *The Peabody Sisters*, 319–26.

20. See Marshall, *The Peabody Sisters*, 319, and Richard Brodhead, *Cultures of Letters*, 15.

21. Mary Tyler Peabody to Elizabeth Palmer Peabody, [1836] (3), *Horace Mann Collection*, microfilm edition, 40 reels (Boston: Massachusetts Historical Society, 1989), reel 4.

22. In her eagerness to help his cause, Peabody had agreed to be his assistant, teaching only two and a half hours a day, and for "such compensation as he could afford to pay." Both Alcott and his wife "said the terms were altogether too small—but it was not a partnership—& he could give me no more possibly—with thirty scholars as his expenses would be great." See Elizabeth Peabody to Mary Tyler Peabody, July 1834, "Cuba Journal," quoted in Ronda, *Elizabeth Palmer Peabody*, 115. His treatment of Elizabeth grew so bad that Mary eventually told her that if she should stay "for the sake of serving Mr. Alcott at the expense of your peace of mind, I shall think you are altogether quixotic & foolish," especially since Alcott could easily find another recorder, "though never such an one as you are"—implying that he would have a difficult time finding someone as supportive as Elizabeth, or as patient with his faults. See Mary Tyler Peabody to Elizabeth Palmer Peabody, [1836] (6), *Horace Mann Collection*, microfilm edition, 40 reels (Boston: Massachusetts Historical Society, 1989), reel 4.

23. Mary Tyler Peabody to Elizabeth Palmer Peabody, [1836] (6), *Horace Mann Collection*, microfilm edition, 40 reels (Boston: Massachusetts Historical Society, 1989), reel 4. As Megan Marshall observes, Peabody would stay up long into the night dutifully copying over the notes she had taken during the day's class, only to have Alcott later alter the dialogue to suit his liking (*The Peabody Sisters*, 322).

24. Mary Tyler Peabody to Elizabeth Palmer Peabody, [1836] (7), *Horace Mann Collection*, microfilm edition, 40 reels (Boston: Massachusetts Historical Society, 1989), reel 4.

25. Mary Tyler Peabody to Elizabeth Palmer Peabody, [1836] (6), *Horace Mann Collection*, microfilm edition, 40 reels (Boston: Massachusetts Historical Society, 1989), reel 4.; emphasis in original. For Fuller's life in the provincial regions of New England, such as Groton or Providence, see Capper, *Margaret Fuller, Vol. 1*.

26. See Marshall, *The Peabody Sisters*, 382.

27. The fervor surrounding the book's appearance is well documented. For instance, Joseph Buckingham, editor of the *Boston Courier*, offered the now-famous, second-hand account of

Andrews Norton, who purportedly claimed that "*one-third* [of the book] *was absurd, one-third was blasphemous, and one-third was obscene.*" Quoted in Larry Carlson, "'Those Pure Pages of Yours:' Bronson Alcott's Conversations with Children on the Gospels," *American Literature* 60.3 (October 1988): 454; italics in original.

28. Several years earlier, before Peabody had won him over with her enthusiasm for his ideas, Alcott recorded this impression of her in his journal: She "may aim perhaps at being 'original' and fail in her attempt, by becoming offensively assertive. On the whole there is, we think, too much of the *man*, and too little of the *woman*, in her familiarity and freedom." See Amos Bronson Alcott, "Journal for 1829," quoted in Ronda, *Elizabeth Palmer Peabody*, 73; emphasis in original.

29. Quoted in Carlson, "'Those Pure Pages,'" 454.

30. Elizabeth Palmer Peabody to Horace Mann, 2 March 1837, in "Biography of Elizabeth Palmer Peabody" [manuscript draft] by Mary Van Wyck Church, page 304, Massachusetts Historical Society.

31. Quoted in "Biography of Elizabeth Palmer Peabody" [manuscript draft] by Mary Van Wyck Church, page 379, Massachusetts Historical Society.

32. Elizabeth Peabody, "Mr. Alcott's Book and School," *Christian Register* (2 April 1838): 1. Subsequent references to this text will appear in parentheses. Mary attributes the "steam-engine" analogy to "Mr. Rodman." See Mary Tyler Peabody to Miss Rawlins Pickman, Thursday Evening July 1835, *Horace Mann Collection*, microfilm edition, 40 reels (Boston: Massachusetts Historical Society, 1989), reel 37.

33. Her article is not all praise; it begins with a lengthy recitation of the book's numerous faults. She grants that "about a dozen of the passages had better have been left in the oblivion into which the Recorder had consigned them," that "the names of the young interlocutors had better been left out of so disputable a book," and that, most significantly, given her own problems with Alcott's methods, it was "unwise" and "unnecessary" to "encumber his already disputed method of Spiritual Culture with questionable matter so extraneous to its great principle, by holding those portions of the Conversations in the first instance (the subjects of which I have observed the children themselves did not introduce)." She then concludes these remarks with the stinging observation that "as an *Exegesis of Scripture*—the book has no value" ("Mr. Alcott's Book," 1; emphasis in original).

34. For the gendered dimensions of the literary publishing industry, see Susan Coultrap-McQuin, *Doing Literary Business, American Women Writers in Nineteenth-Century America* (Chapel Hill: University of North Carolina Press, 1990), 27–48.

35. Ronda, *Elizabeth Palmer Peabody*, 182. As one might imagine, this has been a source of consternation and speculation to biographers and critics. Organizing his aunt's papers in 1904, Benjamin Pickman Mann struggles to "formulate a statement" on the "transition" between what he calls her "teaching period" of 1822–36 and the "business period" of 1840–52. See Benjamin Pickman Mann to Mary Van Wyck Church, 2 January 1904, in the Biography of Elizabeth Palmer Peabody Archive, Massachusetts Historical Society. More recently, Leslie Perrin Wilson has offered "personal and family financial need" as a practical answer to the question of what "brought Peabody—first and foremost a teacher—to the decision to enter commercial life" ("'No Worthless Books,'" 124, 123). Yet these articulations, over 90 years apart, both posit an anachronistic dichotomy between teaching and commerce; if anything, the Temple School controversy had taught Peabody that teachers were never *out* of the marketplace, especially when they "depended on the goodwill and active support of parents [or other customers] for [their]

livelihood" (*Elizabeth Palmer Peabody*, 155). Her decision, therefore, to abandon her position and retreat to Salem for the sake of her reputation made good business sense, even if she resented the provincial expectations that made such an exile necessary, just as her choice to open a bookstore was not a "transition" away from the business of teaching, so much as an educational enterprise (with all the economic connotations this word carries) in yet another form.

36. *Elizabeth Palmer Peabody*, 87.

37. Theodore Parker refers to Peabody writing a "History of the Anglo-Saxons for the School Library." See Theodore Parker to Elizabeth Palmer Peabody, 3 October 1839, *Theodore Parker Papers*, microfilm edition, 4 reels (Boston: Massachusetts Historical Society, 1986), reel 2. A notice for the *The School Library* in the 1 April 1840 *Common School Journal* also lists "Miss E. P. Peabody" as a contributor.

38. Horace Mann to Elizabeth Palmer Peabody, 10 March 1838, *Horace Mann Collection*, microfilm edition, 40 reels (Boston: Massachusetts Historical Society, 1989), reel 5.

39. See the advertisement entitled "E. P. Peabody's Book Room" in the 10 and 11 August and 7, 21, and 24 September 1840 editions of the *Boston Morning Post*. In a trade bill printed that August announcing the opening of her store, Peabody mentions she has the "choicest editions" for sale in her shop, and that she has "already ordered a choice selection" of texts for her circulating library as well, playing upon both the quality of printed materials and the superiority of her own methods of choosing texts for her establishment. For more, see "New Bookstore and Foreign Library" (Boston: Elizabeth Palmer Peabody, 1840), Massachusetts Historical Society. For further discussion of Peabody's advertisements, see Wilson, "'No Worthless Books.'"

40. Elizabeth Palmer Peabody to Samuel Gray Ward, 13 September 1841, Samuel Gray Ward Papers MS Am 1465 (955), Houghton Library, Harvard University.

41. For sale of *The School Library*, see "New Bookstore and Foreign Library" (Boston: Elizabeth Palmer Peabody, 1840), Massachusetts Historical Society.

42. Elizabeth Palmer Peabody to Samuel Gray Ward, 13 September 1841, Samuel Gray Ward Papers MS Am 1465 (955), Houghton Library, Harvard University; emphasis in original.

43. Peabody, *Record*, v.

44. Peabody, *Reminiscences*, 320. Bulwer-Lytton was a common target in the press at the time. For more on antebellum American responses to his writing, see Baym, *Novels, Readers, and Reviewers*.

45. Ronda, *Elizabeth Palmer Peabody*, 81.

46. "Influence of Fictitious Writings," *American Annals of Education* 8.2 (February 1838): 60; emphasis in original.

47. Quoted in "Discussion on School Libraries," *American Annals of Education* 6.12 (December 1836): 550–51.

48. Elizabeth Palmer Peabody, "Journal," 11–15 April 1836, as quoted in Bruce Ronda, "Elizabeth Palmer Peabody's Views of the Child," *Emerson Society Quarterly* 23.2 (1977): 110; emphasis in original. Even "at the utmost of his liberality," Peabody laments, Alcott can do little more than merely "*endure* the suggestion of a contrary view," and he "rather avoids than seeks any communication with persons who differ from himself" (110; emphasis in original). Unlike him, she believed that books, as manifestations of the "thought and views of other minds" or the historical record of the human mind's progress as it unfolded throughout the ages, were important to self-culture precisely because they demonstrated the operations of human nature in vastly differing circumstances and could offer the provocation for an individual's further development.

49. "Newspaper Education," *American Annals of Education* 7.8 (August 1837): 373.

50. Proprietary shares cost $300, and were hereditary, easily transferred or willed to other family members. See Story, "Class and Culture in Boston," 179, 192.

51. Kaser, *A Book for a Sixpence*, 19.

52. Ronda, *Elizabeth Palmer Peabody*, 94. Women were not merely the targets of new circulating libraries but were also their proprietors. For instance, Marty Sprague of Boston ran the "New Circulating Library" out of her millinery shop from 1802 through 1806, where, an advertisement in the *Independent Chronicle* tells us, "mingling useful with the musing," she "flatter[ed] herself she shall receive the patronage of her Sex." Quoted in Charles Bolton, "Circulating Libraries in Boston, 1765–1865," *Publications of the Colonial Society in America* 11 (February 1907): 205. Also see Kaser, *A Book for a Sixpence*, 68. Similarly, in 1804 Boston milliner Kezia Butler opened a circulating library in her own millinery shop. See Bolton, "Circulating Libraries," 205–6. To name but a few other ventures run by local women, N. Nutting operated a successful "Ladies Circulating Library" at 45 ½ Newbury Street in Boston during the 1820s, while Hannah Harris's "Central Circulating Library" in Salem (Elizabeth Peabody's hometown) during the same period flourished with an estimated 4,000 volumes. See Kaser, *A Book for a Sixpence*, 69.

53. Kaser, *A Book for a Sixpence*, 66, 86.

54. Bolton, "Circulating Libraries," 206.

55. Parker does concede that, having learned "more of the scheme through Miss Ripley, the plan strikes me as much better and the more I think of it, the more feasible it does appear." Ultimately, he embraces the idea, declaring: "I should think you might now fill a vacancy and supply a want that has been long felt in Boston." Theodore Parker to Elizabeth Palmer Peabody, 1 July 1840, *Theodore Parker Papers*, microfilm edition, 4 reels (Boston: Massachusetts Historical Society, 1986), reel 2.

56. Elizabeth Palmer Peabody to William Ellery Channing, 10 July 1840, in "Biography of Elizabeth Palmer Peabody" [manuscript draft] by Mary Van Wyck Church, page 402, Massachusetts Historical Society; emphasis in original.

57. Elizabeth Palmer Peabody to William Ellery Channing, August 1840, in "Biography of Elizabeth Palmer Peabody" [manuscript draft] by Mary Van Wyck Church, page 405, Massachusetts Historical Society. Not only had she "learned to keep books in a week," but she also saw the "advantages I possess in knowing something of the interior of books. Especially in this importing business I can detect mistakes made by even the shrewd house in New York which I shall never be liable to, although I will undoubtedly to many others" (405.1, 405). Channing was never quite convinced. He tells Peabody: "I rejoice in your bright prospects. If heroic endurance entitles one to success, you may put in a claim. I cannot judge of the facts you give me as proofs of your prospering or of your business talent; but it is so pleasant to believe, that I start no objection" (*Reminiscences*, 413).

58. As Leslie Perrin Wilson suggests, Peabody offered a selection "deliberately tailored" to her cosmopolitan-minded transcendentalist customers. See "'No Worthless Books,'" 134.

59. Elizabeth Palmer Peabody to William Ellery Channing, August 1840, in "Biography of Elizabeth Palmer Peabody" [manuscript draft] by Mary Van Wyck Church, pages 405–5(1), Massachusetts Historical Society.

60. For more on Burditt, see footnote 2 in *LMF*, 2: 120. See also Rollo Silver, *The Boston Book Trade: 1800–1825* (New York: New York Public Library, 1949), 22.

61. Elizabeth Peabody, "Plan of the West Roxbury Community," *The Dial* 2.3 (January 1842): 371–72; emphasis in original.

62. Elizabeth Peabody, "A Glimpse of Christ's Idea of Society," *The Dial* 2.2 (October 1841): 227–28.

63. As Leslie Perrin Wilson has already demonstrated, the bookstore and circulating library contained two different sets of books; Peabody maintained costlier editions for sale in the bookstore, while the circulating library, having been assembled for "content rather than high-end elegance," was more practical, disseminating foreign knowledge at relatively minor cost to subscribers. See Wilson, "'No Worthless Books,'" 142.

64. The 1840 catalogue is reproduced in Madeleine Stern, "Elizabeth Peabody's Foreign Library (1840)," in *Books and Book People in Nineteenth-Century America* (New York: R. R. Bowker, 1978), 121–35.

65. Many of Peabody's friends would help her stock the circulating library by lending their books to the business. For instance, see Elizabeth Peabody's letter to Channing from August 1840:

> The Library I have more and more hopes of. At first I scarcely expected to more than clear myself of danger xxx Mr. George Bancroft lends me Italian books—nearly enough to begin with during which time I can test how much they are wanted and what is wanted. If any of them circulate enough to become injured, they will become necessary to me, and I can import others for Mr. Bancroft. His generosity therefore will not impair his library in the end, but this does not take from the liberal character of his offer, which was made impulsively, because he thought whoever undertook the enterprise would need assistance at first. Before long the library would create its own clientele. Miss [Lee?] and Mr. Waldo Emerson have also given and lent me many desirable and expensive works in German and English.

See Elizabeth Palmer Peabody to William Ellery Channing, August 1840, in "Biography of Elizabeth Palmer Peabody" [manuscript draft] by Mary Van Wyck Church, page 405, Massachusetts Historical Society.

66. Traditionally, antebellum publishers acted as agents for writers, hiring out the tasks of printing and binding, negotiating with distributors and booksellers to place the texts in stores, and advertising them to consumers. See Charvat, *Literary Publishing in America*, 51–55. Besides the *Grandfather's Chair* series (1841), Peabody issued numerous educational texts in her first few years as a publisher: Anna Cabot Lowell's *Theory of Teaching* (1841), *A Method of Teaching Linear Drawing Adapted to Public Schools* (1841), and Mary Peabody's *Primer of Reading and Drawing* (1841) and *The Flower People* (1842). A sampling of other releases includes Theodore Parker's *A Discourse on the Transient and Permanent in Christianity* (third edition, 1841), an edition of St. Augustine's *Confessions* (1842), her own translation of Guillaume Oegger's *True Messiah* (1842), Felix Paul Wierzbicki's *The Ideal Man* (1842), J. A. Weisse's *Key to the French Language* (1842), Fuller's translation of Bettina von Arnim's *Gunderode* (1842), *The Dial* (from 1842 to 1843), and, later, *Aesthetic Papers* (1849), *First Nursery Reading Book* (1849), and *The Polish-American System of Chronology* (1850). For more, see Marshall, *The Peabody Sisters*, 423 and 562 fn. 395; Ronda, *Elizabeth Palmer Peabody*, 206, and 366 fn. 41; Dowling, *Business of Literary Circles*, 137 and 267 fn. 56; and Phillip Gura, *American Transcendentalism: A History* (New York: Hill and Wang, 2007), 126–27.

67. She notes elsewhere that, almost from the moment she set up shop, the "book-publishers combined against me, and though my friend Dr. Channing gave me his 'Emancipation' and

Hawthorne his 'Grandfather's Chair,' yet I could not fight them all successfully, and finally relinquished business." Quoted in Cooke, *Historical and Biographical Introduction,* 1:148. She would in fact go on to publish other texts throughout the decade, but it seems she would have to temper her hopes for financial success in that business.

68. For "shrewd business," see Dowling, *Business of Literary Circles,* 133. Dowling identifies the book as Channing's *Slavery* (Boston: James Munroe, 1835), but the edition Peabody published is a later treatise, *Emancipation,* inspired by Joseph John Gurney's account of the emancipated British West Indies, *Familiar Letters to Henry Clay of Kentucky.* See references to "Emancipation" in *Reminiscences,* 410, 420; for the book's genesis, see also "Introductory Remarks" in *Emancipation* (Boston: E. P. Peabody, 1840), iii–iv, and Jack Mendelsohn, *Channing: The Reluctant Radical* (Boston: Little, Brown, & Co. 1971), 248.

69. Coultrap-McQuin, *Doing Literary Business,* 34.

70. Ibid., 47, 38.

71. Even Channing, who confessed to Peabody his "great desire to see a variety of employments thrown open to women," registers the conventional gender proprieties of his day when he expounds upon the scope he envisions for her enterprise. Declaring that he saw "nothing in the business inconsistent with [her] sex," he yet imagined it as a strictly female affair: a "bookstore kept by a lady would become a favored resort of your sex. The ladies want a literary lounge, and good might come from the literary intercourse that would spring out of such a place of meeting." See William Ellery Channing to Elizabeth Palmer Peabody, 22 June 1840, quoted in Peabody, *Reminiscences,* 408–9.

72. Elizabeth Palmer Peabody to William Ellery Channing, June 1841, in "Biography of Elizabeth Palmer Peabody" [manuscript draft] by Mary Van Wyck Church, page 410, Massachusetts Historical Society.

73. For her arrangements with Wiley and Putnam, see Marshall, *The Peabody Sisters,* 393, 424, and 561 fn. 393, as well as Wilson, "'No Worthless Books,'" 125.

74. Elizabeth Palmer Peabody to William Ellery Channing, June 1841, in "Biography of Elizabeth Palmer Peabody" [manuscript draft] by Mary Van Wyck Church, page 411, Massachusetts Historical Society. "Perhaps I may make some plan to go on," she concludes, "but I should abandon it for anything worth five hundred dollars a year. It has only paid itself and a very little over, hitherto, and this is not enough with an employment whose highest results are in the purse. I thought at least to fill the requisitions of a life asking so little as mine" (411). For a time, Peabody also tried renting a second office on Washington Street, which was just around the corner on Boston's publishers' row, in the hopes that a new location might help business. For example, she tells Sam Ward: "I have removed to no. 109 Washington Street, and already see that I shall have a great deal more custom from persons whom I have not previously known as well those I did know to whom I am more accessible—& I do desire to make some effort to get upon my counter what will attract them in frequently—or at least to ascertain I am to give this up finally." See Elizabeth Palmer Peabody to Samuel Gray Ward, 13 September 1841, Samuel Gray Ward Papers MS Am 1465 (955), Houghton Library, Harvard University.

75. Elizabeth Palmer Peabody to William Ellery Channing, June 1841, in "Biography of Elizabeth Palmer Peabody" [manuscript draft] by Mary Van Wyck Church, pages 410–11, Massachusetts Historical Society.

76. Zboray and Zboray, *Literary Dollars,* 141–42.

77. In a 9 April 1842 letter, Fuller tells Emerson: "As to pecuniary matters, Miss Peabody I have found more exact and judicious than I expected" (*LMF,* 3:58).

78. Ralph Waldo Emerson to Frederick Henry Hedge, 23 March 1842, quoted in Joel Myerson, *The New England Transcendentalists and the "Dial"* (Rutherford, NJ: Fairleigh Dickinson University Press, 1980), 74.

79. Myerson, *New England Transcendentalists*, 76, and 244 fn. 93.

80. Ralph Waldo Emerson to Thomas Carlyle, 29 April 1843, quoted in Myerson, *New England Transcendentalists*, 90.

81. Theodore Parker to Ralph Waldo Emerson, 7 April 1842, quoted in Myerson, *New England Transcendentalists*, 77. Ironically, Munroe would hurry *The Dial* into the ground within the year; as George Willis Cooke explains, he

> led Emerson to believe that with a more careful business management, and in connection with his own publishing business, the *Dial* could be made to succeed . . . but the subscription list did not increase, while the expenses did. Monroe [*sic*] charged one-third of the selling price for its management, and the result was the abandonment of the enterprise at the end of the first year under his control.

Quoted in Frank Luther Mott, *A History of American Magazines, Vol. 1*, 709.

82. Edward Everett Hale, ed., *James Freeman Clarke: Autobiography, Diary, and Correspondence* (Boston: Houghton Mifflin Company, 1891), 143–44.

83. Bradford, *Memorial History of Boston*, 4:329.

Chapter 4

1. *Memoirs*, 1:168. Charles Capper identifies the letter's recipient as Elizabeth Peabody. See *Margaret Fuller*, 1:175.

2. Christina Zwarg, *Feminist Conversations: Fuller, Emerson, and the Play of Reading* (Ithaca, NY: Cornell University Press, 1995), 2.

3. The list of scholarly work on Fuller's conversational style is too long to recount. For a sampling, see Annette Kolodny, "Inventing a Feminist Discourse: Rhetoric and Resistance in Margaret Fuller's *Woman in the Nineteenth Century*," *New Literary History* 25.2 (Spring 1994): 355–82; Marie Mitchell Olesen Urbanski, "'Woman in the Nineteenth Century': Genesis, Form, Tone, and Rhetorical Devices," in *Margaret Fuller: Visionary of the New Age* (Orono, ME: Northern Lights, 1994); Sandra Gustafson, "Choosing a Medium: Margaret Fuller and the Forms of Sentiment," *American Quarterly* 47 (1995): 34–65; James Perrin Warren, *Culture of Eloquence: Oratory and Reform in Antebellum America* (University Park: Pennsylvania State University Press, 1999); Peter Gibian, *Oliver Wendell Holmes and the Culture of Conversation* (New York: Cambridge University Press, 2001); and Vásquez, *Authority and Reform*.

4. C. Michael Hurst, "Bodies in Transition: Transcendental Feminism in Margaret Fuller's *Woman in the Nineteenth Century*," *Arizona Quarterly* 66.4 (Winter 2010): 3.

5. Stephen Fink, "Antebellum Lady Editors and the Language of Authority," in *Blue Pencils and Hidden Hands: Women Editing Periodicals, 1830–1910*, ed. Sharon Harris and Ellen Gruber Garvey (Boston: Northeastern University Press, 2004), 207.

6. Anne Rose, *Voices of the Marketplace* (New York: Twayne Publishers, 1994), xvii. As Rose argues, attached to "neither specific institutions nor traditional beliefs," capitalist culture "took

shape preeminently in words, particularly in the written words of mass-marketed fiction, advice literature, and periodicals" (61–62).

7. For "age of conversation," see Capper, *Margaret Fuller,* 1:296; for conversation as a transcendental art, see Lawrence Buell, *Literary Transcendentalism: Style and Vision in the American Renaissance* (Ithaca, NY: Cornell University Press, 1973); also see Noelle Baker, "Conversations," in *The Oxford Handbook of Transcendentalism,* ed. Joel Myerson et al. (Oxford: Oxford University Press, 2010), 341–60; for Channing's conversations, see Peabody's *Reminiscences;* for Peabody's, see Charlene Avallone, "Elizabeth Palmer Peabody and the 'Art' of Conversation," in *Reinventing the Peabody Sisters,* eds. Monika Elbert, Julie Hall, and Katharine Rodier (Iowa City: University of Iowa Press, 2006), 23–44. Although Fuller's, like Peabody's, time with Alcott at the Temple School left her skeptical of his methods, the experience nonetheless provided her with "many valuable thoughts" (*LMF,* 1:279).

8. For Fuller's experiences at the Greene Street School, see Capper, *Margaret Fuller,* 1:206–51. For comparison between the Greene Street and Temple schools, see Judith Albert Strong, "Transition in Transcendental Education: The Schools of Bronson Alcott and Hiram Fuller," *Educational Studies* 11 (Fall 1980): 209–19.

9. For more on these girls, see Judith Albert Strong, "Margaret Fuller and Mary Ware Allen: 'In Youth an Insatiate Student'—A Certain Kind of Friendship," *Thoreau Quarterly Journal* 12 (July 1980): 9–22; Strong, "Margaret Fuller's Row at the Greene Street School: Early Female Education in Providence, 1837–1839," *Rhode Island History* 42 (May 1983): 43–55; Frank Shuffelton, "Margaret Fuller at the Greene Street School: The Journal of Evelina Metcalf," *Studies in the American Renaissance* (1985): 29–46; Laraine R. Fergeson, "Margaret Fuller as a Teacher in Providence: The School Journal of Anne Brown," *Studies in the American Renaissance* (1991): 59–118; Paula Kopacz, "The School Journal of Hannah (Anna) Gale," *Studies in the American Renaissance* (1996): 67–113; and Daniel Shealy, "Margaret Fuller and her 'Maiden': Evelina Metcalf's 1838 School Journal," *Studies in the American Renaissance* (1996): 41–65. Subsequent references to these texts will appear in parentheses.

10. For journal-keeping practices at the school, see Judith Albert Strong, "Transcendental School Journals in Nineteenth-Century America," *Journal of Psychohistory* 9 (Summer 1981): 105–26, and Lesley Ginsberg, "'Our Children are Our Best Works': Mary Ware Allen's Transcendental Education," in *The Worlds of Children, 1620–1920,* ed. Peter Benes and Jane Montague Benes (Boston: Boston University Press, 2004), 78–92.

11. Shuffelton, "Margaret Fuller at the Greene Street School," 31; Kopacz, "The Journal of Hanna (Anna) Gale," 69.

12. [Elizabeth Palmer Peabody], "Journal of Margaret Fuller's 'Conversations,'" in Nancy Craig Simmons, "Margaret Fuller's Boston Conversations: The 1839–1840 Series," *Studies in the American Renaissance* (1994): 222. Subsequent references to this text will appear in parentheses.

13. Mary Ware Allen, "School Journal," 4 vols., in Allen-Johnson Family Papers, 1759–1992, American Antiquarian Society, 3:57, 97. Subsequent references to this archive will appear in parentheses.

14. Fuller, *Woman,* 102. For Fuller's sea-captain as a metaphor for "unimpeded opportunity," see Hurst, "Bodies in Transition," 15.

15. For "chiefly conversational" and "required *thought,*" see Allen, "School Journal," 1: 30; emphasis in original. "So different" is quoted in Harriet Hall Johnson, "Margaret Fuller as Known

by her Scholars," rpt. in *Critical Essays on Margaret Fuller,* ed. Joel Myerson (Boston: G. K. Hall & Company, 1980), 139. Subsequent references to this text will appear in parentheses.

16. Jamie S. Crouse, "'If They Have a Moral Power': Margaret Fuller, Transcendentalism, and the Question of Women's Moral Nature," *American Transcendental Quarterly* 19.4 (2005): 271.

17. See Laraine Fergenson, "Margaret Fuller in the Classroom: The Providence Period," *Studies in the American Renaissance* (1987): 134.

18. Ibid.

19. Bell Gale Chevigny, *The Woman and the Myth: Margaret Fuller's Life and Writings* (Boston: Northeastern University Press, 1994), xxxii–xxxiii.

20. Fergenson, "Fuller in the Classroom," 132.

21. Kolodny, "Inventing a Feminist Discourse," 356, 359, 360; emphasis in original.

22. Kolodny, "Inventing a Feminist Discourse," 375; Elizabeth Hewitt, *Correspondence and American Literature* (New York: Cambridge University Press, 2004), 69.

23. Hewitt, *Correspondence and American Literature,* 69, 65.

24. Theodore Parker to Elizabeth Palmer Peabody, 30 August 1839, *Theodore Parker Papers,* microfilm edition, 4 reels (Boston: Massachusetts Historical Society, 1986), reel 2.

25. Thomas Wentworth Higginson, *Margaret Fuller Ossoli* (Boston: Houghton, Mifflin and Company, 1884), 117.

26. Higginson, *Margaret Fuller Ossoli,* 118; Capper identifies the passage as one of Fuller's journal entries from 1844, after she had given her final Conversations series. See *Margaret Fuller,* 1:297.

27. Julie Ellison, *Delicate Subjects: Romanticism, Gender, and the Ethics of Understanding* (Ithaca, NY: Cornell University Press, 1990), 241–42.

28. For a survey of scholarship on Fuller's views of life as art, see Thomas Mitchell, *Hawthorne's Fuller Mystery* (Amherst: University of Massachusetts Press, 1998), 205–6.

29. Similarly, Jeffrey Steele suggests that Fuller's "profoundly dialogic imagination" sought "reflective surfaces . . . to inspect the self she was fashioning." See "Keys to 'the labyrinth of my own being': Margaret Fuller's Epistolary Invention of the Self," in *Letters and Cultural Transformations in the United States, 1760–1860,* ed. Theresa Strouth Gaul and Sharon Harris (Burlington, VT: Ashgate Publishing, 2009), 100.

30. Ellison, *Delicate Subjects,* 218.

31. Gustafson, "Choosing a Medium," 45.

32. Ibid., 50.

33. Ibid., 46, 47.

34. Zwarg, *Feminist Conversations,* 178.

35. Larry Reynolds characterizes *The Dial,* and Fuller's contributions to it, as an "intertextual conversation," quite literally the printed extension of the "ongoing discussion or dialogue" that Fuller's circle was having on topics such as friendship, love, and marriage. See Reynolds, "From *Dial* Essay to New York Book: The Making of *Woman in the Nineteenth Century,*" in *Periodical Literature in Nineteenth-Century America,* ed. Kenneth Price and Susan Belasco Smith (Charlottesville: University of Virginia Press, 1995), 19–20. Similarly, Tiffany Wayne calls the magazine "another forum for 'conversation' among and between friends." See *Feminism and Transcendentalism in Nineteenth-Century America* (New York: Lexington Books, 2005), 28. Rather than retracing any of these topics, my interest in *The Dial* lies in the theory and practice of conversation informing Fuller's editorship, especially as they grow out of earlier teaching enterprises.

36. While Christina Zwarg argues that Emerson constructs "Waldo" as a parodic caricature of a man unable to assimilate Fuller into his masculine perspective, I am inclined to view Emerson as merely capitulating to nineteenth-century gender proprieties. See *Feminist Conversations*, 238–68.

37. For $500, see Packer, "The Transcendentalists," 444; for $600, see Capper, *Margaret Fuller*, 2: 50; for $200, see Packer, "The Transcendentalists," 449; for lack of payment, see Vol. 3 of *The Letters of Ralph Waldo Emerson*, ed. Ralph L. Rusk (New York: Columbia University Press, 1939), 36. All subsequent references to Emerson's letters are to this edition, hereafter cited in parentheses as *LRWE* with volume and page number. For $1,000, see *LMF*, 1:280.

38. See Kelley, *Private Woman, Public Stage*.

39. *Memoirs*, 1:323. Emerson implies that *The Dial*'s average contributor was male and loath to give the periodical "his best work" because, given its private, feminine character under Fuller, it would not offer "paying employment" for contributions (*Memoirs*, 1:323). Perhaps Emerson is projecting, as Fuller seemed to think *he* reserved his best work for other avenues: "From Mr Emerson we may hope good literary criticisms, but his best thoughts must, I suppose take the form of lectures for the present" (*LMF*, 2:126).

40. Fuller's description is closer to the sentiments expressed in George Ripley's "Prospectus": "The purpose of this work is to furnish a medium for the freest expression of thought on the questions which interest earnest minds in every community. It aims at the discussion of principles, rather than the promotion of measures; and while it will not fail to examine the ideas which impel the leading movements of the present day, it will maintain an independent position with regard to them." "Prospectus" for *The Dial*, in *Transcendentalism: A Reader*, ed. Joel Myerson (New York: Oxford University Press, 2000), 290.

41. For the problem of calling, see Henry Nash Smith, "Emerson's Problem of Vocation: A Note on 'The American Scholar,'" *New England Quarterly* 12.1 (1939): 52–67. For its gendered aspects, see Elizabeth Peabody's notes on Fuller's first series of Conversations, where Fuller suggests that the reason there are so few women artists is that traditional gender roles often precluded it: "Miss Fuller said it troubled her to think there was no great musical composer among women. It is true that at the period of life when men gave themselves to their pursuit most women became mothers—but there were some women who never married. I suggested that these too often spent the rest of their lives in mourning over this fact—& society spoke so uniformly of woman as more respectable for being married—that it was [not] long before she entirely despaired" ("Journal," 215). For a discussion of later transcendental feminists and the problem of vocation, see also Wayne, *Woman Thinking: Feminism and Transcendentalism in Nineteenth-Century America* (New York: Lexington Books, 2005), 79–105.

42. Vásquez, *Authority and Reform*, 200.

43. Price and Smith, "Introduction: Periodical Literature," 5–6; Aleta Feinsod Cane and Susan Alves, eds., "American Women Writers and the Periodical: Creating a Constituency, Opening a Dialogue," in *"The Only Efficient Instrument": American Women Writers and the Periodical, 1837–1916* (Iowa City: University of Iowa Press, 2001), 1–2.

44. Price and Smith, "Introduction," 9–10.

45. Fuller's *Dial* notebook, [ca. April 1840], as quoted in Capper, *Margaret Fuller*, 2:56.

46. For more on the literary dialogue, see Capper, *Margaret Fuller*, 2:56; for "considerably more versatile," see Sylvia Jenkins Cooke, *Working Women, Literary Ladies: The Industrial Revolution and Female Aspiration* (New York: Columbia University Press, 2008), 78. The essay was Emerson's chosen form. Pointing to differences in their rhetorical styles, James Perrin Warren

contrasts Emerson's and Fuller's notions of eloquence: "For Emerson, eloquence takes the form of the secularized sermon—the lecture or address," while for Fuller it "develops from the give-and-take of conversation, not from the oracular utterances of a divinely inspired speaker." See *Culture of Eloquence*, 102. It is also a gendered distinction, founded in the discourse of self-reliant manhood and the other-centered language of nineteenth-century womanhood.

47. Reynolds, "From *Dial* Essay," 20. Myerson's seminal study undervalues Fuller's agency in shaping *The Dial*, tending to reinforce conventional depictions of Fuller as an egotist (an image unfairly passed on by contemporaries more often than not threatened by the presence of such female intellect). He suggests, for instance, that her decision to accept the journal's editorship was little more than "her own natural desire to be at the center of attention coincid[ing] with her wish to help the Transcendentalists." See Myerson, *New England Transcendentalists*, 37.

48. As Capper observes, in "Fuller's *Dial*, seasoned Transcendentalists . . . shared the stage with literary novices like Dwight, James Russell Lowell, and Caroline Sturgis; female reformers such as Peabody and Sophia Ripley; and a medley of Unitarian, Trinitarian, Transcendentalist, Quaker, and even, occasionally, Calvinist seekers. If such a cacophony approached at times incoherence, it had one saving grace: it projected Transcendentalism as something more than either simply a circle of Unitarian renegades, or, as it would largely be in Emerson's *Dial*, a literary vehicle for himself and his young literary protégés." See Capper, *Margaret Fuller*, 2: 14. Sylvia Cooke remarks that, while Emerson's *Dial* would continue to publish a "good deal" of Fuller's work after her departure, fewer women were published in its pages, and even fewer of its contributors evinced much interest in the concerns of gender. See Cooke, *Working Women*, 75–76, 90.

49. Capper, *Margaret Fuller*, 1: 340.

50. Quoted in Cooke, *Historical and Biographical Introduction*, 1:75–76.

51. For Alcott's, Parker's, and Ripley's responses to the first issue, see Myerson, *New England Transcendentalists*, 49–50.

52. Margaret Fuller to James Freeman Clarke, 1 January 1840, Fuller Papers, Massachusetts Historical Society, as cited in Capper, *Margaret Fuller*, 1:345.

53. See Myerson, *New England Transcendentalists*, 43, 39.

54. Fuller, "To Contributors," *Dial* 2.1 (July 1840): 136.

55. For "crowded out" see Emerson to William Emerson, 30 June 1840, in *LRWE*, 2:308; for "large" see Emerson to Fuller, 7 & 8 June 1840 in *LRWE* 2:303. In the letter to Fuller, he estimates that the essay is 63 pages long. In her response, Fuller admits that the printers had printed a "good deal before finding it would be too long." She thus dropped his essay until the next issue and instead inserted a few poems by herself and Sarah Clarke in the final two pages. See *LMF*, 2:146, and 148 fn. 3.

56. For her worries about the small number of subscribers, see *LMF*, 2:136; for complaints about quality, see, for instance, her comment that the first issue was far from the "eaglet motion" she had hoped. See *LMF*, 2:146.

57. For example, Fuller excoriates the "contemptuous" attitude displayed in such commonplace expressions as "women and children"—disparagements even used "in no light sally of the hour, but in works intended to give a permanent statement of the best experiences" (*Woman*, 20). For Emerson's view of *The Dial* and his anxieties over the effeminate, imitative character of (American) art, see Packer, "The Transcendentalists," 447. For Fuller's own move away from this kind of masculine language in her *Dial* writings, see Cooke, *Working Women*, 77–87.

58. For more on Hedge's about-face regarding the journal, and the dismay among his old friends, see, Myerson, *New England Transcendentalists,* 156–62, and Capper, *Margaret Fuller,* 1:342–43.

59. Steven Fink, "Margaret Fuller: Evolution of a Woman of Letters," in *Reciprocal Influences: Literary Production, Distribution, and Consumption in America,* ed. Steven Fink and Susan Williams (Columbus: The Ohio State University Press: 1999), 63–64. For a discussion of Thoreau in Fuller's *Dial,* see Fink, *Prophet in the Marketplace* (Columbus: The Ohio State University Press, 1992), 11–37, and pp. 26–33 for "The Service" in particular; for Fuller's response to Thoreau's submissions, see Capper, *Margaret Fuller,* 2:16–17; for a highly critical reading of Fuller's editorship, see Bernard Rosenthal, "The *Dial,* Transcendentalism, and Margaret Fuller," *English Language Notes* 8 (1970): 28–36. While Fink suggests that Fuller's attitude in her letter to Emerson masks "the real pleasure she took . . . in the exercise of literary and professional power," and is an example of her "deep-seated ambivalence about her role and values as she shaped herself as a woman of letters in a complex and evolving literary marketplace" (Fink, "Evolution," 64), Rosenthal calls her editorship "intensely possessive," and claims that "what has been taken as the journal of a community of men was . . . primarily the journal of one woman" (Rosenthal, "The *Dial,*" 29) who was egotistical, more interested in representing her "exotic" tastes (35) than in offering a "panoramic view of the American transcendentalist milieu" (36).

60. For "objection," see Vol. 7 of *Emerson's Journals and Miscellaneous Notebooks,* ed. William Gilman et al. (Cambridge, MA: Belknap Press of Harvard University Press, 1969), 293; for Clarke's opinion of the essay as poorly written, see Myerson, *New England Transcendentalists,* 49; for "foolish," see 10 August 1840, in Parker's journal, 1:35, as quoted in *LRWE,* 2:324, fn 326. Parker adds: Emerson said Thoreau's essay "was full of life. But alas the life is Emerson's, not Thoreau's, & so it had been lived before. . . . I hope he will write for the newspapers more & less for the Dial" (324).

61. Charvat, *Literary Publishing in America,* 17–37. In 1845, Hawthorne wrote of Emerson's reputation: "His reputation is still, I think, provincial, and almost local partly owing to the defects of the New England system of publication." See Nathaniel Hawthorne to E. A. Duyckinck, 1 July 1845, quoted in *Literary Publishing,* 29.

62. Fuller's accusation might also be read as exasperation at what David Dowling calls her fellow editor's "incapacity for expansion outward into the commercial world of resources." Indeed, even those innovations Emerson adopted to encourage *The Dial*'s success, like the "New Poetry" section soliciting "submission of works in progress that might otherwise have been hidden in private journals," tended to enact an "anticommercial poetics" whose effects were to make the magazine more "provincial and idiosyncratic," and to direct its "social trajectory . . . inward rather than outward toward expansion into a cosmopolitan marketplace." See Dowling, *Business of Literary Circles,* 106, 109–10, 112.

63. Specifically, Emerson is thinking of Thoreau's poem "Sympathy," which he calls the "Elegy" (*LRWE,* 2:311).

64. Fuller initially tried to put off the changes, telling Emerson "now we have begun so I should think it undesirable to make changes this year, as the first vol should be uniform" (*LMF,* 2:146), but then simply did not make them. See *LRWE,* 2:311 fn 270 for more. Bernard Rosenthal, however, notes that Fuller would take some of Emerson's advice, incorporating his suggestion to include clear lines separating individual pieces from each other. See Rosenthal, "*The Dial,*" 33.

65. For comparison, see Fuller's *Dial* 1.1 (July 1840) and Emerson's *Dial* 4.13 (July 1843).

66. Theodore Parker to Ralph Waldo Emerson, 7 April 1842, quoted in Myerson, *New England Transcendentalists*, 77.

67. "Miss Dial" is quoted in Capper, *Margaret Fuller*, 2: 10; "beard" is quoted in Higginson, *Margaret Fuller Ossoli*, 161.

68. Thomas Carlyle to Ralph Waldo Emerson, 14 November 1841, in *The Correspondence of Emerson and Carlyle*, ed. Joseph Slater (New York: Columbia University Press, 1964), 312–13; emphasis in original. Emerson was acutely sensitive to these sorts of imputations of unmanliness with regard to the journal. See Packer, "The Transcendentalists," 447–48, and Cooke, *Working Women*, 77.

69. Zwarg, *Feminist Conversations*, 14, 61.

70. Ibid., 86. Extrapolating to *The Dial*, Zwarg suggests that Fuller's editorial control of the 1842 issue, in which her translations of *Tasso* and *Gunderode* appeared, "became her ultimate act of translation, a grafting of complexities of [her authors] onto her own relationship with Emerson, all in the service of a useable model of feminist conversation" (86). But if her conversations with Emerson manifested in a theory of translation put into practice in *The Dial*, I suggest that they also shaped her attitude toward her role as editor and the aims of the journal itself.

71. Ibid., 15, 16. In "Storied Facts," Zwarg describes Fuller's theory of translation as

> a sustained interpretive strategy . . . less about a conquest of meaning, a mastery that subdues and potentially annihilates an alien set of values (hence everything that gets lost in translation), than . . . about the proliferation of meaning, or everything that might be *found* when new values open to view within both languages. In criticism, as in translation, the task is to allow one's own language to be powerfully affected by the alien one, rather than to hold it constant. Thus Fuller's interest in translation guides her thinking through many cultural issues because she sees that a hermeneutic maneuver deriving its authority from a struggle for mastery over meaning has violent *historical* consequences.

See "The Storied Facts of Margaret Fuller," *The New England Quarterly* 69.1 (March 1996): 132–33; emphasis in original.

72. Wayne, *Woman Thinking*, 24; for Emerson's involvement in the mixed-company sessions, see Caroline Healy Dall, *Margaret and her Friends; or, Ten Conversations with Margaret Fuller upon the Mythology of the Greeks and its Expression in Art* (Boston: Roberts Brothers, 1895).

73. Hewitt, *Correspondence and American Literature*, 68.

74. Ripley, "Prospectus," 290.

75. For the rich tradition of nineteenth-century female editorship and the magazine's power to "explode" limiting definitions of what women could do, see Patricia Okker, *Our Sister Editors: Sarah J. Hale and the Tradition of Nineteenth-Century American Women Editors* (Athens: University of Georgia Press, 1995), 6–37.

76. "Newspaper Education," *American Annals of Education* 7.8 (August 1837): 373–74.

77. Ibid., 373. Such assertions demonstrate that antebellum Americans understood the periodical's efficacy in terms very similar to what Richard Brodhead posits as the exclusive province of the nineteenth-century novel; he argues that the novel was uniquely suited to disciplinary functions, because it could "arouse" a sense of "peculiar intimacy" in readers and "transpose its orderings into [their] felt understanding" through seemingly "invisible persuasion." See Brodhead, *Cultures of Letters*, 46.

78. "Newspaper Education," 375; Kett, *Pursuit of Knowledge under Difficulties*, 67–68.

79. Capper, *Margaret Fuller,* 2: 7.

80. Emerson, "Self-Reliance," 29; Fuller, "A Short Essay on Critics," *Dial* 1.1 (July 1840): 5. Subsequent references to this essay will appear in the text in parentheses. For Fuller critiquing Emerson in similar terms, see Jeffrey Steele, "The Limits of Political Sympathy: Emerson, Fuller, and Woman's Rights," in *The Emerson Dilemma: Essays in Emerson and Social Reform,* ed. T. Gregory Garvey (Athens: University of Georgia Press, 2001), 122–23.

81. Okker, *Our Sister Editors,* 22–23.

82. For discussion of these three documents—Ripley's "Prospectus," Emerson's "Editors to the Reader," and Fuller's "Short Essay"—see Fink, *Prophet in the Marketplace,* 18–22.

83. For "sisterly," see Okker, *Our Sister Editors,* 23; for "manliness" and "man to man," see Cooke, *Working Women,* 78–79, and Fuller, "Short Essay," 10.

84. It is not a coincidence that such comments come after she had been hired at the *New York Tribune.* For more on Fuller's conversational ethic at the newspaper, particularly in a cosmopolitan, transnational context, see Leslie Eckel, "Margaret Fuller's Conversational Journalism: New York, London, Rome," *Arizona Quarterly* 63.2 (2007): 27–50.

Coda

1. Dowling, *The Business of Literary Circles,* 2, 5.

2. Patricia Ard, "Transcendentalism for Children: Mary Peabody Mann's *The Flower People,*" in *Reinventing the Peabody Sisters,* ed. Monika Elbert et al. (Iowa City: University of Iowa Press, 2006), 220; Gillian Brown, "Hawthorne's American History," 121–42.

3. For gender and home as transcendent value systems, see Amy Schrager Lang, *The Syntax of Class: Writing Inequality in Nineteenth-Century America* (Princeton, NJ: Princeton University Press, 2003), 14–42.

4. Robert Milder, "The Radical Emerson?", 59.

5. See Martin Bickman, *Minding American Education: Reclaiming the Tradition of Active Learning* (New York: Teachers College Press, 2003).

6. See Ben McGrath, "Food Groups," *The New Yorker,* 7 May 2012, http://www.newyorker.com, and Rachel Monahan, "Talking Pineapple Question on State Exam Stumps . . . Everyone," *New York Daily News,* 19 April, 2012, http:www.nydailynews.com.

7. For student responses to the exam questions, see Anemona Hartocollis, "When Pineapple Races Hare, Students Lose," *New York Times,* 20 April 2012, http://www.nytimes.com.

8. Quoted in McGrath, "Food Groups."

9. Quoted in "Biography of Elizabeth Palmer Peabody" [manuscript draft] by Mary Van Wyck Church, page 379, Massachusetts Historical Society.

10. Daniel Pinkwater, "Pineapple idiots! Who knew my book would be used for the world's dumbest test question," *New York Daily News,* 21 April 2012, http://articles.nydailynews.com.

11. For "Child's Budget," see *CE,* 16:417; "advocate of nonsense" is quoted in Lisa Fleisher, "Test Question Flunks" (includes an interview with Daniel Pinkwater), *The Wall Street Journal,* 20 April 2012, http://online.wsj.com.

12. Pinkwater, "Pineapple idiots!"

13. Paul Theroux, "Introduction," in Henry David Thoreau, *The Maine Woods,* ed. Joseph Moldenhauer (Princeton, NJ: Princeton University Press, 2004), xxi–xxii.

14. Pinkwater, "Pineapple idiots!"

15. Quoted in Fleisher, "Test Question Flunks."

16. Pinkwater, "Pineapple idiots," *New York Daily News,* April 21, 2012.

17. Zboray and Zboray, *Literary Dollars,* 190–94, 197–200; for "school-master," see Adams, *Richard Henry Dana,* 1:119.

18. For "small" see Adams, *Richard Henry Dana,* 1: 119–20; "A lot of authors," quoted in Fleisher, "Test Question Flunks."

19. For this oft-cited aversion, see, for instance, Arthur Versluis, *American Transcendentalism and Asian Religions* (New York: Oxford University Press, 1993), 177; Packer, *The Transcendentalists,* 424; Cooke, *Working Women,* 78; for enshrinement of child-like vision as one of its legacies, see Buell, "Transcendentalist Literary Legacies," 613.

20. See Robert Richardson, *William James: In the Maelstrom of American Modernism* (Boston: Houghton Mifflin, 2006), 20.

21. Greta D. Little and Joel Myerson, eds., "Introduction," in *Three Novels by Christopher Pearse Cranch* (Athens: University of Georgia Press, 2010), xvi.

22. For German literature in antebellum Boston, see Zboray and Zboray, "Transcendentalism in Print," 344.

23. David Kesterson, "Margaret Fuller on Hawthorne," in *Hawthorne and Women: Engendering and Expanding the Hawthorne Tradition,* ed. John Idol, Jr., and Melinda Ponder (Amherst: University of Massachusetts Press, 1999), 68–69; Catherine Mitchell, ed., "A Journalist at the Tribune, 1844–46," in *Margaret Fuller's New York Journalism* (Knoxville: University of Tennessee Press, 1995), 25.

24. "Dandyism" cited in Little and Myerson, "Introduction," xviii; for Locke, see Gillian Brown, "The Metamorphic Book: Children's Print Culture in the Eighteenth Century," *Eighteenth Century Studies* 39.3 (2006): 351–62; for Pestalozzi, see Monaghan and Monaghan, "Schoolbooks," 312–18; Margaret Fuller, "Children's Books," Rpt. in *Essays on American Life and Letters,* ed. Joel Myerson (Lanham, MD: Rowman and Littlefield, 2003), 268.

25. For "wellspring of social inspiration," see Zboray and Zboray, *Literary Dollars,* xxi; for "friends of education," see E. B. H., "Art. VI. The School Library," 387; for 30 to 40 percent, see Tebbel, *History of Book Publishing,* 222; for literary series, see Howsam, "Sustained Literary Ventures," 11; for Ticknor and Fields, see Winship, *Ticknor and Fields;* for "autonomous," see Jonathan Arac, "Narrative Forms," in *The Cambridge History of American Literature, Volume Two,* ed. Sacvan Bercovitch (New York: Cambridge University Press, 1994), 724; for "sun," see Thoreau, *Walden,* 334.

BIBLIOGRAPHY

Primary Sources

Adams, Charles. *Richard Henry Dana: A Biography.* 2 vols. Boston: Houghton Mifflin, 1890.

Alcott, Amos Bronson. *Conversations with Children on the Gospels.* 2 vols. Boston: James Munroe, 1836–37. Reprinted in *The Romantic Tradition in American Literature.* New York: Arno Press, 1972.

Allen, Mary Ware. "School Journal." 4 vols. Allen-Johnson Family Papers, 1759–1992. American Antiquarian Society.

"Art. IX. The School Library." *North American Review* 50.107 (April 1840): 505–15.

Boswell, James. *Life of Johnson.* Oxford: Oxford University Press, 1980.

Bradford, George. "Philosophic Thought in Boston." In Vol. 2 of *The Memorial History of Boston: Including Suffolk County, Massachusetts, 1630–1880.* Edited by Justin Winsor. Boston: J. R. Osgood and Company, 1880.

Brown, Anne. "School Journal." Published in Laraine R. Fergenson. "Margaret Fuller as a Teacher in Providence: The School Journal of Anne Brown." *Studies in the American Renaissance* (1991): 59–118.

Brownson, Orestes. "The School Library." *Boston Quarterly Review* 3.2 (April 1840): 225–37.

Capen, Nahum. *Memorial of Nahum Capen, of Boston, Massachusetts, on the subject of international copyright,* 28th cong., 1st sess., 15 Jan 1844, H. Doc. 61.

Channing, William Ellery. *Emancipation.* Boston: E. P. Peabody, 1840.

Church, Mary Van Wyck. "Biography of Elizabeth Palmer Peabody" [manuscript draft]. Massachusetts Historical Society.

"Common School Library." *Common School Journal* 1.2 (15 January 1839): 29–30.

Cooke, George. *An Historical and Biographical Introduction to Accompany The Dial.* 2 vols. Cleveland: The Rowfant Club, 1902.

Cranch, Christopher Pearse. *Last of the Huggermuggers* and *Koboltozo.* In *Three Novels by Christopher Pearse Cranch.* Edited by Greta D. Little and Joel Myerson. Athens: University of Georgia Press, 2010.

Dall, Caroline Healy. *Margaret and her Friends: Ten Conversations with Margaret Fuller.* Boston: Roberts Brothers, 1895.

The Dial: A Magazine for Literature, Philosophy, and Religion. Boston, 1841–44.
"Discussion on School Libraries." *American Annals of Education* 6.12 (December 1836): 549–54.
E. B. H. "Art. VI. The School Library." *Christian Examiner* 27.3 (January 1840): 386–96.
"Editor's Table." *Godey's Lady's Book* 21.10 (October 1840): 189–91.
Edward Everett Papers. Microfilm edition. 54 reels. Boston: Massachusetts Historical Society, 1972.
Embury, Emma. *Pictures of Early Life.* Boston: Marsh, Capen, Lyon, and Webb, 1839.
Emerson, Ralph Waldo. Vol. 7 of *Journals and Miscellaneous Notebooks.* Edited by William Gilman et al. Cambridge, MA: Belknap Press of Harvard University Press, 1969.
———. Vols. 2 & 3 of *The Letters of Ralph Waldo Emerson.* Edited by Ralph L. Rusk. New York: Columbia University Press, 1939.
———. "Self-Reliance." In Vol. 2 of *The Collected Works of Ralph Waldo Emerson.* Edited by Joseph Slater, et al. Cambridge, MA: Belknap Press of Harvard University Press, 1979.
———, and Thomas Carlyle. *The Correspondence of Emerson and Carlyle.* Edited by Joseph Slater. New York: Columbia University Press, 1964.
Fowle, William B. "The Last Number." *Common School Journal* 14.25 (15 December 1852): 369–70.
Fuller, Margaret. "American Literature." In Vol. 2 of *Papers on Literature and Art.* New York: Wiley and Putnam, 1846.
———. "Children's Books." In *Essays on American Life and Letters.* Edited by Joel Myerson. Lanham, MD: Rowman and Littlefield, 2003.
———. Vols. 1–4 of *The Letters of Margaret Fuller.* Edited by Robert N. Hudspeth. Ithaca, NY: Cornell University Press, 1983, 1984, and 1987.
———. *Memoirs of Margaret Fuller Ossoli.* Edited by Ralph Waldo Emerson et al. 2 vols. Boston: Phillips, Sampson and Company, 1852.
———. "A Short Essay on Critics." *Dial* 1.1 (July 1840): 5–11.
———. "To Contributors." *Dial* 2.1 (July 1841): 136.
———. *Woman in the Nineteenth Century.* Edited by Larry Reynolds. Norton Critical Editions. New York: Norton, 1998.
Gale, Hannah. "School Journal." Published in Paula Kopacz. "The School Journal of Hannah (Anna) Gale." *Studies in the American Renaissance* (1996): 67–113.
George Bancroft Papers. Massachusetts Historical Society.
Goodrich, Samuel. *Recollections of a Lifetime.* 2 vols. New York: C. M. Saxton, 1859.
Hale, Edward Everett, ed. *James Freeman Clarke: Autobiography, Diary, and Correspondence.* Boston: Houghton Mifflin Company, 1891.
Hale, Sarah J. *The Juvenile Budget Opened, being Selections from the Writings of Dr. John Aiken. With a Sketch of his Life, by Mrs. S. J. Hale.* Boston: Marsh, Capen, Lyon, and Webb, 1840.
———. *The Juvenile Budget Reopened, being further Selections from the Writings of Dr. John Aiken, with copious Notes.* Boston: Marsh, Capen, Lyon, and Webb, 1840.
———. *Things By Their Right Names, and Other Stories, Fables, and Moral Pieces in Prose and Verse: Selected and Arranged from the Writings of Mrs. Barbauld, with a Sketch of her Life, by Mrs. S. J. Hale.* Boston: Marsh, Capen, Lyon, and Webb 1840.
Hale, Sarah P. E. *The Lives of Christopher Columbus, the Discoverer of America, and Americus Vespucius, the Florentine.* Boston: Marsh, Lyon, Capen, and Webb, 1840.
———. *Lives of Vasco Nunez de Balboa, the Discoverer of the Pacific Ocean, Hernando Cortes, the Conquerer of Mexico, and Francisco Pizaro, the Conquerer of Peru.* Boston: Marsh, Lyon, Capen, and Webb, 1840.

Hale Family Papers. Sophia Smith Collection. Smith College. North Hampton, Mass.

Hawthorne, Julian. *Nathaniel Hawthorne and His Wife.* 2 vols. Boston: Houghton Mifflin Company, 1884.

Hawthorne, Nathaniel. Vols. 6–11 and 15–16 of *The Centenary Edition of the Works of Nathaniel Hawthorne.* Edited by William Chavat et al. Columbus: The Ohio State University Press, 1972, 1974, 1985, 1989, and 1991.

———. *Peter Parley's Universal History on the Basis of Geography, for the Use of Families.* Boston: American Stationers' Company, 1837.

Higginson, Thomas Wentworth. *Cheerful Yesterdays.* Boston: Houghton, Mifflin, and Company, 1898.

———. *Margaret Fuller Ossoli.* Boston: Houghton, Mifflin, and Company, 1884.

Horace Mann Collection. Microfilm edition. 40 reels. Boston: Massachusetts Historical Society, 1989.

"Influence of Fictitious Writings." *American Annals of Education* 8.2 (February 1838): 57–66.

"Instruction and Education in Families: Influence of Sisters." *American Annals of Education* 8.10 (October 1838): 444–48.

Irving, Washington. Letters III, 1839–1845. Volume 25 of *The Complete Works of Washington Irving.* Edited by Ralph Alderman et al. Boston: Twayne Publishers, 1982.

———. *The Sketch-Book of Geoffrey Crayon.* Edited by Haskell Springer. Boston: Twayne Publishers, 1978.

Longfellow, Henry Wadsworth. Vol. 2 of *The Letters of Henry Wadsworth Longfellow, 1814–43.* Edited by Andrew Hilen. Cambridge, MA: Belknap Press of Harvard University Press, 1967.

Mann, Horace. "Conclusion of Introduction." *Common School Journal* 3.1 (1 January 1841): 15–16.

———. "District School Libraries." *Common School Journal* 2.5 (2 March 1840): 65–72.

———. "An Historical View of Education." In *Lectures on Education.* Reprinted in *American Education: Its Men, Ideas, and Institutions Series.* Edited by Lawrence Cremin. New York: Arno Press, 1969. 215–67.

———. "Necessity of Education in a Republican Government." In *Lectures on Education.* Reprinted in *American Education: Its Men, Ideas, and Institutions Series.* Edited by Lawrence Cremin. New York: Arno Press, 1969. 117–62.

———. "On District School Libraries." In *Lectures on Education.* Reprinted in *American Education: Its Men, Ideas, and Institutions.* Edited by Lawrence Cremin. New York: Arno Press, 1969. 269–301.

Mann, Mary Peabody. *The Flower People.* Boston: E. P. Peabody, 1842.

———. *Life of Horace Mann.* Boston: Lee and Shepard, 1904.

Massachusetts Board of Education. *First Annual Report of the Board of Education, together with the First Annual Report of the Secretary of the Board.* Boston: Dutton and Wentworth, 1838.

———. *Second Annual Report of the Board of Education, together with the Second Annual Report of the Secretary of the Board.* Boston: Dutton and Wentworth, 1839.

———. *Third Annual Report of the Board of Education, together with the Third Annual Report of the Secretary of the Board.* Boston: Dutton and Wentworth, 1840.

———. *Fourth Annual Report of the Board of Education, together with the Fourth Annual Report of the Secretary of the Board.* Boston: Dutton and Wentworth, 1841.

———. *Sixth Annual Report of the Board of Education, together with the Sixth Annual Report of the Secretary of the Board.* Boston: Dutton and Wentworth, 1843.

Mather, Cotton. *Magnalia Christi Americana, Books I & II*. Edited by Kenneth Murdock. Cambridge, MA: Belknap Press of Harvard University Press, 1977.

Metcalf, Evelina. "School Journal, 23 April 1838–16 May 1838." Published in Daniel Shealy. "Margaret Fuller and her 'Maiden': Evelina Metcalf's 1838 School Journal." *Studies in the American Renaissance* (1996): 41–65.

———. "School Journal." Published in Frank Shuffelton. "Margaret Fuller at the Greene Street School: The Journal of Evelina Metcalf." *Studies in the American Renaissance* (1985): 29–46.

"The Moral of the Crisis." *United States Magazine and Democratic Review* 1.1 (October 1837): 108–22.

"Newspaper Education." *American Annals of Education* 7.8 (August 1837): 372–75.

"Notices and Intelligence: The School Library." *Christian Examiner* 27.1 (September 1839): 132–34.

Peabody, Andrew Preston. "Twice-Told Tales." *Christian Examiner and General Review* 24.2 (November 1838): 182–90. Reprinted in *Nathaniel Hawthorne: The Contemporary Reviews*. Edited by John Idol, Jr. and Buford James. Cambridge: Cambridge University Press, 1994.

Peabody, Elizabeth Palmer. "E. P. Peabody's Book Room." *Boston Morning Post* (10 August 1840).

———. "A Glimpse of Christ's Idea of Society." *Dial* 2.2 (October 1841): 214–29.

———. *Letters of Elizabeth Palmer Peabody, American Renaissance Woman*. Edited by Bruce A. Ronda. Middletown, CT: Wesleyan University Press, 1984.

———. "Mr. Alcott's Book and School." *Christian Register* (2 April 1838): 1.

———. "New Bookstore and Foreign Library." Boston: Elizabeth Palmer Peabody, 1840. Broadside, Massachusetts Historical Society.

———. "Plan for the West Roxbury Community." *Dial* 2.3 (January 1842): 361–73.

———. *Record of a School*. Boston: James Munroe, 1835.

———. *Reminiscences of William Ellery Channing*. Boston: Roberts Brothers, 1880.

[Elizabeth Palmer Peabody]. "Journal of Margaret Fuller's 'Conversations.'" Published in Nancy Craig Simmons. "Margaret Fuller's Boston Conversations: The 1839–1840 Series." *Studies in the American Renaissance* (1994): 195–266.

Peabody, William B. O. *Life of Mather*. Vol. 7 of *Sparks' American Biography*. Edited by Jared Sparks. Boston: Hill, Gray, and Company, 1836.

"The Periodical Press, Generally." *American Annals of Education* 8.6 (June 1838): 286.

"Preparatory Study of History." *American Annals of Education* 8.3 (March 1838): 103–7.

[Ripley, George]. "Prospectus for *The Dial: A Magazine for Literature, Philosophy, and Religion*." In *Transcendentalism: A Reader*. Edited by Joel Myerson. Oxford: Oxford University Press, 2000. 289–90.

Samuel Gray Ward and Anna Hazard Barker Ward Papers (MS Am 1465). Houghton Library. Harvard University.

The School Advertiser No. II. "The School Library." In Horace Mann. *Lecture on Education*. Boston: Marsh, Capen, Lyon, and Webb, 1840.

"The School Library." *Common School Journal* 1.12 (15 June 1839): 177–81.

"The School Library." *Common School Journal* 2.7 (1 April 1840): 106–7.

"The School Library." *Common School Journal* 4.7 (1 April 1842): 106–7.

"The School Library." *Connecticut Common School Journal* 3.10 (15 March 1841): 1.

"The School Library." In *Third Annual Report of the Board of Education, together with the Third Annual Report of the Secretary of the Board*. Boston: Dutton and Wentworth, 1840. 24–32.

"The School Library. Introductory Essay, Explanatory of the Plan." *Life and Voyages of Christopher Columbus.* Boston: Marsh, Capen, Lyon, and Webb, 1839.

"Schools in Massachusetts." *American Annals of Education* 7.3 (March 1837): 97–103.

Tappan, Caroline Sturgis. *The Magician's Show Box.* Boston: Ticknor and Fields, 1856.

———. *Rainbows for Children.* Edited by Lydia Maria Child. New York: Harper & Brothers, 1848.

Theodore Parker Papers. Microfilm edition. 4 reels. Boston: Massachusetts Historical Society, 1986.

Thoreau, Henry D. *Walden.* Edited by J. Lyndon Shanley. Princeton, NJ: Princeton University Press, 2004.

Secondary Sources

Anthony, David. *Paper Money Men: Commerce, Manhood, and the Sensational Public Sphere in Antebellum America.* Columbus: The Ohio State University Press, 2009.

Arac, Jonathan. "Narrative Forms." In *The Cambridge History of American Literature, Volume Two.* Edited by Sacvan Bercovitch. New York: Cambridge University Press, 1994. 605–777.

Ard, Patricia. "Transcendentalism for Children: Mary Peabody Mann's *The Flower People.*" In *Reinventing the Peabody Sisters.* Edited by Monika Elbert, Julie E. Hall, and Katharine Rodier. Iowa City: University of Iowa Press, 2006. 216–31.

Augst, Thomas. *The Clerks' Tale: Young Men and Moral Life in Nineteenth-Century America.* Chicago: University of Chicago Press, 2003.

Avallone, Charlene. "Elizabeth Palmer Peabody and the 'Art' of Conversation." In *Reinventing the Peabody Sisters.* Edited by Monika Elbert, Julie E. Hall, and Katharine Rodier. Iowa City: University of Iowa Press, 2006. 23–44.

Babb, Valerie. *Whiteness Visible: The Meaning of Whiteness in American Literature and Culture.* New York: New York University Press, 1998.

Baker, Noelle. "Conversations." In *The Oxford Handbook of Transcendentalism.* Edited by Joel Myerson, Sandra Harbert Petrulionis, and Laura Dassow Walls. New York: Oxford University Press, 2010. 348–61.

Baym, Nina. "The Ann Sisters: Elizabeth Peabody's Millennial Historicism." *American Literary History* 3.1 (Spring 1991): 27–45.

———. *Novels, Readers, and Reviewers: Responses to Fiction in Antebellum America.* Ithaca, NY: Cornell University Press, 1984.

———. *The Shape of Hawthorne's Career.* Ithaca, NY: Cornell University Press, 1976.

Belasco, Susan. "'The Animating Influences of Discord': Margaret Fuller in 1844." *Legacy* 20.1–2 (2003): 76–93.

Bickman, Martin. *Minding American Education: Reclaiming the Tradition of Active Learning.* New York: Teachers College Press, 2003.

Bolton, Charles. "Circulating Libraries in Boston, 1765–1865." *Publications of the Colonial Society in America* 11 (February 1907): 196–207.

Boylan, Anne. *Sunday-School: Formation of an American Institution, 1790–1880.* New Haven, CT: Yale University Press, 1988.

Brodhead, Richard. *Cultures of Letters: Scenes of Reading and Writing in Nineteenth-Century America.* Chicago: University of Chicago Press, 1993.

———. *The School of Hawthorne*. New York: Oxford University Press, 1986.
Brown, Gillian. "Hawthorne's American History." In *The Cambridge Companion to Nathaniel Hawthorne*. Edited by Ricard H. Millington. New York: Cambridge University Press, 2004. 121–42.
———. "The Metamorphic Book: Children's Print Culture in the Eighteenth Century." *Eighteenth Century Studies* 39.3 (2006): 351–62.
Buell, Lawrence. "American Civil War Poetry and the Meaning of Literary Commodification: Whitman, Melville, and Others." In *Reciprocal Influences: Literary Production, Dissemination, and Consumption in America*. Edited by Steven Fink and Susan Williams. Columbus: The Ohio State University Press, 1999. 123–38.
———. "Transcendentalist Literary Legacies." *In Transient and Permanent: The Transcendentalist Movement and its Contexts*. Edited by Charles Capper and Conrad Wright. Boston: Massachusetts Historical Society, 1999. 605–19.
Cane, Aleta Feinsod, and Susan Alves, eds. "American Women Writers and the Periodical: Creating a Constituency, Opening a Dialogue." In *"The Only Efficient Instrument": American Women Writers and the Periodical, 1837–1916*. Iowa City: University of Iowa Press, 2001. 1–19.
Capper, Charles. "'A Little Beyond': Transcendentalism in American History." In *Transient and Permanent: The Transcendentalist Movement and Its Contexts*. Edited by Charles Capper and Conrad Wright. Boston: Massachusetts Historical Society, 1999. 3–45.
———. *Margaret Fuller: An American Romantic Life*. 2 vols. New York: Oxford University Press, 1992 and 2007.
Carlson, Larry. "'Those Pure Pages of Yours': Bronson Alcott's Conversations with Children on the Gospels." *American Literature* 60.3 (October 1988): 451–60.
Charvat, William. *Literary Publishing in America, 1790–1850*. Amherst: University of Massachusetts Press, 1993.
———. *The Profession of Authorship in America, 1800–1870*. Edited by Matthew Bruccoli. New York: Columbia University Press, 1992.
Chevigny, Bell Gale. *The Woman and the Myth: Margaret Fuller's Life and Writings*. Boston: Northeastern University Press, 1994.
Colacurcio, Michael. *The Province of Piety: Moral History in Hawthorne's Early Tales*. Durham, NC: Duke University Press, 1995.
Cooke, Sylvia Jenkins. *Working Women, Literary Ladies: The Industrial Revolution and Female Aspiration*. New York: Columbia University Press, 2008.
Coultrap-McQuin, Susan. *Doing Literary Business: American Women Writers in Nineteenth-Century America*. Chapel Hill: University of North Carolina Press, 1990.
Crain, Patricia. *The Story of A: The Alphabetization of America from the New England Primer to The Scarlet Letter*. Stanford, CA: Stanford University Press, 2000.
Crouse, Jamie. "'If They Have a Moral Power': Margaret Fuller, Transcendentalism, and the Questions of Woman's Moral Nature." *American Transcendental Quarterly* 19.4 (December 2005): 259–79.
Crowley, J. Donald. "Historical Commentary." In Vol. 9 of *The Centenary Edition of the Works of Nathaniel Hawthorne*. Edited by William Charvat et al. Columbus: The Ohio State University Press, 1974. 485–533.
Culver, Raymond B. *Horace Mann and Religion in the Massachusetts Public Schools*. New York: Arno Press, 1969.

Deutsch, Helen. *Loving Dr. Johnson*. Chicago: University of Chicago Press, 2005.
Douglas, Ann. *The Feminization of American Culture*. New York: Alfred Knopf, 1977.
Dowling, David. *The Business of Literary Circles in Nineteenth-Century America*. New York: Palgrave Macmillan, 2011.
Eckel, Leslie. "Margaret Fuller's Conversational Journalism: New York, London, Rome." *Arizona Quarterly* 63.2 (2007): 27–50.
Elbert, Monika. "Elizabeth Peabody's Problematic Feminism and the Feminization of Transcendentalism." In *Reinventing the Peabody Sisters*. Edited by Monika Elbert, Julie E. Hall, and Katharine Rodier. Iowa City: University of Iowa Press, 2006. 199–215.
Ellison, Julie K. *Delicate Subjects: Romanticism, Gender, and the Ethics of Understanding*. Ithaca, NY: Cornell University Press, 1990.
Erlich, Gloria. *Family Themes and Hawthorne's Fiction*. New Brunswick, NJ: Rutgers University Press, 1984.
Everton, Michael J. *The Grand Chorus of Complaint: Authors and the Business Ethics of American Publishing*. New York: Oxford University Press, 2011.
Exman, Eugene. *The Brothers Harper*. New York: Harper & Row, 1965.
Ezell, Margaret. *Social Authorship and the Advent of Print*. Baltimore: Johns Hopkins University Press, 1999.
Felker, Christopher. *Reinventing Cotton Mather in the American Renaissance: Magnalia Christi Americana in Hawthorne, Stowe, and Stoddard*. Boston: Northeastern University Press, 1993.
Fergenson, Laraine. "Margaret Fuller as a Teacher in Providence: The School Journal of Anne Brown." *Studies in the American Renaissance* (1991): 59–118.
———. "Margaret Fuller in the Classroom: The Providence Period." *Studies in the American Renaissance* (1987): 131–42.
Fink, Stephen. "Antebellum Lady Editors and the Language of Authority." In *Blue Pencils and Hidden Hands: Women Editing Periodicals, 1830–1910*. Edited by Sharon Harris and Ellen Gruber Garvey. Boston: Northeastern University Press, 2004. 205–21.
———. "Margaret Fuller: The Evolution of a Woman of Letters." In *Reciprocal Influences: Literary Production, Distribution, and Consumption in America*. Edited by Steven Fink and Susan S. Williams. Columbus: The Ohio State University Press, 1999. 55–74.
———. *Prophet in the Marketplace*. Columbus: The Ohio State University Press, 1992.
Fleisher, Lisa. "Test Question Flunks" (includes an interview with Daniel Pinkwater). *The Wall Street Journal*. 20 April 2012. http://online.wsj.com.
Freeman, Robert. "Harper & Brothers' Family and School District Libraries, 1830–1846." In *Libraries to the People*. Edited by Robert Freeman and Robert Hovde. Jefferson, NC: McFarland & Company, 2003. 26–49.
Gibian, Peter. *Oliver Wendell Holmes and the Culture of Conversation*. Cambridge: Cambridge University Press, 2001.
Gilkes, Lillian B. "Hawthorne, Park Benjamin, and S. G. Goodrich: Three-Cornered Imbroglio." *Nathaniel Hawthorne Journal 1971*. Middletown, CT: Microcard Edition Books, 1971. 83–112.
Gilmore, Michael. *American Romanticism and the Marketplace*. Chicago: University of Chicago Press, 1985.
Ginsberg, Lesley. "Hawthorne, Grace Greenwood, and the Culture of Pedagogy." *Nathaniel Hawthorne Review* 36.1 (Spring 2010): 47–71.
———. "'Our Children are Our Best Works': Mary Ware Allen's Transcendental Education." In

The Worlds of Children, 1620–1920. Edited by Peter Benes and Jane Montague Benes. Boston: Boston University Press, 2004. 78–92.

Goodenough, Elizabeth. "Grandfather's Chair: Hawthorne's 'Deeper History' of New England." *Lion & the Unicorn* 15 (1991): 27–42.

Griffin, C. S. *Ferment of Reform, 1830–1860*. New York: Crowell, 1967.

Groves, Jeffrey D. "Judging Books by their Covers." In *Reading Books: Essays on the Material Text and Literature in America*. Edited by Michele Moylan and Lane Stiles. Amherst: University of Massachusetts Press, 1996. 75–100.

Gura, Phillip. *American Transcendentalism: A History*. New York: Hill and Wang, 2007.

Gustafson, Sandra. "Choosing a Medium: Margaret Fuller and the Forms of Sentiment." *American Quarterly* 47 (1995): 34–65.

Hall, David. "The Uses of Literacy in New England, 1600–1850." Reprinted in *Cultures of Print: Essays in the History of the Book*. Amherst: University of Massachusetts Press, 1996. 36–78.

Hartocollis, Anemona. "When Pineapple Races Hare, Students Lose." *New York Times*. 20 April 2012. http://www.nytimes.com.

Herbert, T. Walter. *Dearest Beloved: The Hawthornes and the Making of the Middle-Class Family*. Berkeley: University of California Press, 1993.

Hewitt, Elizabeth. *Correspondence and American Literature*. New York: Cambridge University Press, 2004.

Hollinger, David. "Ethnic Diversity, Cosmopolitanism, and the Emergence of the American Liberal Intelligentsia." *American Quarterly* 27.2 (May 1975): 133–51.

Howsam, Leslie. "Sustained Literary Ventures: The Series in Victorian Book Publishing." *Publishing History* 31 (1992): 5–26.

Hurst, C. Michael. "Bodies in Transition: Transcendental Feminism in Margaret Fuller's *Woman in the Nineteenth Century*." *Arizona Quarterly* 66.4 (Winter 2010): 1–32.

Idol, John, Jr. "Elizabeth Palmer Peabody: A Tireless Hawthorne Booster." In *Hawthorne and Women: Engendering and Expanding the Hawthorne Tradition*. Edited by John Idol, Jr. and Melinda Ponder. Amherst: University of Massachusetts Press, 1999. 36–44.

Irons, Susan. "Channing's Influence on Peabody: Self-Culture and the Danger of Egoism." *Studies in the American Renaissance* (1992): 121–35.

Jackson, Leon. *The Business of Letters: Authorial Economies in Antebellum America*. Stanford, CA: Stanford University Press, 2008.

Johnson, Harriet Hall. "Margaret Fuller as Known by her Scholars." Reprinted in *Critical Essays on Margaret Fuller*. Edited by Joel Myerson. Boston: G. K. Hall & Company, 1980. 134–40.

Jones, Diane Brown. "Elizabeth Palmer Peabody's Transcendental Manifesto." *Studies in the American Renaissance* (1992): 195–207.

Jones, Wayne Allen. "Sometimes Things Just Don't Work Out: Hawthorne's Income from *Twice-Told Tales* 1837, and Another 'Good Thing' for Hawthorne." *Nathaniel Hawthorne Journal* (1975): 21–23.

Kaestle, Carl. *Pillars of the Republic: Common Schools and American Society, 1780–1860*. New York: Hill and Wang, 1983.

Kaser, David. *A Book for a Sixpence: The Circulating Library in America*. Pittsburgh: Beta Phi Mu, 1980.

Kelley, Mary. "Introduction" to "Section III. Educating the Citizenry." In *A History of the Book in America, Volume 2: 1790–1840*. Edited by Robert Gross and Mary Kelley. Chapel Hill: University of North Carolina Press, 2010. 269–72.

———. *Learning to Stand and Speak: Women, Education, and Public Life in America's Republic.* Chapel Hill: University of North Carolina Press, 2006.

———. *Public Woman, Private Stage: Literary Domesticity in Nineteenth-Century America.* New York: Oxford University Press, 1984.

Kett, Joseph. *The Pursuit of Knowledge under Difficulties.* Stanford, CA: Stanford University Press, 1994.

Kolodney, Annette. "Inventing a Feminist Discourse: Rhetoric and Resistance in Margaret Fuller's *Woman in the Nineteenth Century.*" *New Literary History* 25.2 (Spring 1994): 355–82.

Kopacz, Paula. "The School Journal of Hannah (Anna) Gale." *Studies in the American Renaissance* (1996): 67–113.

Laffrado, Laura. *Hawthorne's Literature for Children.* Athens: University of Georgia Press, 1992.

Lamoreaux, Naomi. *Insider Lending: Banks, Personal Connections, and Economic Development in Industrial New England.* New York: Cambridge University Press, 1994.

Lang, Amy Schrager. *The Syntax of Class: Writing Inequality in Nineteenth-Century America.* Princeton, NJ: Princeton University Press, 2003.

Lehuu, Isabelle. *Carnival on the Page: Popular Print Media in Antebellum America.* Chapel Hill: University of North Carolina Press, 2000.

Levin, David. *History as Romantic Art.* Stanford, CA: Stanford University Press, 1959.

Little, Greta D., and Joel Myerson, eds. "Introduction." In *Three Novels by Christopher Pearse Cranch.* Athens: University of Georgia Press, 2010. ix–xxxvi.

Marshall, Megan. *The Peabody Sisters: Three Women Who Ignited American Romanticism.* New York: Houghton Mifflin, 2005.

Matthews, Samantha. "Gems, Texts, and Confessions: Writing Readers in Late-Victorian Autographic Gift-Books." *Publishing History* 62 (207): 53–80.

McGill, Meredith L. *American Literature and the Culture of Reprinting, 1834–1853.* Philadelphia: University of Pennsylvania Press, 2003.

McGrath, Ben. "Food Groups." *The New Yorker.* 7 May 2012. http://www.newyorker.com.

Mellow, James. *Hawthorne in His Times.* Baltimore: Johns Hopkins University Press, 1998.

Mendelsohn, Jack. *Channing: The Reluctant Radical.* Boston: Little, Brown, & Company, 1971.

Messerli, Jonathan. *Horace Mann: A Biography.* New York: Alfred A. Knopf, Inc., 1971.

Milder, Robert. "The Radical Emerson?" In *The Cambridge Companion to Ralph Waldo Emerson.* Edited by Joel Porte and Saundra Morris. Cambridge: Cambridge University Press, 1999. 49–75.

Miller, Perry. *The Transcendentalists: An Anthology.* Cambridge, MA: Harvard University Press, 1950.

Mitchell, Thomas. *Hawthorne's Fuller Mystery.* Amherst: University of Massachusetts Press, 1998.

Monaghan, Charles, and E. Jennifer Monaghan. "Schoolbooks." In *A History of the Book in America, Volume 2: 1790–1840.* Edited by Robert Gross and Mary Kelley. Chapel Hill: University of North Carolina Press, 2010. 304–17.

Monahan, Rachel. "Talking Pineapple Question on State Exam Stumps . . . Everyone." *New York Daily News.* 19 April 2012. http://www.nydailynews.com.

Moran, Gerald, and Maris Vinovskis. "Schools." In *A History of the Book in America, Volume 2: 1790–1840.* Edited by Robert Gross and Mary Kelley. Chapel Hill: University of North Carolina Press, 2010. 286–303.

Mott, Frank Luther. *A History of American Magazines, Vol. 1.* New York: D. Appleton and Company, 1930.

Mott, Wesley T. "Education." In *The Oxford Handbook of Transcendentalism*. Edited by Joel Myerson et al. New York: Oxford University Press, 2010. 153–71.

Myerson, Joel. *The New England Transcendentalists and the "Dial": A History of the Magazine and Its Contributors*. Rutherford, NJ: Fairleigh Dickinson University Press, 1980.

Nord, David Paul. *Faith in Reading*. New York: Oxford University Press, 2004.

Okker, Patricia. *Our Sister Editors: Sarah J. Hale and the Tradition of Nineteenth-Century American Women Editors*. Athens: University of Georgia Press, 1995.

Packer, Barbara. "The Transcendentalists." In *The Cambridge History of American Literature, Volume Two: Prose Writing, 1820–1860*. Edited by Sacvan Bercovitch. New York: Cambridge University Press, 1994. 329–604.

Parille, Ken. "Allegories of Childhood Gender: Hawthorne and the Material Boy." *Nathaniel Hawthorne Review* 36.1 (Spring 2010): 112–37.

———. *Boys at Home: Discipline, Masculinity, and the "Boy Problem" in Nineteenth-Century American Literature*. Knoxville: University of Tennessee Press, 2009.

Pearce, Roy Harvey. "Historical Introduction." In Vol. 6 of *The Centenary Edition of the Works of Nathaniel Hawthorne*. Edited by William Charvat et al. Columbus: The Ohio State University Press, 1972. 287–311.

Person, Leland. "Hawthorne's Early Tales: Male Authorship, Domestic Violence, and Female Readers." In *Hawthorne and the Real: Bicentennial Essays*. Edited by Millicent Bell. Columbus: The Ohio State University Press, 2005. 125–43.

Pinkwater, Daniel. "Pineapple idiots! Who knew my book would be used for the world's dumbest test question." *New York Daily News*. 21 April 2012. http://articles.nydailynews.com.

Post-Lauria, Sheila. *Correspondent Colorings: Melville in the Marketplace*. Amherst: University of Massachusetts Press, 1996.

———. "Magazine Practices and Melville's Israel Potter." In *Periodical Literature in Nineteenth-Century America*. Edited by Kenneth W. Price and Susan Belasco Smith. Charlottesville: University of Virginia Press, 1995. 115–32.

Price, Kenneth, and Susan Belasco Smith, eds. "Introduction: Periodical Literature in Social and Historical Context." In *Periodical Literature in Nineteenth-Century America*. Charlottesville: University of Virginia Press, 1995. 3–16.

Reynolds, Larry. "From *Dial* Essay to New York Book: The Making of *Woman in the Nineteenth Century*." In *Periodical Literature in Nineteenth Century America*. Edited by Kenneth M. Price and Susan Belasco Smith. Charlottesville: University Press of Virginia, 1995. 17–34.

———. "'Strangely Ajar with the Human Race': Hawthorne, Slavery, and the Question of Moral Responsibility." In *Hawthorne and the Real: Bicentennial Essays*. Edited by Millicent Bell. Columbus: The Ohio State University Press, 2005. 40–69.

Richardson, Robert. *William James: In the Maelstrom of American Modernism*. Boston: Houghton Mifflin Company, 2006.

Robbins, Sarah. *Managing Literacy, Mothering America: Women's Narratives on Reading and Writing in the Nineteenth Century*. Pittsburgh: University of Pittsburgh Press, 2004.

———. "Re-Making Barbauld's Primers: A Case Study in the Americanization of British Literary Pedagogy." *Children's Literature Association Quarterly* 21.4 (Winter 1996–97): 158–69.

Roberts, Josephine. "Elizabeth Peabody and the Temple School." *New England Quarterly* 15.3 (September 1942): 497–508.

Ronda, Bruce A. *Elizabeth Palmer Peabody: A Reformer on Her Own Terms*. Cambridge, MA: Harvard University Press, 1999.

---. "Elizabeth Palmer Peabody's Views of the Child." *Emerson Society Quarterly* 23.2 (1977): 106–13.

---. "Elizabeth Peabody and the Fate of Transcendentalism." In *Reinventing the Peabody Sisters*. Edited by Monika Elbert, Julie E. Hall, and Katharine Rodier. Iowa City: University of Iowa Press, 2006. 232–47.

---. "Print and Pedagogy: The Career of Elizabeth Peabody." In *A Living of Words: American Women in Print Culture*. Edited by Susan Albertine. Knoxville: University of Tennessee Press, 1995. 35–48.

Rose, Anne. *Transcendentalism as a Social Movement, 1830–1850*. New Haven, CT: Yale University Press, 1981.

---. *Voices of the Marketplace: American Thought and Culture, 1830–1860*. New York: Twayne Publishers, 1994.

Rosenthal, Bernard. "The *Dial*, Transcendentalism, and Margaret Fuller." *English Language Notes* 8 (1970): 28–36.

Rowland, William, Jr. *Literature and the Marketplace: Romantic Writers and their Audiences in Great Britain and the United States*. Lincoln: University of Nebraska Press, 1996.

Sánchez, María Carla. *Reforming the World: Social Activism and the Problem of Fiction in Nineteenth-Century America*. Iowa City: University of Iowa Press, 2008.

Sánchez-Eppler, Karen. *Dependent States: The Child's Part in Nineteenth-Century American Culture*. Chicago: University of Chicago Press, 2005.

---. "Hawthorne and the Writing of Childhood." In *The Cambridge Companion to Nathaniel Hawthorne*. Edited by Richard H. Millington. New York: Cambridge University Press, 2004. 143–61.

Shealy, Daniel. "Margaret Fuller and her 'Maiden': Evelina Metcalf's 1838 School Journal." *Studies in the American Renaissance* (1996): 41–65.

Shuffelton, Frank. "Margaret Fuller at the Greene Street School: The Journal of Evelina Metcalf." *Studies in the American Renaissance* (1985): 29–46.

Silver, Rollo. *The Boston Book Trade: 1800–1825*. New York: New York Public Library, 1949.

Simmons, Nancy Craig. "Margaret Fuller's Boston Conversations: The 1839–40 Series." *Studies in the American Renaissance* (1994): 195–225.

Smith, Henry Nash. "Emerson's Problem of Vocation: A Note on 'The American Scholar.'" *New England Quarterly* 12.1 (March 1939): 52–67.

Sorby, Angela. *Schoolroom Poets: Childhood, Performance, and the Place of American Poetry, 1865–1917*. Durham: University of New Hampshire Press, 2005.

Steele, Jeffrey. "Keys to 'the labyrinth of my own being': Margaret Fuller's Epistolary Invention of the Self." In *Letters and Cultural Transformations in the United States, 1760–1860*. Edited by Theresa Strouth Gaul and Sharon Harris. Burlington, VT: Ashgate Publishing, 2009. 99–116.

---. "The Limits of Political Sympathy: Emerson, Fuller, and Woman's Rights." In *The Emerson Dilemma: Essays in Emerson and Social Reform*. Edited by T. Gregory Garvey. Athens: University of Georgia Press, 2001. 115–35.

Stern, Madeleine. "Elizabeth Peabody's Foreign Library (1840)." In *Books and Book People in Nineteenth-Century America*. New York: R. R. Bowker, 1978. 121–35.

Story, Ronald. "Class and Culture in Boston: the Athenaeum, 1807–1860." *American Quarterly* 27.2 (May 1975): 178–99.

Strong, Judith Albert. "Margaret Fuller and Mary Ware Allen: 'In Youth an Insatiate Student'—A Certain Kind of Friendship." *Thoreau Quarterly Journal* 12 (July 1980): 9–22.

———. "Margaret Fuller's Row at the Greene Street School: Early Female Education in Providence, 1837–1839." *Rhode Island History* 42 (May 1983): 43–55.

———. "Transcendental School Journals in Nineteenth-Century America." *Journal of Psychohistory* 9 (Summer 1981): 105–26.

———. "Transition in Transcendental Education: The Schools of Bronson Alcott and Hiram Fuller." *Educational Studies* 11 (Fall 1980): 209–19.

Tamarkin, Elisa. *Anglophilia: Deference, Devotion, and Antebellum America*. Chicago: University of Chicago Press, 2007.

Tebbel, John. *A History of Book Publishing in the United States, Vol. 1*. New York: R. R. Bowker Company, 1972.

Tharp, Louise Hall. *Until Victory: Horace Mann and Mary Peabody*. Boston: Little, Brown and Company, 1953.

Theroux, Paul. "Introduction." In Henry David Thoreau, *The Maine Woods*. Edited by Joseph Moldenhauer. Princeton, NJ: Princeton University Press, 2004. ix–xxv.

Urbanski, Marie Mitchell Olsen. "'Woman in the Nineteenth Century': Genesis, Form, Tone, and Rhetorical Devices." In *Margaret Fuller: Visionary of the New Age*. Orono, ME: Northern Lights, 1994. 160–80.

Valenti, Patricia. "'None But Imaginative Authority': Nathaniel Hawthorne and the Progress of Nineteenth-Century (Juvenile) Literature in America." *Nathaniel Hawthorne Review* 36.1 (Spring 2010): 1–24.

Vásquez, Mark G. *Authority and Reform: Religious and Educational Discourses in Nineteenth-Century New England Literature*. Knoxville: University of Tennessee Press, 2003.

———. "Declaration and Deference: Elizabeth Palmer Peabody, Mary Peabody Mann, and the Complex Rhetoric of Mediation." In *Reinventing the Peabody Sisters*. Edited by Monika Elbert, Julie E. Hall, and Katharine Rodier. Iowa City: University of Iowa Press, 2006. 45–65.

Versluis, Arthur. *American Transcendentalism and Asian Religions*. New York: Oxford University Press, 1993.

Wadsworth, Sarah A. *In the Company of Books: Literature and Its "Classes" in Nineteenth-Century America*. Amherst: University of Massachusetts Press, 2006.

Walters, Ronald G. *American Reformers, 1815–1860*. New York: Hill and Wang, 1997.

Warren, James Perrin. *Culture of Eloquence: Oratory and Reform in Antebellum America*. University Park: Pennsylvania State University Press, 1999.

Wayne, Tiffany. *Woman Thinking: Feminism and Transcendentalism in Nineteenth-Century America*. New York: Lexington Books, 2005.

Wilson, John B. "A Transcendentalist Minority Report." *New England Quarterly* 29.2 (June 1956): 141–58.

Wilson, Leslie Perrin. "'No Worthless Books:' Elizabeth Peabody's Foreign Library, 1840–1852." *Papers of the Bibliographical Society of America* 99.1 (March 2005): 113–52.

Winship, Michael. *American Literary Publishing in the Mid-Nineteenth Century: The Business of Ticknor and Fields*. Cambridge: Cambridge University Press, 1995.

———. "Manufacturing and Book Production." In *A History of the Book in America, Volume 3: The Industrial Book, 1840–1880*. Edited by Scott Casper et al. Chapel Hill: University of North Carolina Press, 2007. 40–69.

———. *Ticknor and Fields: The Business of Literary Publishing in the United States of the Nineteenth Century*. Chapel Hill: University of North Carolina Press, 1992.

———. "The Transatlantic Book Trade." In *Reciprocal Influences: Literary Production, Distribution, and Consumption in America*. Edited by Steven Fink and Susan S. Williams. Columbus: The Ohio State University Press, 1999. 98–122.

Zboray, Ronald. *A Fictive People: Antebellum Economic Development and the American Reading Public*. New York: Oxford University Press, 1993.

Zboray, Ronald, and Mary Saracino Zboray. *Literary Dollars and Social Sense: A People's History of the Mass Market*. New York: Routledge, 2005.

———. "Transcendentalism in Print: Production, Dissemination, and Common Reception." In *Transient and Permanent: The Transcendentalist Movement and Its Contexts*. Edited by Charles Capper and Conrad Wright. Boston: Massachusetts Historical Society, 1999. 310–81.

Zwarg, Christina. *Feminist Conversations: Fuller, Emerson, and the Play of Reading*. Ithaca, NY: Cornell University Press, 1995.

———. "The Storied Facts of Margaret Fuller." *The New England Quarterly: A Historical Review of New England Life and Letters* 69.1 (March 1996): 128–42.

INDEX

Abbott, Jacob: *Rollo* books, 76
Abbott, John: *Child at Home*, 153n25
abolition: 5, 7, 11, 15, 39, 100. *See also* Channing, William Ellery; Mann, Horace
Aikin, John: 17, 19. *See also* Barbauld, Anna Laetitia
Alcott, Bronson, 9, 123, 129; egotism, 85, 86, 89, 90, 165n14, 168n48; on books and school libraries, 93–94, 96; relationship with Elizabeth Peabody, 83–90, 165n15, 167n28; Temple School, 83–90, 99–108, 138–39, 140, 166n18, 166n19, 167n33, 167n35, 173n7; *Conversations with Children upon the Gospels* (with Peabody), 4, 83, 85–86, 87–90, 140, 166n23; *Record of a School* (Peabody), 84. *See also* Peabody, Elizabeth
Alcott, William, 9. *See also American Annals of Education*
Alexandrian Library, 1, 7, 8, 10, 13, 50–51
Allen, Mary Ware, 109–10, 111–12, 132, 140
American Annals of Education (Alcott, ed.), 6, 9, 10–11, 69
"American Literature" (Fuller), 12, 134, 135–36
American Stationers' Company, 53, 61. *See also* Goodrich, Samuel
Anglophilia, 37–38. *See also* transatlantic literary influences

annual gift books, 43, 44, 45, 53
Anthony, David, 162n44
Atlantic Monthly (Lowell, ed.), 141
authorship, professional and the desire for remuneration, 2, 3, 5, 7, 9, 11–12, 14, 15, 18, 22, 24–27, 48, 51, 53–55, 56–57, 60–61, 66, 70–78, 90–91, 136, 137–39, 140, 141, 142, 147n9, 154n28, 154n31, 158n76, 159n9, 159n10, 160n19, 162n44m 163n45, 175n39. *See also* Hawthorne, Nathaniel
autographs, 30, 31

Bancroft, George, 21, 27, 58, 155n35, 170n65; *History of the United States,* 27
Barbauld, Anna Laetitia, 17–18, 43; *Evenings at Home,* 18, 36; *Hymns in Prose,* 18; *Lessons for Children,* 18; *Things by their Right Names* (ed. Hale), 17–18, 19, 34, 35, 36–38, 39, 40, 41, 42; "The Manufacture of Paper," 36–37; "On Manufactures," 42. *See also* Hale, Sarah J.
Baym, Nina, 63–64, 159n7, 164n7
Belcher, Jonathan, 60
The Bible, 14, 43
bibliomania, 51, 158n2
Bigelow, Jacob: *The Useful Arts*, 19, 29
Biographical Stories for Children (Hawthorne), 13, 70–75, 76, 138, 163n46

Bliss, Elizabeth David, 91
The Blithedale Romance (Hawthorne), 162n44
books, cost of, 8, 14, 21, 23, 24, 30, 43, 54, 94, 97, 99, 152n18, 153n19, 153n21
Boston, 4, 6, 9, 15, 20, 21, 24, 47, 64–65, 67, 70, 79, 80, 81, 82, 83, 84, 86, 87, 91, 93, 94, 96, 97, 99, 100, 101, 102, 103, 104, 106, 113–18, 123, 125, 128, 144, 153n22, 165n11, 169n52, 169n55, 171n74
Boston Morning Post, 168n39
Boston Athenaeum, 94, 97, 169n50. *See also* libraries
Boston Courier, 166n27
Boston News Letter, 62
Boston Quarterly, 99
Boswell, James, 4, 71, 148n11; *Life of Johnson*, 72, 163n47. *See also* Johnson, Samuel
Boys' and Girls' Magazine, 75
Bradford, George, 103, 165n11
British literature, 12, 13, 17–18, 32, 34, 37–38, 42, 54, 70–75, 93, 99, 103, 118, 144, 153n19, 170n65. *See also* Barbauld, Anna Laetitia; Boswell, James; Bulwer-Lytton, Edward; Johnson, Samuel; transatlantic literary influences
Brodhead, Richard, 63, 64, 156n41, 161n25, 162n43, 178n77
Brown, Ann, 130–31
Brown, Gillian, 59, 69
Brown, James, 155n35
Buckingham, Joseph, 166n27
Buell, Lawrence, 10
Bulwer-Lytton, Edward, 93, 168n44; *Henry Pelham*, 93; *Paul Clifford*, 93

Capen, Nahum, 22, 42–43, 47, 158n70, 160n16
capitalism, 15, 92, 172n4
Capper, Charles, 123, 172n1, 174n26, 176n48
Carey, Matthew, 128
Carové, Friedrich Wilhelm, 144

Carlyle, Thomas, 99, 129, 165n13
Channing, William Ellery, 83–84, 87, 97, 101, 107, 166n18, 166n19, 170n65; on circulating libraries, 95; doubts about Peabody's business plans, 96, 103, 169n57, 171n71; and transcendentalism, 83, 164n7, 165n13; *Emancipation*, 11, 99–100, 170n67, 171n68; *Slavery*, 171n68
Channing, William Henry, 113, 116, 119, 120, 121, 122, 123, 124, 126
Charvat, William, 147n9
Cheever, Ezekiel, 62, 63, 64, 67, 161n34
Chevigny, Bell, 112
Child at Home (Abbot), 153n25
children's literature, 4, 49, 59, 143–44. *See also* Cranch, Christopher; Embury, Emma; Fuller, Margaret; Hale, Sarah J.; Hawthorne, Nathaniel; Mann, Horace; Tappan, Caroline Sturgis
The Christian Examiner, 1, 27, 29, 30, 49, 99
Clarke, James Freeman, 114, 115, 123, 124, 127
Clarke, Sarah, 114, 124, 176n55
Coleman, Samuel, 75–76
Combe, George, 47
Common School Journal, 6, 46, 47, 157n68
Connecticut, 27
Conversations with Children upon the Gospels (Alcott and Peabody), 4, 83, 85–86, 87–90, 140, 166n23
Cooke, George Willis, 172n81
copyright, 18, 25, 27, 42–43, 54, 99, 100, 153n19
corporal punishment, 63, 64, 85, 138–39, 161n32
coterie, 2, 5, 22, 80, 82, 97, 98, 100, 103, 117, 122, 123, 124–25, 133, 137–38, 148n13. *See also* Fuller, Margaret; Peabody, Elizabeth
Coultrap-McQuin, Susan, 100
Crain, Patricia, 28
Cranch, Christopher Pearse, 143–44; *Koboltozo*, 143; *Last of the Huggermuggers*, 143
culture, American antebellum, 2, 3, 5, 7, 13,

14–16, 32, 34, 37, 38, 40, 42, 44–46, 53, 59, 94, 97, 103, 105, 108, 117, 118, 119, 137, 144, 145, 161n32, 172n4
"culture of reprinting." *See* McGill, Meredith; piracy, transatlantic

Dana, Richard Henry Jr., 25, 142, 151n4, 155n35; *Two Years before the Mast*, 142, 155n35
Democratic party, 47, 48, 67; "hard" democrats & metallic currency vs. paper currency debate, 61–62, 63, 70, 73, 161n30
The Dial, 4, 5, 8, 12, 81, 82, 84, 97–99, 102–6, 107, 113, 114, 118–32, 133–34, 135, 143, 147n9, 170n65, 171n77, 172n81, 174n35, 175n36, 175n39, 175n46, 176n47, 176n48, 176n55, 176n56, 176n57, 177n59, 177n60, 177n61, 177n62, 177n63, 177n64, 178n68, 178n70. *See also* Emerson, Ralph Waldo; Fuller, Margaret; Peabody, Elizabeth; Thoreau, Henry David
"District School Libraries" (Mann), 21, 26, 32, 38, 154n31
Dowling, David, 5, 171n68, 177n62

education, democratic, 2, 5, 7, 13, 10, 15, 18, 106, 107, 113, 122, 134, 137
Elbert, Monika, 164n8
Ellison, Julie, 115, 116
Emancipation (Channing), 11, 99–100, 170n67, 171n68
Embury, Emma: *Pictures of Early Life*, 19, 43; "A Day's Pleasure," 44–46
Emerson, Lidian, 112
Emerson, Ralph Waldo, 3, 5, 8, 81, 82, 84, 104, 107, 113, 114, 143, 147n9, 170n65, 175n36, 175n46, 177n61, 177n63; and *The Dial*, 5, 102–3, 106, 118–32, 133–34, 135, 171n77, 172n81, 174n35, 175n39, 176n47, 176n48, 176n55, 176n56, 176n57, 177n59, 177n60, 177n62, 177n64, 178n68, 178n70; at mixed-company Conversations, 130–31; *Memoirs of Margaret Fuller Ossoli*, 111, 112, 113, 114, 115, 116, 118, 119–20, 121–22, 123, 125, 135, 136, 141, 143, 144, 175n39; "Conversations in Boston," 119, 138; *Nature*, 3; "Self-Reliance," 16, 125; "The Editors to the Reader," 133; "Thoughts on Modern Literature, 124." *See also* Fuller, Margaret
Evenings at Home (Barbauld), 18, 36
Everett, Edward, 19, 152n16, 155n34, 155n35

Family Library, 153n19
Famous Old People (Hawthorne), 50–51, 53, 60, 62–65, 77, 160n17, 161n34
"festive discipline," 28–29
fiction, uses for and criticisms of, 7, 9, 10, 28, 43, 50, 51, 53, 55, 57, 58, 66, 72, 93, 95, 143, 168n44
Fink, Steven, 107, 126, 177n59
The Flower People (Mann), 138, 170n66
Fowle, William, 157n68
Franklin, Benjamin, 71
French literature, 12, 80, 96, 99, 103
Froebel's kindergarten model, 5
Fuller, Hiram, 108, 112
Fuller, Margaret, 2, 4–5, 7, 13–14, 15, 87, 97, 104, 105–36, 137, 141, 142, 143–44, 170n66, 173n7, 174n29, 175n36; and children's literature, 143–44, 170n66; and "multi-vocality," 106, 122, 172n3; Conversations in Boston, 4, 81, 106, 113–18, 130–31, 175n41, 176n46; feelings on coterie, 5–6, 117, 122, 133; and Emerson, 5, 104, 106, 107, 111, 112, 114; and Greene Street School, 14, 106, 107–13, 114, 115–16, 117, 120, 130, 132, 140; and the *New York Tribune*, 15, 106, 134, 135, 136, 144, 179n84; as editor of *The Dial*, 4, 5, 12, 14, 102, 103, 105–7, 118–32, 133–34, 135, 136, 144, 170n66, 171n77, 174n35, 175n39, 175n40, 176n47, 176n55, 176n56, 177n62, 177n64m 178n68, 178n70;

as periodicalist, 1-, 106, 134–36, 144, 179n84; as translator, 12, 81, 113, 130, 131, 143–44, 178n70; 178n71; "American Literature," 12, 134, 135–36; "A Short Essay on Critics," 133–34; "The Great Lawsuit," 106; *Memoirs,* 111, 112, 113, 114, 115, 116, 118, 119–20, 121–22, 123, 125, 135, 136, 141, 143, 144, 175n39; *Woman in the Nineteenth Century,* 14, 106, 107, 109, 110, 117, 125, 130, 135

Gale, Anna, 108
German literature, 12, 80, 96, 97, 99, 103, 105, 107, 113, 143–44, 170n65
Gilmore, Michael, 147n9
Ginsberg, Lesley, 7, 159n3
Godey's Lady's Book, 10, 18, 48
Goethe, Johann Wolfgang von, 107, 113
Goodenough, Elizabeth, 161n34
Goodrich, Samuel, 53–54, 76, 159n9, 159n20; *Recollections of a Lifetime,* 8–9; *The Token,* 53, 159n8
Grandfather's Chair series (Hawthorne): 56, 57, 60, 63–70, 71, 76, 92, 160n17. See also *Grandfather's Chair; Famous Old People; The Liberty Tree*
Grandfather's Chair (Hawthorne), 4, 13, 56, 57, 58, 59, 61, 62, 63–64, 69–70, 144, 160n17, 160n19, 171n67
Graves, Juliet, 116
Gurney, Joseph John, 171n68
Gustafson, Sandra, 116

Hale, Edward Everett, 103
Hale, Sarah J., 17–18, 19; *Juvenile Budget Opened,* 17, 19, 40; *Juvenile Budget Reopened,* 18, 19, 40; "Sketches of American Character," 34, 35; "Sketch of Barbauld's Life," 34, 35, 36; *Things by Their Right Names* (Barbauld), 17, 18, 34, 35, 36–38, 39, 41, 42
Hale, Sarah P. E., 19, 25, 46–47, 48, 152n16, 158n76

Harper & Brothers, 15, 23, 24, 27, 47, 48, 153n19, 158n76
Harper's *School District Library,* 24, 48, 152n18
Harrison, William Henry, 67, 68
Hawthorne, Elizabeth, 4
Hawthorne, Louisa, 53–54
Hawthorne, Nathaniel, 2, 3, 5, 7, 11, 14, 15, 25, 49, 50–78, 81, 82, 102, 137, 142, 143, 161n29, 161n30, 161n34, 162n35, 162n41, 162n43, 162n44, 177n61; and the Boston customhouse, 55, 56, 160n16, 160n19; and Brook Farm, 56–57; and children's literature, 4, 5, 10, 11–12, 13, 49, 51–78, 140, 159n3, 160n16, 160n24, 162n44, 163n48; and collaboration with Longfellow / "Boys' Wonder-Horn," 56, 76, 159n5, 160n18; and desire for financial success, 51, 53–55, 56–57, 60–61, 66, 70–78, 90–91, 147n9, 159n8, 159n9, 159n10, 160n19, 162n44, 163n45; and the "fountain of youth," 12, 55; and Mary Silsbee, 57; editor of *The American Magazine of Useful and Entertaining Knowledge,* 53; *Biographical Stories for Children,* 13, 71, 74, 76, 138, 163n46; preface to *Biographical Stories,* 71; "Samuel Johnson," 70–75; *The Blithedale Romance,* 162n17; *Famous Old People,* 60, 64, 160n17; "Devil in Manuscript," 50–51, 53, 77; "The Old-Fashioned School," 62–64, 67, 161n34; "The Rejected Blessing," 64–65; *Grandfather's Chair* series (also known as *The Whole History of Grandfather's Chair*), 56, 60, 63–70, 71, 76, 92, 160n17; *Grandfather's Chair* (first volume of series), 4, 13, 56, 57, 59, 61, 62, 63–64, 144, 160n17, 160n19, 171n67; preface to *Grandfather's Chair,* 58, 59; "Lady Arbella," 69–70; "New England Historical Sketches," 22, 160n16; *Peter Parley's Universal History,* 54, 59, 159n10, 163n45; *The House of the Seven Gables,* 163n44; *The Liberty Tree,* 68, 160n17; "Boston Tea Party," 68; "Grandfather's Dream," 69;

"The Hutchinson Mob," 67–68; "The Tory's Farewell," 68; *The Scarlet Letter*, 76; *Tanglewood Tales*, 4, 76, 143; *True Stories from History and Biography*, 76, 77; *Twice-Told Tales*, 22, 53, 54, 57, 61, 160n16; *A Wonder Book for Girls and Boys*, 4, 59, 76–78, 143
Hawthorne, Sophia (née Peabody), 3, 51, 52, 56, 57, 60, 61, 66, 70, 74, 160n16, 162n44, 163n45
Hedge, Frederick Henry, 4, 84, 125, 126
Henry Pelham (Bulwer-Lytton), 93
Herbert, T. Walter, 162n43
Hewitt, Elizabeth, 113, 131–32
Higginson, Thomas Wentworth, 80
Hillard, George, 159n3
history, 9, 17, 22, 27, 55, 58, 59, 60, 69, 71, 81, 108, 109
Hollinger, David, 164n8
Holmes, Oliver Wendell, 6, 77
Houghton Mifflin, 78
House of the Seven Gables (Hawthorne), 163n44
Howe, Samuel Gridley, 22
Howsam, Leslie, 151n4
Hutchinson, Thomas, 67–68
Hymns in Prose (Barbauld), 18

illustrations and engravings, 29, 30, 39, 143, 144, 155n32, 156n44
Indiana, 27
Ingraham, Joseph, 36–37, 42, 44
Iowa, 27
Irving, Washington, 8, 18; *Life and Voyages of Columbus*, 19, 26–27; *The Sketch-Book of Geoffrey Crayon*, 11, 51
Italian literature, 99, 170n65

James, Henry, 82
James, William, 143
Johnson, Harriet Hall, 109, 112, 115
Johnson, Samuel, 13, 70–75, 163n47
The Juvenile Budget Opened (Hale), 17, 19, 40

The Juvenile Budget Reopened (Hale), 18, 19, 40

Kelley, Mary, 150n41
Koboltzo (Cranch), 143
Kolodny, Annette, 113

Laffrado, Laura, 52, 59, 62, 163n46
Last of the Huggermuggers (Cranch), 143
Lee, Chloe, 39
Lessons for Children (Barbauld), 18
The Liberty Tree (Hawthorne), 67–68, 69, 160n17
libraries, 8, 16, 32, 43, 44; circulating, 79, 94–95, 96, 99, 101, 169n53; college, 94, 97; public, 6, 24, 27, 153n23; school, 1, 4, 9, 17, 20, 21, 23, 24–26, 27, 47, 77–78; social, 24, 94. *See also* Boston Athenaeum; Peabody, Elizabeth
Life and Voyages of Columbus (Irving), 19, 26–27
Life of Johnson (Boswell), 72, 163n47
literary marketplace, antebellum, 2, 3, 5, 7, 8, 9, 10, 11, 12, 13, 14, 15, 16, 18, 20, 22, 24, 27, 28, 30, 32, 34, 38, 42, 46–49, 50–51, 52–54, 60, 62, 73–74, 76–78, 81, 82, 90–91, 92–93, 101, 107, 120, 121, 132–33, 136, 138, 141, 142, 144–45, 147n9, 163n2, 170n66, 160n67, 177n59. *See also* authorship, professional and the desire for remuneration
literature, popular and mass market, 2, 7, 8, 13, 18, 28, 29, 32, 34, 38, 39, 52, 54, 56, 58, 62, 63, 67, 79, 82, 134, 173n4
Lives of Eminent Individuals (Sparks), 19, 30, 31,
Locke, John and *tabula rasa* / theories of education, 109–10, 140, 144
Longfellow, Henry Wadsworth, 25, 26, 54, 55, 56, 76, 77, 155n52, 160n16, 160n18, 160n19. *See also* Hawthorne, Nathaniel
Lowell, MA, 46
Lowell, James Russell, 127, 141, 176n48

Magician's Show Box (Sturgis Tappan), 143
Magnalia Christi Americana (Mather), 162n44
Maine Woods (Thoreau), 141
Mann, Benjamin Pickman, 167n35
Mann, Charlotte, 4
Mann, Horace, 1, 2, 3, 4, 5, 7, 8, 11, 12, 14, 15, 17–49, 50–51, 53, 59, 76, 77, 88, 91, 92, 137, 142, 151n4, 152n18, 153n25, 154n26, 154n28, 155n35, 158n16, 161n25, 162n43; on annuals and gift books, 43; feud with Edward Newton, 158n69; on diversity of schoolbooks, 9, 13, 38; on fiction and novels, 43, 55, 58; on history books, 58; Mann-Packard controversy, 24, 153n25, 159n69; response to Hawthorne's writings, 55–56, 57; "District School Libraries," 21, 26, 32, 38, 154n31; *First Annual Report*, 20; *Fourth Annual Report*, 38; *Lectures on Education*, "On District School Libraries," 13, 21–22, 28, 55; "The School Library," 4, 10, 142; *Second Annual Report*, 28, 92, 153n22; *Sixth Annual Report*, 47; *Third Annual Report*, 23, 24, 27, 43, 44, 58, 153n22, 153n23
Mann, Mary Peabody (née Tyler Peabody), 4, 34, 39, 87, 93, 143; on Alcott's manipulations at the Temple School, 85, 86, 166n22, 167n32; *The Flower People*, 138, 170n66
Marsh, Capen, Lyon, and Webb, 21, 22, 23, 28, 35, 41, 46, 154n31, 157n68
Marshall, Megan, 166n23
Massachusetts Board of Education, 1, 17, 18, 20–22, 23, 24, 25, 27, 28, 43, 47, 48, 91, 92, 152n16, 153n22, 154n31, 158n69, 158n70
The Massachusetts School Library, 47–48, 158n76
Mather, Cotton, 13, 64–65, 66; and smallpox epidemic, 64–65; *Magnalia Christi Americana*, 162n44
Mathews, Cornelius, 135
McGill, Meredith, 12, 20, 34, 54, 55
Means and Ends (Sedgwick), 19, 25

Memoirs of Margaret Fuller Ossoli (Emerson and Fuller), 111, 112, 113, 114, 115, 116, 118, 119–20, 121–22, 123, 125, 135, 136, 141, 143, 144, 175n39
Melville, Herman, 77, 147n9
Metcalf, Evelina, 110
Michigan, 24–25, 27
Milder, Robert, 15, 139
Miller, Perry, 3
"moral enterprise," 2, 4, 11, 12, 13, 14, 20, 22, 46, 55
Morton, Marcus, 47
"Mr. Alcott's Book and School" (Peabody), 89–90, 167n33
Munroe, James, 61, 70, 74, 102, 129, 163n45, 172n81
Murray's *English Reader*, 149n27
Murray's Family Library, 27
Myerson, Joel, 122, 124, 176n47

nationalism, bibliographic, 17–49
nationalism, literary, 12–13, 16, 34, 48, 69
Natural Theology (Paley), 19, 29, 32
Nature (Emerson), 3
New England Magazine, 4
New York, 15, 27, 48, 97, 100, 101, 102, 139, 141
New York Tribune, 15, 106, 134, 144, 179n84. *See also* Fuller, Margaret
Newton, Edward. *See* Mann, Horace
"No Child Left Behind," 137
North American Review, 29, 32, 134–35
novel, American, 43, 48, 57, 58, 95, 122, 178n77

O'Sullivan, John, 160n19; as editor of *The United States Magazine and Democratic Review*, 161n30
Ohio, 27, 77
"On District School Libraries" (Mann), 13, 21, 22, 28, 55

Packard, Frederick, 24, 153n25, 158n69

Packer, Barbara L., ix, 148n10, 175n37, 176n57, 178n68, 180n19
Paley, William: *Natural Theology*, 19, 29, 32
Palmer, Edward, 126
Palmer, Theodore, 154n28; *Teacher's Manual*, 154n28
Panic of 1837, 46, 60–61, 161n30
paper currency, 60–62, 63, 70, 161n30, 163n44
paper making, 8, 36–37
Parker, Theodore, 95, 103, 114, 123, 127, 129, 131, 148n11, 164n7, 169n55, 170n66, 177n60
Paul Clifford (Bulwer-Lytton), 93
Peabody circle, 3–7, 10, 15–16, 81, 82, 138, 143, 145, 148n11, 164n7
Peabody, Andrew Preston, 57
Peabody, Elizabeth, 2, 3, 4, 7, 10, 13–14, 16, 66, 79–104, 105, 107, 108, 116, 117–18, 137, 142, 143, 160n16, 164n7, 165n11, 165n13, 175n41; and Boston (West Street) bookstore and foreign circulating library, 4, 5, 12, 15, 61, 80–104, 164n8, 165n14, 168n35, 168n39, 169n57, 170n63, 170n65, 171n71, 171n74; Bronson Alcott and the Temple School, 83–90, 99, 108, 140, 165n14, 165n15, 166n18, 166n19, 166n22, 167n28, 167n35, 168n46; on coterie, 5–6, 80, 82, 97, 98, 103; and *The Dial*, 97, 98, 102, 119, 123, 128, 129, 170n66, 171n77; on *The School Library*, 10; as promoter and "faithful booster" of Hawthorne and others, 4, 5, 11–12, 53, 55, 57, 71, 81, 92, as publisher, 11, 99–103, 170n66, 170n67; *Conversations with Children on the Gospels* (with Alcott), 4, 83, 85–86, 87–90, 140, 166n23; "A Glimpse of Christ's Idea of Society;" 98; "Mr. Alcott's Book and School," 89–90, 167n33; "Plan for the West Roxbury Community," 97; *Record of a School*, 84, 92–93; *Reminiscences*, 83, 93, 95, 96, 100, 103, 165n13
Pearson PLC, 139, 140, 141, 142
Penn, William, 1, 49

periodical culture, 8, 9, 10, 16, 18, 54, 63, 97, 99, 102, 103, 105, 106, 118, 119, 122, 127, 132–33, 134–35, 173n4. See also *The Dial*
"Persius Flaccus" (Thoreau), 126, 127
Person, Leland, 162n35
Pestalozzi curriculum, 144, 149n15
Peter Parley's Universal History (Hawthorne), 54, 59, 159n10, 160n24, 163n48
Philadelphia, 100, 128
Phips, William, 70
Pictures of Early Life (Embury), 19, 43, 44–46
Pierce, John D., 24–25
Pinkwater, Daniel, 139–41, 142
Post-Lauria, Sheila, 10
Prescott, William, 58
print culture, antebellum, 1, 3, 5, 6, 12, 13, 22, 51, 52, 62, 79, 80, 81, 82, 92, 93, 98, 122, 138. See also "culture of reprinting;" literary marketplace, antebellum
print technology; 8, 18, 23, 30, 37, 42–43, 54. See also paper making
Providence, 106, 107, 108, 111, 112, 113, 116, 117, 120, 140
public schools, American, 6, 17, 20, 24–25, 27, 137
Puritans, 62, 63, 64, 65, 69
Putnam, George Palmer. See Wiley and Putnam

Rainbows for Children (Sturgis Tappan), 143
Record of a School (Peabody), 84, 92–93
reformers, educational, 2, 4, 5, 6, 9, 14, 18, 22, 29, 46, 51, 55, 58, 63, 64, 142, 145, 149n15, 161n25, 161n34
reformers, literary, 2, 5, 7, 10, 12, 14, 15, 16, 92, 94, 121, 142, 176n48
Reminiscences (Peabody), 83, 93, 95, 96, 100, 103, 165n13
Reynolds, Larry, 122–23, 174n35
Rhode Island, 27
Ripley, George, 123, 131; and Brook Farm, 81, 97, 98; "Prospectus" to *The Dial*, 132, 134, 175n40

Ripley, Sophia, 117, 123, 169n55, 176n48
Riverside Literature Series, 78
Robbins, Sarah, 18
Rollo books (Abbot), 76
Romanticism, 3, 12, 17, 29, 99, 110, 115, 116, 140, 141, 144, 147n9
Ronda, Bruce, 91, 164n7, 166n19
Rose, Anne, 15, 172n4
Rosenthal, Bernard, 177n64
Rowland, William, 148n9

Salem, MA, 83, 87, 90, 91, 168n35, 169n52
Sánchez-Eppler, Karen, 156n41
Sánchez, María Carla, 7
The Scarlet Letter (Hawthorne), 76
schoolbooks, 6, 9, 25, 38, 45, 51, 76, 77, 91, 145, 154n26
The School Library (Mann), 1, 2, 5, 7, 13, 17–49, 91, 142, 151n4, 153n19, 154n28, 155n35, 156n68, 158n69, 160n16; *Adult Series*, 19, 26, 33; *Juvenile Series*, 19, 21, 22, 39, 40, 41; advertisements for and reviews of, 1–2, 22, 29–30, 32, 46, 92, 156n43, 156n44, 156n16; bindings ("plainly and substantially bound"), 20, 32, 33, 40, 45; contents, 19, 152n16; frontispiece to, 39, 41; price of, 20–21, 23; "Introductory Essay," 1, 17, 23, 27, 28–29, 49. *See also* Mann, Horace
Sedgwick, Catherine Maria, 7–8, 10, 19, 25–26; *Means and Ends*, 25
Sedgwick, Charles, 25–26
self-culture, 2, 5, 6, 7, 13, 29, 63, 80, 83, 84, 85, 86, 95, 102, 109, 111
"Self-Reliance" (Emerson), 16, 125
sentiment / sentimentality and sympathy, 10, 43, 52, 64, 66, 69–70, 110, 111, 112, 114, 116, 119, 140
"The Service" (Thoreau), 126
Shealy, Daniel, 110, 111, 114
"A Short Essay on Critics," (Fuller), 133–34
Shuffelton, Frank, 109
The Sketch-Book of Geoffrey Crayon (Irving), 11, 51

slavery, 37. *See also* abolition; Channing, William Ellery
smallpox epidemic, Boston. *See* Mather, Cotton
Sparks, Jared, 152n16; *Lives of Eminent Individuals*, 19, 30, 31
Sprague, Mary, 169n52
Stamp Act, 67
Steele, Jeffrey, 174n29
Story, Ronald, 158n2
"Sympathy" (Thoreau), 126, 177n63

Tamarkin, Elisa, 37–38
Tappan and Dennet, 71
Tappan, Caroline Sturgis (née Sturgis), 107, 176n48; *Magician's Show Box*, 143; *Rainbows for Children*, 143
Tanglewood Tales (Hawthorne), 4, 76, 143
Teacher's Manual (Palmer), 154n28
Tebbel, John, 153n21
Tennyson, Alfred Lord, 127
textbook industry, 6, 9, 10, 11, 13, 15, 20, 24–27, 28, 47–49, 91, 137, 142, 145
Things by their Right Names (Barbauld; Hale, ed.), 17, 18, 34, 35, 36–38, 39, 41, 42
Thoreau, Henry David, 95, 141, 143, 163n2; and *The Dial*, 126–27, 128, 129, 177n60; *Maine Woods*, 141; "Persius Flaccus," 126, 127; "The Service," 126; "Sympathy," 126, 177n63; *Walden*, 79–80
"Thoughts on Modern Literature" (Emerson), 124
Tieck, Ludwig, 97, 143
Ticknor and Fields, 15, 32, 77, 143
The Token (Goodrich), 53, 159n8
transatlantic literary influences; 12, 13, 17–18, 19, 20, 27, 28, 32, 34, 36–38, 42, 44, 54, 70–75, 80, 82, 93, 96–97, 98–99, 103–4, 105, 118, 144, 170n65. *See also* Anglophilia; British literature; French literature; German literature; Italian literature; Peabody, Elizabeth and the West Street bookstore
transatlantic piracy, 18, 34, 37, 42, 54, 153n19

transcendentalism, 3, 4, 5, 6, 7, 9, 12, 14, 15, 16, 53, 68, 69, 80, 81, 82, 83–84, 89, 91, 97–98, 99, 103–4, 105, 107, 113, 123, 124, 125, 127, 135, 136, 137, 138, 139, 140, 143, 144, 164n7, 164n8, 165n11, 165n13, 165n14, 175n41, 176n47, 176n48, 177n59
True Stories from History and Biography (Hawthorne), 76, 77
Twice-Told Tales (Hawthorne), 22, 53, 54, 57, 61, 160n16
Two Years before the Mast (Dana), 142, 155n35

Unitarianism, 4, 6, 63, 82, 83, 95, 153n25, 176n48
United States Magazine and Democratic Review (O'Sullivan, ed.), 161n30
The Useful Arts (Bigelow), 19, 29

Valenti, Patricia, 160n24
Vásquez, Mark, 6, 122

Wadsworth, Sarah, 10, 59, 159n10, 160n24, 163n48

Walden (Thoreau), 79–80
Ward, Samuel Gray, 92–93, 126, 171n74
Warren, James Perrin, 175n46
Washington, George, 68
Wayne, Tiffany, 130, 174n35
Webb, Thomas, 26, 46–47, 48
Weeks and Jordan, 102, 129
Western Messenger, 99
Whitman, Sarah Helen, 97
Wiley and Putnam, 101, 102
Wiley, John. *See* Wiley and Putnam
Wilson, Leslie Perrin, 81, 167n35, 170n63
Winship, Michael, 12
Woman in the Nineteenth Century (Fuller), 14, 106, 107, 109, 110, 117, 125, 130, 135
women writers, 14, 48, 81, 82, 87, 90, 101, 102, 103–4, 132, 175n41, 176n57. *See also* Fuller Margaret; Peabody, Elizabeth
A Wonder Book for Girls and Boys (Hawthorne), 4, 59, 76–78, 143

Zboray, Ronald, 23
Zboray, Ronald and Mary Saracino, 3, 148n13
Zwarg, Christina, 117, 130, 175n36, 178n70, 178n71

www.ingramcontent.com/pod-product-compliance
Lightning Source LLC
Chambersburg PA
CBHW021757230426
43669CB00006B/109